'The Bad Times'

Waterford Country Houses

During the Revolutionary Period

William Fraher

Series Editor Willie Whelan

for Waterford County Museum

Cover Design by Martin Whelan

Foreword

For people of my generation, the teaching of Irish history in school stopped at the 1916 Rising. Even when I studied history in UCD in the 1970s, our lecturer began his talk on the Civil War by saying he was conscious that we might have had family members who took part on one side or the other, and that he would respect the sensitivities involved. One of the great virtues of the Decade of Centenaries has been the encouragement it has given to historians to explore that era in some depth, casting new light on previously hidden corners.

While most of us know in general terms about "the burning of the big houses" during the War of Independence, it is only recently that publications such as Terence Dooley's book of the same name, painting the picture at national level, and Willie Fraher's book dealing with Co. Waterford, have covered the issue in the detail it deserves.

Willie has a formidable knowledge of the architectural history of the county, both urban and rural. To this he has added a vivid account of the people who lived through the revolutionary period, whether as occupants of the country houses (both large and small), their servants, members of the IRA or the Free State army, or ordinary people living in the countryside caught up in the tides of war. His research is meticulous and is based on an extraordinarily wide range of sources, both published and unpublished, including compensation claims in the National

Archives, witness statements given to the Bureau of Military History, and contemporary Irish and UK newspapers.

One of the most valuable sources is the family archives of the owners of some of those houses, particularly the correspondence of Emily Ussher of Cappagh House and the diary of Mary de la Poer of Gurteen le Poer. Their contemporary accounts enable us to witness through their eyes what it was like to experience raids on their homes, sometimes accompanied by a demand to provide accommodation, but sometimes ending in a warning to evacuate before the house was set on fire.

The immediacy of these and similar stories is complemented by an outline of the wider historical context, such as the economic impact of the Land Acts 1881 to 1909 on both landlords and tenant farmers, and the loss of confidence among Anglo-Irish unionists as Home Rule appeared imminent. The impacts of both the IRA levy on big houses in 1921 and the farm labourers' strike of 1922 are analysed. There are also wonderfully evocative black-and-white photos showing not only the damage caused to the houses but also the social life of the owners, including family gatherings, hunt meetings and balls, and their indoor and outdoor staff.

I welcome additions such as a map and an index to this second edition of the book, which will enhance its value as a work of reference. For anyone with an interest in the local history of Co. Waterford, particularly during the dramatic events of a century ago, this book is essential reading.

John Martin
October 2022

Acknowledgements

T his research would not have been possible without the assistance of the following individuals and institutions who allowed me to examine original documents and images in their archives or assisted with advice or other sources.

The late Ambrose Congreve, Mount Congreve, and Geraldine Critchley. The late Major Hugh Dawnay, Maria Ines Dawnay for documents relating to Whitfield Court. The Marquis of Waterford for permission to quote from letters and documents in the Curraghmore Archive. Sir Charles Keane for access to documents relating to the reconstruction of Cappoquin House. The late Henrietta, Lady Staples for permission to quote from the unpublished memoir of Emily Ussher and to Jackie Pullen for providing the images of Arland and Emily Ussher. To Count Anthony de la Poer for permission to quote from his grandmother's unpublished diary and for transcribing entries from the diary of Rivallon de la Poer. Henry Wilks for permission to quote from Mildred Dobbs's memoir. The late Jim Russell, Seafield House. Waterford County Museum for permission to use images from their image archive, and to Barry Moore, image archivist. Gregory McReynolds for information on Rockmount and the Hunt family.

I am indebted to Julian Walton for advice on the text, for his ongoing support for this book over the years, and for drawing my attention to correspondence in the archives of Mount Congreve and Curraghmore House. Seán and Síle Murphy for the images of Rockmount and Comeragh and to Brian Fitzelle for the images of Ballynatray and the defence of the country house booklet. Jenny

Hunt for the images of Rockmount and the Hunt family. The late Tom Hunt for his valuable eye-witness account of the burning of Rockmount. John Galloway for permission to quote from the letters relating to Annestown House and to the late Emily Villiers-Stuart and to Barbara Grubb for information on the Dromana visitor's book for 1921. The National Archive of Ireland. Joanne Rothwell, Waterford City & Co Council Archivist, for drawing my attention to the criminal injuries' compensation claim book. Brendan O'Brien for information on his grandfather's link with Glenaheiry Lodge. Particular thanks to Cian Flaherty for reading the text and for his assistance with queries and observations on the compensation claim files and allowing me to consult his unpublished thesis on unrest in Co Waterford during the Civil War period. Committee members and staff of Waterford County Museum past and present. Thanks to Anthony de la Poer and Brian Fitzelle for making suggestions for additions and amendments to the text of this second edition. I'm grateful to Stephanie Edwards for her work in compiling the index and to John Martin for his foreword. A special thank you to Martin Whelan for the cover design and Willie Whelan for preparing the text and images for the publication of this second edition.

Introduction

T he aim of this book is to focus on the impact of the War of Independence/Civil War on the owners of big houses in County Waterford. Most of these houses were modest in size and some were hunting lodges. Mark Bence-Jones's book *Twilight of the Ascendancy*[1] was probably the first to give an account of this period from the point of view of the owners of country houses. Terence Dooley's *The Decline of the Big House in Ireland*[2] examined the topic in more detail concentrating on the larger country houses. The destruction of country houses during the revolutionary period has recently been the subject of more detailed investigation by Gemma Clark in her study concentrating on Tipperary, Waterford and Limerick.[3] Ciaran J Reilly has written on the burning of country houses in Co Offaly[4], and J.R. Donnelly on the destruction of houses in Co Cork.[5] Since the publication of the first edition of this book three further publications on the topic have been released: *Burning the Big Houses* by Terence Dooley, *Left Without a Handkerchief* by Robert

---

[1] Mark Bence-Jones, *Twilight of the Ascendancy* (London, 1987).
[2] Terence Dooley, *The Decline of the Big House in Ireland – A study of Irish Landed Families 1860-1960* (Dublin, 2001).
[3] Gemma Clark, *Everyday Violence in the Irish Civil War* (Cambridge, 2014).
[4] C.J. Reilly, 'The Burning of Country Houses in Co Offaly during the Revolutionary Period – 1920-1923,' in Terence Dooley/Christopher Ridgeway (eds), *The Irish Country House: its Past, Present and Future* (Dublin, 2011) pp 110-33.
[5] J.S. Donnelly Jr, 'Big House Burnings in County Cork During the Irish Revolution, 1920-21' *Eire-Ireland*, Vol 47, Nos. 3-4, 2012. pp 141-97.

O'Byrne, and Doomed Inheritance - *Mitchelstown Castle Looted and Burned 1922* by Bill Power.

Glascott Symes compiled the first detailed case study of the burning and subsequent restoration of a Waterford country house during the revolutionary period – Cappoquin, the residence of Sir John Keane.[6] Cian Flaherty has researched why relatively few big houses were burned in Co Waterford during the revolutionary period.[7] Tommy Mooney's *Cry of the Curlew* and *The Deise Divided* provide a valuable month by month account of events in Co Waterford for the War of Independence and Civil War periods.[8] Seán and Síle Murphy's book *The Comeraghs - Gunfire & Civil War* records the Civil War period in mid Co Waterford. Pat McCarthy's comprehensive overview of the period in *The Irish Revolution, 1912-23, Waterford*, is invaluable.

This book approaches the subject from the viewpoint of the owners of the Big House and how it impacted on their lives and their attitudes to England and the new emerging Ireland. The role of the house and estate staff is also examined. It will look at the efforts of the owners to obtain compensation to rebuild their houses which were burned or damaged. Fortunately, a number of primary sources became available during my research which have now been brought together for the first time.

---

[6] Glascott Symes, *Sir John Keane and Cappoquin House in time of war and revolution* (Dublin, 2016).
[7] Cian Flaherty, 'Lucky escapes, rising damp or something else entirely? Why so few County Waterford 'big houses' were burned during the Irish Revolution'. 'The triple misfortune of Richard Poer O'Shee: aspects of Civil War unrest in Waterford, 1922-23'. Unpublished MPhil thesis, Trinity College, Dublin, 2019.
[8] Tommy Mooney, *Cry of the Curlew* (Dungarvan, 2012), *The Deise Divided* (Kilkenny, 2014).

I will also be looking at how the period is covered in unpublished local eye-witness accounts written by Anglo-Irish women. These are key primary sources by Emily Ussher of Cappagh House, Mildred Dobbs of Camphire House, the Hon. Mary Olivia de la Poer of Gurteen le Poer, Beatrix, Lady Waterford of Curraghmore and Frida Keane of Cappoquin. These all offer insightful observations on the period and are significant for their detailed content. Mary de la Poer's diary is of particular interest as it was compiled on an almost daily basis throughout the conflict. It also covers the Clonmel/south Tipperary area which also features in the letters between Lord Osborne ('Obby') de Vere Beauclerk, later 12th Duke of Saint Albans, of Newtown Anner and his wife Lady Osborne Beauclerk (formerly the wife of the 6th Marquis of Waterford). I have also examined letters from the owners and staff of the big houses, the Compensation Claim files in the National Archive, republican witness statements, and newspapers.

One house was burned during the War of Independence, Glenahiery Lodge, owned by Lord Ashtown. Ballycoe House near Dungarvan was owned by the Catholic Dunlea family. It was not burned but completely wrecked by the Black and Tans in 1921 as a reprisal for a local ambush. Six big houses were burned during the Civil War, Comeragh, Rockmount, Annestown, Gardenmorris, Tay Lodge, and Cappoquin. Other houses such as Lismore Castle were set for burning by Republicans but were saved by chance. Its interior was badly damaged, and it took over a year to make it habitable again. Curraghmore House was under threat of looting or possibly burning during the farm labourers' strike in 1922. The reasons for the destruction of certain houses are more obvious such as Cappoquin which was the home of a Senator. The motivation behind the destruction of others such as Gardenmorris, owned by the Catholic Power O'Shees, is unclear.

Gurteen le Poer the home of the Catholic De la Poers, was also marked for destruction. I will examine the previous history of the houses destroyed or damaged to see if any actions of the owners before the revolutionary period contributed to the motivation of the incendiaries.

The subject has been covered in novels by authors such as Molly Keane, Elizabeth Bowen, Una Troy and Barbara Fitzgerald. I have concentrated on one novel *The Trail of the Black and Tans* by Emily Ussher. While it does not feature a substantial country house as such, she does incorporate the true story of the destruction of a modest gentry house, Ballycoe, near Dungarvan.

The main title of this book 'The Bad Times' was a phrase which was unknown to me but was the title often given to this period by many of the owners of Irish country houses.

Photographs

1 Staff at Cappagh House c.1920s. Image courtesy Waterford County Museum

2 Staff at Ballyssaggartmore House 1905. Image courtesy Sarah Kerr.

3 Ambrose Congreve with his nurse Miss Mayhew in the garden at Mount Congreve.

4 House staff, Curraghmore House, c.1905. Image courtesy National Library of Ireland.

TO THE
ELECTORS
OF THE
COUNTY OF WATERFORD.

Gentlemen,

Her Majesty having signified her inte[...]dissolve Parliament on the Twenty-fourth of March, I take the e[...]opportunity of coming before you again to solicit your suffrages at the approaching General Election

I come forward on the same Conservative principles upon which you returned me at the head of the Poll more than six years ago, during which time I hope I have merited your confidence as your Representative. When I remind you that the Family of which I am a member is one well known to you all, and which has proved its affection for our common Country by a constant residence within its borders, and a determination to provide for the welfare of all those with whom it has been connected, I feel confident I am advancing an additional claim to your support.

I have always been of opinion that the question of the Education of the People in Ireland should be ultimately and finally arranged with a due regard to the religious convictions of the various sects of the population. You need not be reminded, that of the Irish Members of the Conservative Party, I was the first to come forward in my place in Parliament to advocate the adoption of the system known as the "Denominational System," which I look upon as the only one which will be complete and worthy of the acceptance of the Irish People.

The Government of the day has given proofs of its desire to meet the wishes of the population of this country in this respect, by passing the "Intermediate Education Act of 1878," and the "Irish Universities Act" of last year. The Intermediate Education Act offers Educational facilities to all Irishmen, without distinction of creed, and that Act I strongly supported both in and out of Parliament. As regards the Universities Act, I consider it a st[...]p in the right direction; but I have already publicly insisted that it can only be [...]ed as an instalment; and if you should do me the honour to re-elect me, I sh[...]ly advocate in the future such an improvement in the existing law as [...]ble the Catholic population of this country to partake of the same a[...]ges as regards University Education as are now enjoyed by the Pr[...]nt portion of the community. I need hardly add, that any propos[...]nange in the Primary System of Education, which tends toward[...]nominationalism, will command my fervent adherence.

The happy experience during many years past of the relations betw[...]ny Family and their Tenantry, will be a guarantee to the Tenant Farmers of the County that I shall always have their best interests at heart.

Owing to a recent domestic affliction, I have been detained in England for a few days, but I hope immediately to be able to wait upon you personally.

I am, Gentlemen,
Your Obedient Servant,

CHARLES BERESFORD.

London, March 11th, 1880.

"STANDARD" Steam-Printing Works, Waterford.

5 Charles Beresford, election poster 1880. Image courtesy Waterford County Museum.

HONEST FARMERS AND THE NATIONAL LEAGUE: TRADESMEN STABBING THE EFFIGY OF MAJOR CHEAMLEY IN THE SQUARE AT DUNGARVAN.

6 Pictorial World, 1886. Image courtesy Waterford County Museum.

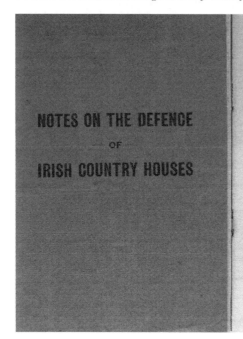

7 Notes on the Defence of Irish Country Houses. Image courtesy Brian Fitzelle Collection.

8 Emily Ussher (nee Jebb). Image courtesy Henrietta, Lady Staples.

9 Cappagh House, garden façade, 24 June 1929. Image courtesy Henrietta, Lady Staples.

10 IRA at Cappagh House August 1922. L to R: Jack Lynch, Liam Power, Jim Ahearne, Mick Small, and John Cahill. The man in the suit has not been identified. Image courtesy Waterford County Museum.

11 *Henrietta Ussher, Emily Ussher, and Beverly Ussher having a haircut from John Power at Cappagh House. Image courtesy Henrietta, Lady Staples.*

12 *Old Cappagh House. Image author's collection.*

13 Photographs of IRA at Cappagh House 1922 by Charles Roden Buxton. Image courtesy Waterford County Museum.

14 Republican graffiti, Cappagh House. Images courtesy Claire Chavasse.

15 *Helvick House, Ring, Co Waterford. Image author's collection.*

16 *Derriheen House, Cappoquin. Image courtesy Sir Charles Keane.*

17 Cappagh Barracks 1922. Image courtesy Waterford County Museum.

18 Ballycoe House, early 1900s. Image courtesy Waterford County Museum.

19 Ballycoe House, 25 March 1921. Image by Edmond Keohan.

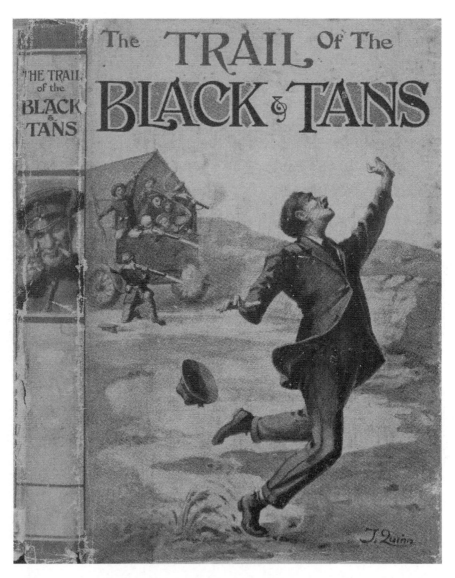

20 Cover design by John Quin. Image from author's collection.

CONFIDENTIAL

TO -

Alice Mansergh
Woodstown

A Chara,

We have permission from G.H.Q. to LEVY you according to Valuation, on as fair a basis as possible.

The blood-hounds of the oppressor are once more let loose on our native soil. For what purpose? - (1). To smash DAIL EIREANN, the Elected GOVERNMENT of the IRISH PEOPLE. Why do they want to drive from our shores so FORMIDABLE A BODY? The common intellect of every IRISH MAN and WOMAN will answer the question quite readily.

Every GOVERNMENT throughout the World has a FORCE to safeguard the Interests of it's Country. To-day IRELAND'S FORCE is the I. R. A. It is the duty of every IRISHMAN and WOMAN to stand by and support IRELAND'S FORCES, who are prepared to make any sacrifice until our INDEPENDENCE is won.

Every form of BARBARITY has been enacted on our People and Forces, in the forms of ARSON, PILLAGE, PLUNDER, & HUMAN TORTURE, but all have failed. The SPIRIT OF A NATION STILL MARCHES ON.

The FORCES of the REPUBLIC hold unlimited appreciation for the general services rendered to them by the FARMERS and PEOPLE of all creeds and denominations in the past.

You may consider yourself hereby duly warned that you are LEVIED the amount of _____'s SHILLINGS IN THE POUND, according to VALUATION. Official Collectors will call on you in the course of a few days.

You are also hereby WARNED that this MANIFESTO is strictly CONFIDENTIAL, and any person REFUSING will be treated as an ENEMY; or giving INFORMATION likely to INTERRUPT our COLLECTORS, will also be treated as an ENEMY, and will be dealt with accordingly.

The AMOUNT required is £ . 10 - 0

Mise le Meas,

X.V.

O/C. WATERFORD NO. 6 BDE. I.R.A.

21 Waterford No.6 Brigade IRA Levy demand letter sent to Alice Mansergh, Woodstown, Co Waterford, undated. Private collection.

22 Dromana House 1960s. Image courtesy Waterford County Museum.

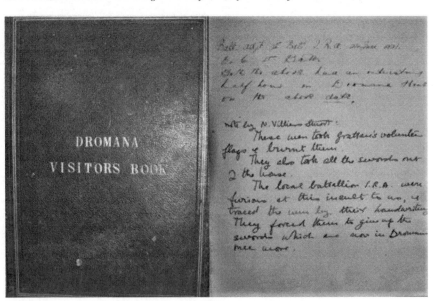

23 Dromana Visitors Book. Image courtesy Barbara Grubb, Dromana House.

24 Glenaheiry Lodge. Lord Ashtown sitting with his gamekeeper (on right) and guarded by two RIC. Denis O'Brien on far right. The Tatler, 17 April 1912. Scrapbook, private collection.

25 Irish Independent, 23 September 1907. Scrapbook, private collection.

26 Glenaheiry Lodge in ruins mid-1920s. Image courtesy Brendan O'Brien.

27 Cloncoskeran House. Image courtesy Waterford County Museum.

28 Charles Nugent Humble. Image courtesy Waterford County Museum

29 Duckspool House c.1953 by Tom Tobin. Image courtesy Waterford County Museum.

Yours Faithfully
E. ARTHUR RYAN.
Nationalist Candidate for West Waterford.
Vote for the Local Man whose principles are : ———
To Defend your right to freely exercise the Franchise.
To Win Home Rule
To Resist over taxation.
To Facilitate Land Purchase.
To Uplift the Labourers.
To Support a United Pledge Bound Party.

E. Keohan.

30 E A Ryan. Image courtesy Waterford County Museum.

31 Gurteen le Poer Castle, exterior and hall. Images courtesy Anthony de la Poer.

32 De la Poer family, Gurteen, c.1907. Back: Patricia, Mary, Edmond, Rivallon (sitting), Front: Yseult and Ermyn. Image courtesy Anthony de la Poer.

33 *Entrance facade Mount Congreve c. 1900. Image courtesy Congreve Archive.*

34 *Mount Congreve Visitors Book 1922. 'Occupation by Irregulars under Commandant Goff'.*

35 Entrance hall, Mount Congreve c.1909. Image courtesy Congreve Archive.

36 The walled garden, Mount Congreve, 1909. Image courtesy Congreve Archive.

Damage to Front Hall.

Bullet through front door broke one pane of glass & lodged in wall opposite.
Bit of ornamentation of ceiling broken off
Marble stand for plant broken
1 mahogany chair broken & 1 scratched
side table scratched, screen torn & scratched
leaves torn out of visitors book.
Cricket bats used 1 broken
Tennis balls used some probably missing
Some books taken from book case & used
5 or 6 missing.

Missing from Hall.

Lady I. C's walking stick & Burberry Hat
Major C's best green felt hat & 3 mackintosh coats
mackintosh rug.
All gloves & scarfs from round table drawes
Handbag torn inside & clasp broken
big watch taken from case.
Master Ambrose's 2 caps & 2 felt hats.
Tweed hat & fishing bag from stand
Field glasses from cupboard.
Baromiter, 2 whips, Hare's Head & fishing rod.

37 Mount Congreve damage report. Image courtesy Congreve Archive.

38 Whitfield Court, entrance façade c. 1913. Image courtesy Waterford County Museum.

LADY SUSAN DAWNAY AND HER SONS

39 Lady Susan Dawnay and family 1920. Image private collection.

40 Whitfield Court, entrance hall c. 1913. Image courtesy Waterford County Museum.

41 Pouldrew House by Hughes & Co, Waterford & Dungarvan. Image from author's collection.

42 Curraghmore House, entrance façade. Image courtesy National Library of Ireland.

43 Annestown House c.1905. Image courtesy Waterford County Museum.

44 Coming of Age of Lord Waterford, Curraghmore 1922. L to R: Capt Lord Osborne Beauclerk, Miss Annesley, Miss Anson, Lady Blanche Beresford, Lady Osborne Beauclerk, Lady Patricia Beresford, Hon. Claud Anson, Lady Catherine Beresford, Marquis of Waterford.

45 Free State army at Curraghmore House 1922. Image courtesy Waterford County Museum.

xl

46 Mr & Mrs Walker, Springfield House, Portlaw. Image courtesy Waterford County Museum.

47 Butlerstown Castle

48 Lackendarra Lodge c.1841. Image courtesy Julian Walton

49 Millfort House, Portlaw. Image author's collection.

50 Glencorran House, Ardmore, 1990s. Image from author's collection.

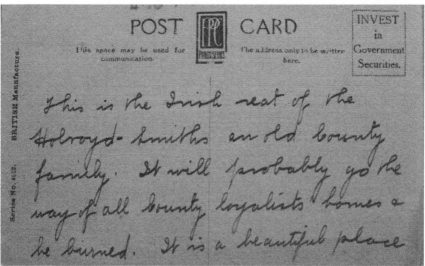

This is the ~~Irish~~ seat of the ~~Holroyd~~ Smiths an old county family. It will probably go the way of all county loyalists' homes & be burned. It is a beautiful place

51 Ballynatray House, undated postcard 1920s. Images from author's collection.

52 *Letter from Patrick J. Reilly, Ballybricken Prison, Waterford, to Mrs Holroyd-Smyth, Ballynatray. Formerly in the collection of Kitty Fleming and recently acquired by the National Library of Ireland.*

53 The Holroyd-Smyths and staff member at the entrance door, Ballynatray House. Image courtesy Brian Fitzelle Collection.

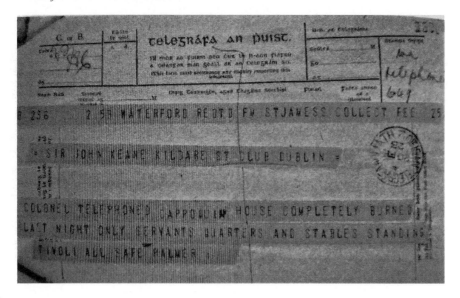

54 Telegram from John D Palmer to Sir John Keane, 2 February 1923. Image courtesy Sir Charles Keane.

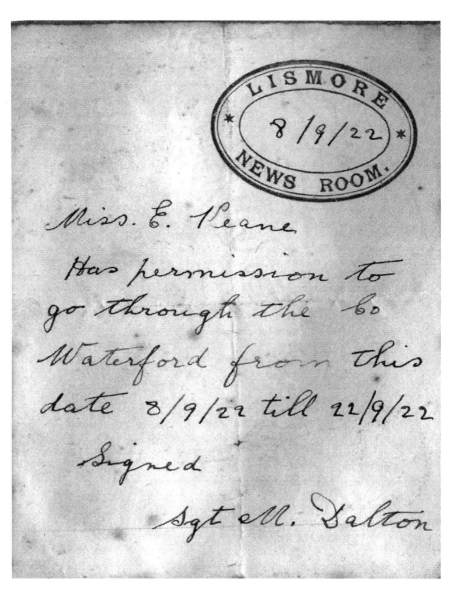

55 IRA pass for Frida Keane, Fortwilliam House. Image courtesy Caroline Palmer.

CAPTAIN SIR JOHN KEANE, Bt., WHO IS
ENGAGED TO THE HON. ELEANOR HICKS-
BEACH.

Photograph by Poole and Co.

56 Sir John Keane from The Sketch, 16 January 1907.

THE HON. ELEANOR HICKS - BEACH, WHO IS ENGAGED TO CAPTAIN SIR JOHN KEANE, Bt.

Photograph by Langfier.

57 Eleanor Hicks-Beach from The Sketch, 16 January 1907.

58 Cappoquin House after restoration. Image courtesy Sir Charles Keane.

59 The west façade of Cappoquin House after the fire in 1923.

60 New concrete beams in the hall, Cappoquin House. Image courtesy Sir Charles Keane.

61 Raising concrete beams Cappoquin House 1925. Image courtesy Sir Charles Keane.

62 Template for proposed plasterwork for Cappoquin House by Michael Creedon, Dublin, c.1913. Image courtesy Sir Charles Keane.

Rebuilding the Ancestral Home of Senator Sir John Keane, In County Waterford, which was burned during the recent trouble in Ireland.

63 'Rebuilding the Ancestral Home' 1923. Image courtesy Sir Charles Keane.

64 Coming-of-Age party at Cappoquin for Richard M Keane. Irish Independent, 8 January 1930.

65 Comeragh House, garden façade c.1900. Image Seán & Síle Murphy / WCM.

66 Comeragh House after the burning in 1923. Image courtesy Seán & Síle Murphy.

67 Gardenmorris House before the fire in 1923. Image, private collection.

68 Miss Russell and Richard Russell of Seafield House, with Col Richard Power O'Shee at Gardenmorris House, February 1927. Image, private collection.

69 Rockmount House before the fire of 1923. Image courtesy Jenny Hunt.

70 Rockmount House after the fire of 1923. Images courtesy Jenny Hunt.

71 Rockmount rebuilt.

72 Arthur Hunt

73 Tom Hunt

74 Lismore Castle in 1903. Scrapbook, private collection.

FROM THE ISLE OF UNREST
And Two Interesting Snapshots in London.

Poole, Waterford

THE MASTER OF THE WATERFORD HOUNDS AND A FAMILY GROUP

The above excellent photograph was taken at Seafield Bonmahon, the residence of Mr. J. R. Russell, the popular master of the Waterford Hounds. Mr. Russell has been master of these hounds since 1914, in which year he succeeded Mr. C. H. Davey. The names, reading from left to right, are—Mr. J. R. Russell, M.P.H., J.P. and High Sheriff for co. Waterford, Mr. Richard Russell, O.T.C., Mrs. Russell, wife of the master, and Miss Russell

75 The Tatler, 13 February, 1918.

76 Tay Lodge. Image courtesy Peter Langley.

77 Camphire House

78 Robert Conway Dobbs, Mildred E Dobbs and Arthur Conway Dobbs, Mitchelstown 1930.

79 Hunt Ball, Curraghmore House, 1939. Image courtesy Waterford County Museum.

80 Shooting party, Gurteen le Poer, Kilsheelan, 1938. Image Courtesy Waterford County Museum.

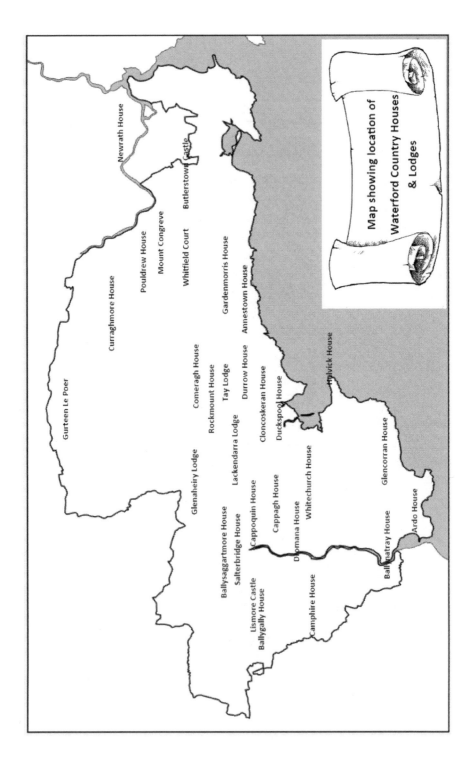

Map showing location of Waterford Country Houses & Lodges

Newrath House

Butlerstown Castle

Pouldrew House

Mount Congreve

Whitfield Court

Gardenmorris House

Curraghmore House

Anniestown House

Gurteen Le Poer

Comeragh House

Tay Lodge

Durrow House

Rockmount House

Cloncoskeran House

Duckspool House

Islyvick House

Glenaheiry Lodge

Lackendarra Lodge

Glencorran House

Ballysaggartmore House

Cappagh House

Whitechurch House

Salterbridge House

Cappoquin House

Diomana House

Ardo House

Ballinatray House

Lismore Castle

Ballygally House

Camphire House

Contents

'A kind of faded feudalism'

Chapter 1

By 1920 the big house owners no longer had the same influence and power as they once had. Their estates were considerably reduced in size and there was no longer a sufficient rental income to make them financially self-sufficient. However, McCarthy[1] notes that although 'a widening of the franchise, disestablishment of the Church of Ireland and land transfers had greatly reduced their power, their status and wealth were undiminished.' This may be true in relation to large estates such as those owned by the Duke of Devonshire at Lismore Castle and the Marquis of Waterford at Curraghmore, but some of the smaller estate owners were finding it difficult to generate the income to run their estates. Even the Curraghmore estate of the Marquis of Waterford had sold off lands in the late 19th century. Under the 1881 Land Act the Marquis received £263,000 for the sale of land in Waterford, Longford, and Londonderry.[2]

The Wyndham Land Act of 1903 encouraged many landowners to sell part of their estates, but this was not compulsory. In October 1903 the Dungarvan Rural District Council wrote to landlords who had property in the area to ascertain if they were willing to sell to their tenants under the terms of the act. Henry P Chearnley, Salterbridge House, felt that it was of no concern of the council but a matter between landlord and tenant; and that it depended

---

[1] Pat McCarthy, (2001) *The Irish Revolution* 1912-23 - Waterford (Dublin, 2001), p.6.

[2] Terence Dooley, *The Decline of the Big House in Ireland* (Dublin, 2001), p.105.

1

entirely on what the tenants offered. Henry C Villiers-Stuart, Dromana House, replied:

> I would rather not part with my property, which has been in my family for many generations...at the same time I have long recognised that the present land system is not the best for inducing people to make the best of their holdings. Therefore, if my tenants are prepared to offer me a sufficient sum, which, when invested in Trustee's securities, would produce an income somewhat approximate to that which I have at present, and which would enable me to reside at Dromana, I will not stand in their way...I will never consent to anything that will involve shutting up this place and leaving the country.

Richard J Ussher, Cappagh House, told the council that none of his tenants had asked to buy their holdings. He said that landlords could not be expected to sell at a loss. John Hunt, agent for Sir John Nugent Humble, Cloncoskeran House, informed the council that they should contact him directly to obtain details of the situation on the Nugent-Humble estate. Nicholas Giles Carew, Coolnagour House, informed them that the matter was in the hands of his solicitor, and he would contact them as soon as all the legal issues relating to the estate were resolved. One of the members of the Rural District Council, Mr McCarthy, J.P., said that it was unfair of landlords to expect their tenants to come up with a purchase figure.[3]

In October 1903 a large number of tenants on the estates of Sir Richard Musgrave, Tourin; the Misses Musgrave, London; Percy Smyth, Headborough House; and Lady Harriet Holroyd- Smyth, Ballynatray, met in Youghal to apply for rent reductions. Lady

---

[3] *Waterford Standard*, 24 October 1903.

Holroyd-Smyth's agents stated that she had agreed to a 15% reduction to which the majority of tenants agreed. Not one tenant appeared to pay rent to Musgraves's agent Thomas H Marmion. They held a meeting and decided to demand a 30% reduction 'as a result of the disastrous harvest'. Percy Smyth of Headborough said he could not agree to any reduction and only a handful of his tenants paid.[4] In July 1904 Sir John Keane returned to Cappoquin House after two years as private secretary to Sir Henry Blake, Governor General of Ceylon. He planned to meet with his tenants 'with a view to purchasing their holdings under the Land Act, as it has been freely stated that Sir John is prepared to sell his estate, provided he can obtain satisfactory terms from his tenants. It is hoped that a conciliatory spirit will be shown on both sides throughout any negotiations'. T H Marmion (Keane agent) acted for Sir John and J.J. O'Shee, MP, for the tenants.[5]

In 1921 the Marquis of Waterford addressed his employees and informed them that due to increased taxation and wage increases he would be forced 'to do things on a greatly reduced scale.'[6] In 1922 the agent claimed that there was insufficient income from the estate to meet the wages of the employees who were demanding 35 shillings a week. There were many impoverished owners who had a country house but not a great deal of productive land from which to obtain an income to run their estate.

Kevin R Shiel, Judicial Commissioner, Dáil Éireann Land Courts 1920-22, gave his opinion on Irish landlords:

---

[4] *Waterford Standard*, 24 October 1903.
[5] *Waterford Standard*, 23 July 1904.
[6] *Irish Times*, 13 September 1921.

There remained...at that time, not a few landlords...living in large, out-of-date mansions (becoming progressively burdensome as to upkeep), with agents, stewards, bailiffs, etc...the proprietors of tenanted land that, for one reason or another had failed to sell out to their tenantry...Those surviving landlords were mainly, but not entirely, Protestant and Unionist. There were Catholics amongst them who were generally as Unionist and, in not a few cases, very much more anti-Irish than they were. Those later-day county magnates clung to a kind of faded feudalism...They failed to see themselves as they really were and hung on, pathetically, to a world that was in its death throes. They were not at all bad fellows...more victims of a system that had long since seen its hey-day...Had they been wiser men, they would have...sold out under the singularly advantageous terms of the Wyndham Act of 1903.[7]

Shiel appears to have no opinion on or interest in the artistic or cultural value of the houses owned by these landlords.

Clark states that by 1923 56% of land in Co Waterford had been purchased by tenants under the Land Acts of 1881-1909. However, 60% of the total acreage lay with only 12% of occupiers.[8]

---

[7] BMH WS 1770, pp 910-912.

[8] Gemma Clark, *Everyday Violence in the Irish Civil War* (Cambridge, 2014), pp 116-117.

Working in the Big House

Chapter 2

These estates did provide considerable employment. What percentage of the staff were local and how many were Catholics? To give some idea I analysed the census returns of 1911 for forty country houses in Co Waterford, large and small. The expectation was that it would show that the majority of staff employed in these houses came from outside County Waterford and were Church of Ireland/England and that the Catholic employees only carried out the menial tasks.

There was a total of 224 staff employed in the sample of forty houses. Of these 134 were Catholic, 31 were Church of Ireland, 32 were Church of England, 20 were Presbyterian and there were 7 of other religious denominations. Of the total seventy were born in Co Waterford. Houses owned by Catholic families such as Gurteen Le Poer and Faithlegg only employed Catholic servants. Twenty house staff were employed at Curraghmore and were all born in England. Three of the staff were Catholic.

The findings show that there was no bias against employing Catholic servants in the majority of Waterford houses, but it does show that Co Waterford-born servants were in the minority. From the sample of forty houses servant roles were evenly divided between Catholic, Church of Ireland/England or other denominations. There is no evidence that non-Catholic servants were given priority by employers. The position of governess was prestigious and was unlikely to be given to a person of Irish Catholic background. In the sample of forty houses there are three governesses listed: at Tourin, a French Catholic, Ballynatray, Church of Ireland, and Ballysaggartmore, Church of England.

What was the relationship between staff and their employers? This is sometimes difficult to gauge. Staff who had been employed for a long period were probably loyal to their employers and would not have supported the campaign of destruction. It would have left them homeless (if residing in the house or on the estate) and without income. What is obvious from looking through the documentation on Waterford houses is that servants often assisted the IRA to gain entry to a number of these houses, particularly during the War of Independence, and provided information on the location of firearms. A number of IRA men in their witness statements recalled how servants assisted them in their search for arms. The following account of a raid on Ballysaggartmore House, near Lismore, the residence of Hon Claud Anson, was made by James Ormond, captain of the Lismore Company IRA and Quarter Master of 5th battalion of Cork No.2 Brigade:

> The year 1919 was mainly noted for raids for arms which were carried out on houses of the gentry. We usually got 'tipped off' by some of the servants in the particular house as to where the guns were kept. I remember one night raiding the house of the Honourable Claud Anson...About twelve other men of the company were with me. On reaching the house one of the maids, who was expecting us, let us into the building through a back window. Searching the house, we came across two shotguns...While we were there, we met the owner. We told him what we wanted. He offered no objection to us taking the arms.[9]

---

[9] BMH WS 1289

The de La Poers of Gurteen were shocked to discover that two of their servants had been despatch carriers for the IRA. While the owners of houses which were burned were genuinely hurt to discover that their 'faithful' servants were involved it showed how out of touch they were with the real feelings of many of the ordinary people who lived in and around their estates.

In June 1921 there was a plan to disarm four British officers who used to visit Ardkeen House, near Waterford city, the home of the De Bromhead family. The officers visited regularly to play tennis. The cook had agreed to 'dope their tea', but the plan was cancelled for fear of reprisals by the British.[10]

Many of those involved on the Republican side were young and wished to overthrow the influence and power of the landlords. A very important aspect of this period was the acquisition of the land attached to the big houses by whatever means possible, burning or threats, and its redistribution amongst local people. Mary de la Poer suggested that it was not just the IRA who burned houses but the 'farmers' sons who want the land and think that if once the houses are burnt, they will take possession of the land'.[11] Their motives were not political but simply concerned with acquiring land for themselves and they saw the political turmoil as the perfect opportunity to strike. Did the Civil War as Clark suggests: 'provide the conditions for the final reckoning of ancient enmities, settling local scores and purging the community of old enemies – tyrannical landlords, ex-Servicemen, southern Unionists and Protestants? Clark in her research on counties Limerick, Waterford and Tipperary found that the 'Loyalist,

---

[10] BMH WS 1132
[11] Diary entry, 12 March 1923.

protestant minority was disproportionately targeted during the Civil War'.[12] Lady Fingal summed up their situation:

> People whose families had lived in the country for three or four hundred years, realised, suddenly that they were still strangers and that the mystery of it was not to be revealed to them – the secret lying as deep as the valleys in the Irish hills, the barrier they had tried to break down standing as strong and immovable as those hills, brooding over an age-long wrong. It was those who tried to atone for that wrong and to break down this barrier, who did most of the paying'. [13]

Kevin O'Higgins wished to make them feel included in the new Irish state: 'These people... are part and parcel of the nation, and we, being the majority and strength of the country...it comes well from us to make a generous adjustment to show that these people are regarded, not as alien enemies, not as planters, but that we regard them as part and parcel of this nation and that we wish them to take their share of its responsibilities'.[14]

It is evident that there are many reasons why houses were burned. In order to obtain a clearer picture more detailed research is required on individual houses. As Dooley states: 'unless the full circumstances of social, political and agrarian activities in the locality - both at the point in time of burning and in the historical past - are explored, one cannot be certain that there were no other underlying reasons'.[15]

---

[12] Gemma Clark, pp 55,89.

[13] Elizabeth, Countess of Fingal, *Seventy Years Young* (Dublin,2009), pp 414-415.

[14] Terence De Vere White, *The Anglo-Irish* (London, 1972), p.259.

[15] Terence Dooley, p.450.

Landowners and Tenants

Chapter 3

The Marquis grew pale and swore with a fury:
He howled for the laws that Cromwell brought o'er;
We'll try them, he said, without judge and jury
And hang them in scores like our fathers before.
They laughed of old Cromwell he couldn't restore;
Oh! If all Ireland combined with those heroes
And banish such tyrants away from our shore![16]

The house owners who feature in this study varied regarding the treatment of their tenants and some, in particular, had poor reputations as landlords. The four largest landowners in Co Waterford were: the Duke of Devonshire, Lismore Castle; the Marquis of Waterford, Curraghmore; Henry Villiers-Stuart, Dromana; and Count de la Poer of Gurteen le Poer. Of the four, the Beresfords, Marquises of Waterford had the least favourable reputation.

The reputation of these families tended to fluctuate over the decades. Sometimes a particular landlord is praised for his treatment of his tenants while at the same time one can read an account in the local newspapers of an eviction carried out by the very same landlord. During the land wars landlord and tenant relations were under strain. O'Ceallacháin in his article on land agitation in Co Waterford notes that 'the Marquess of Waterford, Henry Villiers-Stuart, the Duke of Devonshire, and Count de la

---

[16] Patrick C Power, *History of Waterford City and County* (Cork,1990) p.208.

Poer...had a very good reputation among their tenants'. When the Waterford Farmers' Club was founded in 1879 it was not welcomed by landlords. Nicholas Power O'Shee of Gardenmorris asked that they provide evidence that the agricultural depression was caused by landlords raising rents. He suggested that farmers should have saved their money during the good times instead of 'squandering their money'.[17] Waterford landlords did offer rent reductions but from 1880 they were not as accommodating, and the situation deteriorated with increased evictions and violent incidents. In October 1881 while cub hunting in Newtown Wood Lord Waterford and his entourage were 'attacked by a mob numbering over two hundred' who pelted them with stones and pitchforked some of the hounds. He and the others in attendance stated that many of the protesters were not local but that they were assisted by local people. Lord Waterford said that the Land League was responsible, and that the local organiser was Peter Wall. The Marquis was forced to suspend the Curraghmore Hunt and moved with his hounds to England. According to Harry Sargent – 'Curraghmore was shut up, and the servants, with many of the stablemen, were discharged.'[18] This must have created tensions locally between members of the Land League and those employed on the Curraghmore estate and local businesses. The Waterfords did not return to Curraghmore full-time until c.1886 according to their daughter Clodagh.[19]

The Rev Thomas Finn P.P. of Newcastle, Co Tipperary published a pamphlet in 1881 giving details of the harsh treatment by two landlords in the area, William Perry and Lord Ashtown at

---

[17] Donnchadh Ó Ceallacháin, 'Land Agitation in County Waterford, 1879-1882' *Decies* 53. 1997, pp 91-131.
[18] Harry R Sargent, *Thoughts upon Sport* (London, 1895), pp 40-54.
[19] Lady Clodagh Anson, *Book-Discreet Memoirs* (London, 1931), p.20.

Glenaheiry. He thought when Lord Ashtown purchased the Glenaheiry estate from Lord Stradbroke matters would improve for the tenants, but this was not the case. New leases were drawn up with higher rents, but all the tenants refused to accept them. They were informed by the agent Uniacke Townsend that if they did not agree they would be evicted.[20]

On 31 January 1889 Edmund Fleming of Clashmore, a tenant of the Villiers-Stuarts, was evicted from his holding at Ballycurrane. The Sub-Sheriff Mr Hudson and his bailiffs, 'reinforced by rangers, rent-warners, and hangers-on of the Dromana estate', arrived led by the agent John Armit. A large police force was in attendance overseeing the eviction along with a crowd of Fleming's family, friends, and supporters.[21]

A county Waterford branch of the Evicted Tenants Association was formed in Dungarvan on 12 December 1922. Many of those who attended were evicted tenants or descended from evicted tenants and were encouraged to make a case to be reinstated in their family holding. The minute book of the association records some details of the meeting and lists the stories of the evicted tenants from throughout the county. The following statement written into the minute book expresses the depth of feeling in relation to evictions and may partly explain the burning of certain country houses, in particular during 1923:

> It is evident from the large number of evicted tenants which assembled at the Town Hall, Dungarvan, on Sunday 12th inst, that the evictions of exterminating landlordism

---

[20] Rev. Thomas Finn, *Notes on the History of Two Irish Estates* (Dublin, 1881). http://opac.oireachtas.ie/Data/Library3/Library3/Batch_5_Delivery/DCT11 7013.pdf [Accessed 2/9/2021].
[21] *The Irish Canadian*, 7 March 1889.

and impossible rents – owing to agricultural depression are well organised and alive to their interests and have no intention of allowing the government to shirk or deviate from their written promises of restoring them legally to homes and farms of their predecessors who were bled white from centuries past by the extortion of impossible rack rents thereby purchasing over and over every sod of their farms to the very subsoil, but when agricultural produce became unsaleable by the preferential facilities given by the Irish Landlords and the British Government to foreign competition, they were forcibly evicted from those homes and farms which were purchased by the very blood of themselves and their antecedents, and are consequently held sacred by them, and nobody but the veriest reptile would dare lay claim to anything so sanctified by the blood of generations'.[22]

The minute book records the landlords who evicted the highest number of families. Surprisingly, the Villiers-Stuarts of Dromana top the list (7) followed by the Nugent Humbles of Cloncoskeran (6). The Villiers-Stuarts were generally considered to be good landlords.

Lismore Castle was the seat of the Duke of Devonshire, an absentee landlord, but the family were conscious of their duty to their tenants. A newspaper report of 1880[23] noted that: 'There is no estate in Ireland which the comforts of the labourer are more studied and looked after than on the Duke of Devonshire's estate'. The estate workers lived in comfortable slate-roofed cottages. In 1883 the duke's agent, Chetwynd Currey, believed that the policy

---

[22] Waterford County Museum Archive, *Co Waterford Evicted Tenant's Association Minute Book,* 1988-3-103.
[23] *Waterford News,* 30 December 1880.

of improvements to the estate over the previous sixty years had helped landlord-tenant relationships. According to Proudfoot only thirteen tenants had their rents reduced by the land court and since 1871 only nine tenants had been evicted for not paying rent.[24] In 1906 a newspaper report noted that the duke was strongly opposed to home rule for Ireland.[25] Some years later he had come to accept the possibility of self-government. The duke was a major symbol of British unionism which made Lismore Castle a prime target for destruction.

The Beresfords at Curraghmore, have often been portrayed as bad landlords, evicting tenants without hesitation. Is this borne out by the historical record? Looking through local newspapers throughout the 19th century there are frequent references to evictions on the Curraghmore estate. However, newspaper articles need to be read with a certain amount of caution. In 1846 the *Waterford Chronicle* published a shocking report on the eviction of hundreds of tenants on the Marquis of Waterford's land at Graigueshoneen, Kilmacthomas. *The Times* reprinted the story and J. O'Connell, M.P. for Kilkenny, demanded an explanation from the marquis in the House of Commons.[26] The *Waterford Mail* came to his defence and explained that the story was not quite as portrayed. It stated that those evicted were not tenants of the marquis. They were from Cork and Kerry and had been allowed by the tenants of the marquis onto their land for a fee where they erected 'miserable hovels'. The 'squatters' were asked by the Curraghmore agent to demolish their habitations and move out with the offer of £2, which they did. The paper

---

[24] Lindsay Proudfoot, 'The Estate System in Mid Nineteenth-Century Waterford', in *Waterford History and Society* (Dublin 1992), p.536.
[25] *The Scotsman* 28 February 1906.
[26] http://api.parliament.uk/historic-hansard/commons/1846/apr/27/the-marquess-of-waterford-alledged [Accessed 4 September 2020].

noted that the marquis was a large employer and was about to make a financial contribution to the local Catholic church and expansion of the cemetery.[27] While the 'squatters' were not tenants of the marquis they were nevertheless deprived of their homes.

The mid-19th century owners, Henry, 3rd marquis and his wife Louisa were well liked and did much to assist their tenants and improve their lives by setting up cottage industries and opening schools and churches. On Henry's death in 1859 his brother Rev John de la Poer Beresford succeeded to the title. He was not popular and undid the positive relationships which Henry and Louisa had cultivated between the family and their tenants.

However, a different impression of tenant relations was given by Finlay Dun writing of Curraghmore in 1881. He commented that the then 5th Marquis, John Henry de la Poer Beresford (1844-1895) had 'expended much thought, personal labour, and expense, in developing his estate and improving his tenantry'. The county Waterford estate then comprised 35,128 statute acres and there were 474 landholders, 94 of whom paid less than £10 annually. At the weekly pay night, he listened to any issues which his tenants had. At least once a year he visited every tenant on his estate. Dun claimed that no tenants were evicted during the marquis's occupation and that improvements to tenants' holdings were paid for without increasing rents. The weekly wage bill for those who worked in the gardens, stables, home farm and woods came to £100. This was in addition to wages for the 'heads of departments', and foremen.[28]

---

[27] *Waterford Mail*, 4 April 1846.
[28] Finlay Dun, *Landlords and Tenants in Ireland* (London, 1881), pp 43-53.

Comments in the minute book for the Rathgormack Tenants National League in 1890 are not complimentary to the Beresfords and others:

> He was delighted to find that the farms from which honest men were unjustly evicted by such tyrants as Lord Waterford and Barron continued derelict, and that no one could be found to act the treacherous part of grabbing them.[29]

An undated [c.1890] printed circular titled: 'A List of Objectionable Persons, with whom it is expected that no true man will have any dealings whatsoever' included a number of the landowners featured in this study. The Marquis of Waterford, 'evictor'; Thomas Hunt, Rockmount, 'grabber and manager of evicted farms'; Major Chearnley, Cappoquin, Sir Richard Musgrave, Tourin, Villiers-Stuart, Dromana, R.H. Power, agent to the Duke of Devonshire are all described as 'evictor'. G.L. Gallwey, Steward at Lismore Castle is described as 'secret manager of evicted farms'. Mr Good, forester to the duke is described as 'assister of emergency men'.[30]

At the coming of age of the 5th Marquis of Waterford in 1896 the Town Commissioners of Carrick presented him with an address in which they quoted Daniel O'Connell: 'He gave them credit as residents for their interest in their country, and he further remarked that absenteeism was unknown in their family'.[31] In 1911 the 6th Marquis announced that he was resigning as Master of the Waterford Hounds. There was widespread regret at his

---

[29] Waterford County Museum, *Minute Book of the Rathgormack Branch of the Tenants National League*, 26 October and 27 April 1890.
[30] Canon P Power scrapbook, Waterford City Library.
[31] *Waterford Standard*, 5 September 1896.

decision and a petition was organised in county Waterford, Tipperary and Kilkenny appealing to him to change his mind. It was presented to the Marquis and Marchioness at Curraghmore in February. The *Waterford Standard* noted that the petition had 'no parallel in Irish history as far as hunting is concerned'. 'This fact speaks much for his lordship's popularity...[and] of the personal regard felt for is lordship and his house, to the anxiety on the part of all to keep at home the nobility and gentry of our country'. After the presentation of the petitions Lord Waterford replied that the goodwill shown towards him would 'show the people all over Ireland and England, too, that in spite of differences of politics and differences of various kinds that there is a substratum of downright common sense and good feeling in Ireland'.[32]

Ballysaggartmore near Lismore was the seat of the Keily family in the 19th century. During the Famine John Keily, the landlord, evicted many of his tenants in a heartless manner. We know much of the harrowing details as the case was reported in the press. The memory of these evictions remained with local people right into the 20th century. It is therefore surprising that Ballysaggartmore, a symbol of landlord oppression, was not targeted for destruction in the War of Independence/Civil War period. It has been erroneously stated by a number of writers that it was burned during the revolutionary period, but this is untrue as the house was still in existence when it was sold by the owner Claud Anson in 1930.[33] Lady Clodagh Anson recalled a story about IRA men who stole some of her husband's clothing: 'The only time that

---

[32] *Waterford Standard*, 25 February 1911.
[33] *Irish Examiner*, 5 April 1930. According to the *Waterford Standard* 10 May 1930, the Duchess of Devonshire and Lady Susan Dawnay were amongst the top bidders at the auction.

Claud felt he had been insulted was when, during the bad times, the Sinn Feiners had raided Ballysaggart and took away all his clothes, returning a few days afterwards to lay a pile of his waistcoats on the doorstep with a note pinned on to say they did not like the cut of them![34] In October 1922 her husband submitted a claim to the Co Council for £150 for the stolen clothing.[35] It was reported in February 1922 that the Hon Claud Anson had received £800 for 'the disappearance of a motor car and damage to a garage'.[36] Clark has noted in her study of Limerick, Tipperary and Waterford that county Waterford had the highest incidence of car theft.[37] At Seafield House, Bonmahon, James Richard Russell (1874-1926), Master of the Waterford Hunt 1914-1923, had his car taken; the owner refused to give it up at first and was hit on the head. One of the men involved was Keohan of Bonmahon.[38] Cars were taken from at least 15 big houses throughout county Waterford in 1922 for which the owners claimed compensation through the Post Truce (Damage to Property (Compensation) Act 1923. Samuel Jervis Power of Affane House claimed for a Ford car purchased in 1916 for £150. He was travelling from Clonmel Fair when the car was taken from him by armed men. He was awarded £75. Col Sampson Roch, Woodbine Hill claimed £200 for a Ford car. Michael Keane was left in charge of the house and two armed men, 'members of the Ardmore I.R.A.' arrived demanding the car. Roch was awarded £135. Harry Keane of Fortwilliam House claimed for a Ford and a

---

[34] Lady Clodagh Anson, *Another Book* (London, 1937), p.92.
[35] WCCA WCC/GWA288
[36] *Irish Examiner*, 15 February 1922.
[37] Clark, p.21
[38] Author interview with Jim Russell, Seafield House, 2017.

Bianchi car, 'a good Italian car' which had cost £398. He was granted £130 for the Ford and £225 for the Italian car.[39]

In July 1922 a local newspaper reported that Henry Winston Barron-Newell, of Woodstown House, had been taken into custody by the Waterford city IRA. A number of IRA men attempted to take his car and Barron shot at them, wounding a member of the Dunmore East IRA in the leg and eye. The newspaper noted that two cars and some arms belonging to Barron-Newell were taken by the IRA.[40]

In 1882 Miss Edith Palliser of Comeragh House was taking part in the Curraghmore hunt and sued a fifteen-year-old boy for assault for throwing a stone at her and setting dogs at her horse while he shouted, 'Down with Curraghmore!' In court she asked to have the charge struck out if the boy confessed, but he declined.[41] In February 1894 a public meeting was held at Mahon Bridge attended by P.J. Power M.P. and organised by the Kilrossanty & Fews branch of the Land League to protest at the 'wholesale evictions' on the Fairholme and Giles estates.[42]

Sir John Nugent Humble lived at Cloncoskeran House, near Dungarvan. In the mid-19th century, there had been evictions on the estate to facilitate new landscaping of the demesne. In March 1906 J.J. O'Shee, MP for Waterford, questioned the sale of part of the Cloncoskeran estate by Sir John Nugent Humble to his brother Charles. He stated that there had been 'a clearance of many tenants off this estate…affected about 50 years ago, and that

---

[39] *Waterford News*, 9 November 1923.
[40] *Waterford News*, 7 July 1922.
[41] Edith Charlotte Bury Palliser (1859-1927). *Waterford Mail*, 2 December 1882.
[42] *Freeman's Journal*, 6 February 1894.

several tenants were also evicted within the past 25 years'.[43] According to the minute book of the Evicted Tenants Association the Nugent Humbles evicted two families in the 1860s – the Terry family who held 150 acres at Cloncoskeran and the Tobins who had a farm of 130 acres in the same area. The reason given was 'for the enlargement of the Demesne' in both instances. [44] The work of laying out the demesne took place from 1858 to 1859: 'The esteemed Baronet [Sir John Nugent Humble] has a large number at work to whom he is paying good wages, and the demesne, in a short time, bids fair to be one of the most picturesque for many miles around...'[45] In 1865 Sir Nugent Humble was accused by Mr Anthony at a meeting of the Poor Law Guardians for Dungarvan of being responsible for a number of the workhouse inmates who were former evicted tenants of his at Ballinroad and Kilminion 'being swept off the face of the earth'.[46] In 1894 the labourers' cottages built on the Nugent Humble estate were described as 'the worst class of labourers' cottages in the county. They were of mud walls, the thatch was like peat, and could be pulled out in fistfuls; the walls were open, and they were badly ventilated'.[47] In 1922 these lands were used as part of a 'grazing ranch' by Charles Nugent Humble which amounted to about 2,000 acres. Between 1875 and 1895 the Nugent Humbles evicted six other families that we are aware of.

The Chearnley family acquired Salterbridge House near Cappoquin through marriage with the Musgrave family in the 18th century. They also had a hunting lodge called Lackendarra Lodge,

---

[43] HC Deb 28 March 1906 Vol 154 CC1243-4

[44] Waterford County Museum archive, *Minute Book of the Co Waterford Evicted Tenant's Association 1925.*

[45] *Limerick Reporter*, 12 August 1859

[46] *Cork Examiner*, 8 June 1865.

[47] *Freeman's Journal*, 31 May 1894.

in Touraneena, Co Waterford. In the 1880s the relationship between the family and their tenants deteriorated. In 1886 five of Major Chearnley's tenants were advised by the National Tenant League to withhold their rent unless they received an abatement. The sub-sheriff, John T Hudson, put their holdings up for auction. They were purchased by friends of the evicted tenants and after the auction a meeting was held in Dungarvan square by the Tenant League. In the speeches Chearnley was compared to the infamous landlord, John Adair and it was noted that there had been more instances of 'landlord tyranny' on his estate than any other in Munster.[48] The meeting was the subject of an engraving in an English publication in 1886 titles: 'Honest farmers and the National League stabbing an effigy of Major Chearnley in the Square at Dungarvan', which shows a number of men stabbing an effigy of Chearnley with pikes.[49] In 1891 Salterbridge House was attacked by a group of six armed men described as 'Moonlighters'. They tried to enter the house through the conservatory, but Major Chearnley confronted them and fired two shots.[50]

On 11 April 1912, the Prime Minister, Herbert Asquith, introduced the third home rule bill in the House of Commons. Nationalists in Ireland were delighted but many of the big house owners were alarmed at the prospect of home rule for Ireland. Unionists were determined to prevent its introduction. In 1912 Thomas O'Callaghan-Westropp (1864-1944) of Coolreagh, Co Clare, published a pamphlet titled: *Notes on the defence of Irish Country Houses.* He recommended that owners be discreet and carry out the works 'without offence to or distrust of respectable neighbours'. He noted that respectable Nationalists would be

---

[48] *Waterford Standard*, 3 February 1886.
[49] *The Pictorial World*, 11 February 1886.
[50] *Nottingham Express*, 21 February 1891.

powerless to protect their Unionist neighbours from the 'secret societies or by the rowdy or criminal elements'. It was noted that the best land was associated with country house demesnes. The author noted the 'greed for land, which, with the help of boycotting and cattle-driving, has been fostered by the present Government, and stimulated by...the low prices at which untenanted land is purchased and resold by Public Departments'. He admitted that the ordinary country house was not capable of being defended in the military sense without major alterations which would be impracticable.

> For convenience, a normal country house will be assumed to contain about sixteen rooms, say twenty-four windows, to be two or three stories high, with three doors. Even with some defensive preparation a house of this kind could not be held against the assault of fifty resolute men by less than six defenders...expert in the use of all firearms...

He felt the defenders required four shot guns, three magazine rifles, six revolvers, twenty hand grenades, searchlights and flares. He suggested six forms of attack by the assailants: treachery, stratagem, sniping, incendiarism, explosion, and famine. The second example could consist of the following scenario: 'Say that by day when some of the defenders are abroad, a 'piano-tuner' arrives and is admitted, while his confederates are in ambush close by. If he be not searched, he may disable the watchman, and engage any other defenders who may be indoors, while the house is rushed'. He recommended that ladders should not be left lying around, and heavy library books would be good for barricading windows. Houses whose owners were under particular threat should be garrisoned by a corporal and three privates.[51]

McCarthy[52] notes that Waterford city in 1912 consisted of various groups:

> At one end of the political spectrum stood the IRB, a small band of nationalists who were committed to the physical force ideal. At the other was the unionist community, predominantly but not completely Protestant, who dreaded the prospect of home rule... Socially there was an equally large divide between the landed aristocracy and the inhabitants of the slums of the city.

The main unionist spokesmen in Waterford city were the Church of Ireland bishop, Henry O'Hara, and Sir William Goff of Glenville. They attended the meeting of Munster unionists in Cork in April 1912. Amongst the speakers was the Duke of Devonshire. Goff planned a similar meeting for Waterford city but was refused permission to use the City Hall. He held the meeting instead at his residence, Glenville, on 13 June 1912. The *Waterford News* claimed that most of those in attendance were 'from the furthest reaches of the county.' The meeting and the signing of the Solemn League and Covenant at Christ Church Cathedral Waterford, were, according to McCarthy, 'the highpoints of unionist resistance in Waterford.'

---

[51] George O'Callaghan-Westropp, *Notes on the Defence of Irish Country Houses*, 1912. I would like to thank Brian Fitzelle for allowing me access to this very rare publication.
[52] McCarthy, op-cit.p.16.

The House of Ussher

E mily Horsley Jebb (1872-1935) was born at The Lyth, Ellesmere, Shropshire, in 1872. She was the eldest of six children. Her parents were 'Anglican Conservatives who instilled a strong social conscience and commitment to public service in their children'.[53] Emily was educated at home and spent a short time in Dresden studying German and art. Her sisters Eglantyne and Dorothy were founders of Save The Children, and her other sister Louisa founded the Women's Land Army during WWI. Dorothy married Charles Roden Buxton, who was at Cappagh in 1922 and took a series of photographs of the IRA in occupation of the house and of the burned-out RIC barracks.[54]

Emily married Beverly Grant Ussher (1867-1956), Inspector of Schools in England.[55] His family's estate was at Cappagh, County Waterford. Their only child, Percival Arland Ussher, was born in Battersea in 1899. They lived in England for the next fifteen years. When Beverly retired in 1914, he returned to Ireland to the family estate at Cappagh.

Beverly became involved in local politics and farming. Emily joined The United Irishwomen Association and hosted industrial

---

[53] Clare Mulley, *The Woman who Saved the Children, A Biography of Eglantyne Jebb: Founder of Save The Children* (London, 2019), p.9.

[54] Charles Roden Buxton (1875-1942). Humanitarian and politician who married Dorothy Jebb in 1904.

[55] *The Cambrian*, 21 October 1898. The paper notes they were married on 15 October at the Quinta Church, Bronygarth.

shows at Cappagh. In 1915 the Irish War Hospital Supply Depot established its headquarters in Dublin.[56] A series of work depots were also established around the country, a number of which were based in country houses. These were mainly run by Anglo-Irish ladies who oversaw the production of Sphagnum moss dressings, shirts, and other item for soldiers on the front. Emily established a depot at Cappagh House where the participants consisted of 'farmers and the cottagers class'. She invited the local gentry to take part, but they all declined. Captain Umfreville and his wife were living in Old Cappagh House within the demesne, and he was suffering from rheumatic fever. Emily invited him to move into the main house to recuperate but he declined her offer on the grounds that he could not share a house with farmer's daughters. However, he did have a change of heart and moved in. Every Wednesday Emily was given the dining room for her work party. Mrs Umfreville held a rival event (tea party) in the drawing room, which had a piano. Emily's group would sing 'The Wearing of the Green' when Mrs Umfreville began her musical soiree. After work Kate Cullinane read the tea leaves for Emily and her group. They produced 900 'swabs' for the war effort.[57]

In August 1918 Emily, assisted by her sister Eglantyne, opened the Cappagh Co-operative Society store which had 170 members.[58] The Jebbs had been involved with the co-operative movement in England.

On settling into Cappagh Emily described the atmosphere as 'electric. Whispers told of arms being smuggled into Ireland,

---

[56] Susan Schreibman, Monika Barget, 'Irish Women's wartime networks: care work and female agency on the first world war home front', *Women's History review* www.tandfonline.com/journals/rwhr20 [Accessed 11/07/2022.
[57] Emily Ussher, pp.7-8.
[58] *Dungarvan Observer*, 15 June 1918.

north and in anticipation of Home Rule.' She noted that General Richardson, of the Grange Volunteers, was busy organising a unionist army. The agent at Cappagh, Colonel Kirkwood,[59] would be first in command, and Colonel Umfreville[60], who lived in Old Cappagh House, would be his second. Emily noted that the three of them were holding regular meetings of the unionist gentry at Old Cappagh House, to which she and her husband were never invited. She states that they were 'known to be Liberals and that was enough'. Old Cappagh was the original Ussher house built in the 18th century which was situated below the later 19th-century house. The Usshers advertised it for sale in September 1920.[61] The sale advert noted that it would be suitable for 'Hunting men, dairy, tillage farmers and others'. The residence 'is approached through a lovely avenue with imposing gate entrance and lodge'. The house comprised of a 'Fine' entrance hall, three reception rooms, eight bedrooms, kitchen, pantries, bathroom, and servant's rooms. The courtyard buildings contained a laundry, garage/coach house, calf house, and could accommodate seven horses and eighteen cows. Included in the sale were the Kennell farm of 30 acres, and lands and cottages at Killieshal where there was a 'valuable plantation' of Larch, Scotch Fir, and Beech.

Emily recalled being invited to a tennis party by the Collisons (at Rockfield House, Cappagh) at which none of the other guests would speak to her. The few comments she made were 'received with hostile silence'. A friend of hers, Mildred Dobbs of Camphire

---

[59] Col. S W Kirkwood, agent to the trustees of the Villiers-Stuart estate at Dromana,1908-1921.Until September 1920 Kirkwood lived at Bleach House, Villierstown when he advertised the sale of his belongings in the *Irish Examiner* on 25 September as he was 'changing his residence'.

[60] Possibly Captain Harry Kirwan Umfreville (1873-1956) who married Enid, daughter of Capt. D'Olier George of Cahore House Co Wexford in 1902.

[61] *Irish Examiner*, 25 September 1920.

House, said to her: 'It is a pity that you publish your opinions; you lose all the influence you might have.' She also informed Emily that it was commonly believed that she and her husband Beverly were government spies sent over by Asquith to report on the Irish situation.

Emily is often critical of her fellow gentry in west Waterford. She was involved in mounting an annual industrial show at Cappagh but received little or no financial support from local gentry. A friend of Emily's, Mrs Walsh of Ballylemon Lodge,[62] commented that they should 'wave a farewell to them all from our shores and never miss them after'. However, Emily later regretted the remark:

> We little dreamt we would live to see them all go and to wish them all back. Every empty house had left the country less able to pay its way and stands desolate in its own little puddle of unemployment. In those days so many, oh so many, seemed to be just unsympathetic pleasure-seeking parasites, and when they began to boast of maintaining their old ascendancy by force, it became only natural to reply in similar accents.

Mildred Dobbs, a member of the unionist gentry who lived at Camphire House, also commented on the situation. She had her own theories on the cause of the development of an 'anti-British' sentiment in the country. According to her there were two actions initiated by Augustine Birrell, the Chief Secretary, which inflamed the situation. The first was the refusal to raise the salaries of National School teachers and the other was the removal of the

---

[62] Kathleen Mary Walsh, widow of John Joseph Walsh M.D. of Suirville, Co Tipperary who died in 1894. She was living in Ballylemon Lodge by 1895. www.willcalendars.nationallibrary.ie

Arms Act. In relation to the teachers, she says they turned to Sinn Féin and 'before long every school was being taught that 'England was the enemy'. She observed that there was no real demand from home rule supporters to have the Arms Act removed: 'There is possibly no record of how many arms were imported into the south, but they were on sale at every fair immediately the restrictions were taken off and reports of bands of men drilling became common.'

She noted that this was long before the formation of the Ulster Volunteers, and the fact that the Liberals intended to pass the Home Rule Bill without an election encouraged unionist resistance: 'The actual destruction of property and assaults on persons by the Suffragettes were numerous and ever-increasing, while the Ulster Organisation acted as an outlet to a people who were ever ready to stand firmly on their rights, who were also genuinely afraid of coming under Popish rule.'

In 1913 she says that few people were involved in politics in the Lismore area. Sir George Richardson,[63] a retired Indian army lieutenant-general, became commander in chief of the Ulster Volunteer Force. He lived with his brother-in-law Colonel Charles Gordon at Tourtane House, near Lismore.[64] Mildred Dobbs states that Sir George, known as 'Jidge'. was popular with everyone and was elected to many local committees.

---

[63] Sir George Lloyd Reily Richardson (1847-1931), army officer and commander of the UVF. Retired from the army in 1908 and moved to Ireland. In July 1913, he was appointed general officer in command of the UVF when he moved from Lismore to Belfast.

[64] Colonel John Charles Frederick Gordon, J.P. (b.1894), married Grace Hay. Appointed Commissioner of the Peace, Co Waterford in 1912.

...we...were electrified, one day, to see that Sir George had been the guest of Sir Edward Carson and had attended a big review. The following afternoon, I happened to be cycling past Lismore when who should walk out of the station but Sir George. I jumped off and exclaimed 'Well, what do you think of the North?' As he shook hands, he said fervently: 'Splendid fellows! I've at last seen people who may save the Empire and I've promised to help them.

Sir George's wife came to tea at Camphire some weeks later and said that her husband's letters to her were being opened. Police protection had to be provided at Tourtane House. Dobbs noted that Sir George returned to Lismore at weekends, 'but finally, as feelings rose high, it was thought best for Lady Richardson to join him in Belfast.' They never returned to Lismore.

There was a fear amongst local unionists about what might happen if Home Rule was passed. Mildred Dobbs commented that one day her father returned from a meeting of the Unionist Defence Committee and told her that it had been agreed to 'warn all Protestants to be ready to fly for shelter to Lismore Castle if a row began, and that, though shotguns would be of great use, it was absolutely necessary to obtain a few Winchesters to ensure the defence; he added that he had been deputised to procure them...' Her father was then over seventy and had a bad heart so he and his wife decided that Mildred should travel to England to obtain the guns.

Mildred began planning for her mission. She arranged with an English friend to order the guns. She made a false bottom to fit in her split-cane cabin-trunk. She covered the false bottom with linen to match that already lining the trunk. On arrival in London, she stayed with her aunt and then with her sister, 'both ardent suffragettes'. She visited the gunsmith and he showed her how to take apart and put the four rifles back together. She was given boxes of ammunition which weighed about two stone.

While in London she went to the House of Commons and listened to speeches from Asquith, Lloyd George, Winston Churchill, and John Redmond. She heard Edward Carson appeal to the government to come to terms which would not force Ulster to leave the Empire.

Mildred began to plan for her return journey to Ireland and how to smuggle the guns and ammunition without being noticed:

> The next day I spent in making long tubes of linen stitched on to the front and sides of my breeches, and into these I pushed cartridges one by one till I had stowed away rather more than half. I then fixed strong tape at certain points in my trunk my means of screws and secured the four Winchester stocks and barrels by tying them down and wedging them so that they could not possibly move. I finished the job by screwing down the false bottom...

She noted that at that point although the importation of arms was forbidden the authorities were not doing any detailed searches of passenger luggage. However, some days later she learned that the government had ordered that all passenger luggage be searched for arms and if any were found, the result would be prison. On the morning of her departure, she had to come up with a way to conceal the remainder of the ammunition. She pushed the cartridges into the lining of her coat and the remaining box of fifty cartridges she tied up in handkerchiefs and covered in white paper and string to make it look like a pack of sandwiches. On arrival at Rosslare, she had to leave the boat without arousing suspicion:

I boldly threw the coat over my left arm and holding my sandwiches in that hand and my handbag in the right, I proceeded down the gangway...a policeman stood at the end of the gangway with two plain-clothes men at each side, who halted the passengers with the question: 'Are you carrying any ammunition?' and something about rifles...but though they asked the lady in front of me and the man behind me, they let me pass...

Mildred's trunk with the rifles also got through and by that evening they were safely delivered to Lismore Castle.

In answer to the establishment of the Ulster Volunteer Force a meeting was held in Dublin on 25 November 1913 at which the Irish Volunteers were established. Early in 1914 groups were formed around the country. On 22 April 1914, a meeting was convened at the Town Hall in Dungarvan. The chairman was J.A. Lynch, the owner of the *Dungarvan Observer* newspaper. The meeting was addressed by The O'Rahilly and Eoin Mac'Neill. Beverly Ussher of Cappagh House attended with his son Percy, and Emily Ussher recorded the event in her memoir:

> Beverly evoked great applause by declaring 'There is at least one Protestant in this room.' Percy, aged 13, in native costume, his young face all aglow, I was told, sat on the platform. On his return he declared with solemn emphasis 'Mother I am a Volunteer.' He attended drill meetings during his Easter holidays, and later on I found myself painting a large wooden target, and Sunday after Sunday we superintended shooting in a gravel pit with two rifles...

In May 1914, a volunteer rally was held at Cappagh attended by five hundred people.

Around this time the elderly Trant sisters lived in Derriheen House, Cappoquin. The family seat was at Dovea House in Co Tipperary. Michael Vincent O'Donoghue recalled an event at Derriheen in 1914. He described the Trants as 'one of the most tyrannical rack-renting Cromwellian planter families in all Tipperary'. He learned that the District Inspector of the RIC used to pay occasional visits to the Trants at Derriheen. In 1914 O'Donoghue along with a friend named Kenny decided to approach the house through a wooded area to pick a good vantage point to shoot the RIC Inspector. O'Donoghue had a Colt 45 with him and after a while he was bored and decided to put a paper target on a tree and fire at it. He then handed the gun to his friend who missed the target. 'He was about to shoot again when I saw the figure of a woman (one of the Misses Trant) about 60 yards away behind the target and walking in our direction, looking curiously all round. Whether she had heard the shots or seen us I could not say. We did not wait to find out'.[65]

On 4 August 1914 Britain declared war on Germany. While home on leave in August 1914 Sir John Keane of Cappoquin gave a public talk on the war. Emily Ussher felt strongly that Irishmen who were fighting in the war were not getting the recognition they deserved. In the spring of 1916, she began a series of public talks around the county, using magic lantern slides, promoting awareness of Irish soldiers at the Front.

> Although mine were not recruiting lectures I had to take refuge in barns and creameries. I was once again surprised that the gentry did not offer so much as a coach house. I got crowded audiences in all the remotest places including Coolnasmear...When I went to Dungarvan where I secured a room in the courthouse, I asked the resident magistrate

---

[65] BMH WS 1741

to put me up...I got a butcher who afterwards became a prominent Sinn Feiner (Michael Brennock) to stand at the door and take the entrance pennies.

Gathering Arms – 'rather ancient and not of much use'

Chapter 5

Witness Statements are a useful source of information concerning raids on country houses for arms. The Bureau of Military History was established in 1947 to 'assemble and co-ordinate material to form the basis for the compilation of the history of the movement for Independence from the formation of the Irish Volunteers on 25 November 1913 to the 11 July 1921'.

Many Waterford houses were raided for arms by volunteers. Michael Vincent O'Donoughue of Lismore commented on raids in the area:

> During the autumn and winter of 1917, the local Volunteer Company in the Cappoquin area did a little bit of searching for weapons. A few big houses in the locality were quietly ransacked at night and some guns and ammunition got. A few others owned by the 'gentry' were raided by masked Volunteers and more stuff was got. These operations were carried out by the officers of the company with the aid of a few men with intimate local knowledge and the inside co-operation of a servant on occasion. Though upwards of a dozen big houses were raided, only one was reported to the R.I.C. and they did no more than make a few cursory inquiries. It looked as if the people raided were

sympathetic, or, at least, wished not to be involved in any way. They kept silent.[66]

It is interesting to note his observation that the owners cooperated and were 'sympathetic.' This seems unlikely and was a naive statement to make; it would probably be more correct to say that they cooperated out of fear.

Tom Kelleher[67] of Cappoquin Company Irish Volunteers recalled raids in the Cappoquin area in 1918:

> Voluntary handing up of shot guns, plus the raids we carried out on loyalist's houses, brought our stock of shot guns up to 32 by the end of 1918. I was one of a small party which raided Villiers-Stuarts of Richmond (near Cappoquin) at the end of this year, where we got two old type game rifles and some small amount of assorted ammunition.

Often the raids yielded very old firearms as James Prendergast[68] of Carriglea recalled:

> In 1919, we began to become more active. Raids for shotguns were made on private houses, mostly those of the so-called gentry class... These raids were carried out at night by about half a dozen men or so. We were successful in getting hold of some guns, some of which were rather ancient and not of much use.

In January 1919 T.F. Wyley, secretary of the Waterford Sinn Féin Executive, issued a directive to Joseph Widger, Albion House, Tramore, Master of the East Waterford Fox Hounds, and to J. R. Russell, Seafield House, Bunmahon, Master of the 'Waterfords': 'it

---

[66]BMH WS 1741
[67]BMH WS 758
[68]BMH WS 1655

was decided that, pending the release of the Irish political prisoners, no hunting will be allowed within the above districts'. The areas listed include Ballygunner, Duagh, Butlerstown, Kilculliheen, Skibbereen and Waterford city. An anonymous commentator observed that 'in most cases the hunting fraternity chuckle over the imprisonment of our leaders and laugh and scorn at the idea of Ireland claiming its independence'.[69]

Emily Ussher recalled a raid on Cappagh some time in 1919:

> I heard leaves rustling outside and when I wet to the window, eight or nine masked men jumped out from under the weeping elm on the terrace. I said, 'what do you want?', 'Arums, arums!' they replied. We had not even our old sporting gun in the house and said so. They were disposed to be gruff if not rough and I told them there was no need – had I not taught them all to shoot in the old days? After some parleying they insisted on coming into the house and searching. They all followed each other into the cupboard under the stairs with their revolvers full cock on. If one had gone off, they would all have been shot in a heap.[70]

Patrick Joseph Whelan recalled a raid on the Hudson residence at Helvick in 1918. One of the servant girls told him that if he saw the owner's yacht out in the bay it would be safe to enter the house and she would show him where the guns were. On a summer evening at around 7 p.m. they saw the yacht and decided this was the opportunity to raid the house. He was accompanied by Dan Terry, and they were both armed with revolvers:

> We were turning in to the door of the Sheriff's house when the son and mother came out. I gave them 'hands up' and told them to go back inside. I asked who was in the house and the son said his father, a bank manager named Going,

---

69 *Waterford News*, 31 January 1919.
70 Emily Ussher, p.34.

and a military officer were there. When the son went inside with his hands up, the others laughed...thinking he was joking; we followed and told them to put their hands up and face the wall. I said that the house was completely surrounded, and, if they didn't obey orders, it would be just too bad for them. I told Dan Terry to keep them covered and to shoot if they took down their hands. I next called Mr Hudson [son] aside and asked where the arms were. He said they had all been sent to Dublin Castle for safety. There was a quantity of ammunition on the table which I took...I told the party not to leave the house for five minutes, but, as we left, I looked around and saw them at the door. I fired a shot over their heads, at which they hastily withdrew.[71]

The Sleady Company IRA raided local hunting lodges between 1918 and 1920. E.N. Power's lodge at Sleady Castle and the Chearnley family lodge at Lackendarra were raided by Jack Whelan, Lar Condon, Thomas Cowmy, Daniel McGrath, Pax Whelan, and others.[72]

In early February 1920 a shocking incident took place at Parkswood House near Passage East which was reported in the press. It was then the residence of retired doctor, Richard Anderson Lambert. The 1911 census described it as a first-class house with nine rooms and twelve windows on the front façade. It was reported that around midnight explosives were placed against the front of the house followed by loud explosions. 'Luckily the occupants, consisting of Dr. Lambert and his housekeeper, escaped without injury, but the front windows were completely shattered. Robbery is the supposed motive for the attack.'[73] The doctor was described as of a 'retiring and

---

[71] BMH WS 1231

[72] Military Activities of Sleady Company, 1 April 1918 to 31 March 1920. Waterford County Museum, 1999-19-84.

[73] *Munster Express*, 7 February 1920.

unassuming disposition' and the incident caused much upset in the area. The police and locals were at a loss to explain why he was targeted. If it was a planned robbery, it was an extreme way to go about it. It would appear that there was another motive but whether it was a grudge against the owner, or he refused to hand over any guns in the house is a matter for conjecture.

In April 1920 the homes of Arthur Hunt at Rockmount, Charles Langley of Tay Lodge and John Hobbs of Briska House (all in the Comeragh district) were raided while the owners were attending service at the Church of Ireland in Comeragh. The raiders obtained 'some guns and quantities of ammunition'.[74] The Hobbs family were Protestant farmers and lived in a modest two-story farmhouse. John V. Hobbs in a recent article recounted events at Briska during the revolutionary period. In one of the raids on the house (possibly that referred to in the above article) a gun was taken and camera equipment:

> Later my grandmother went to Pat Keating (Captain of the Kilrossanty Company IRA) who was working at Durrow Creamery and appealed for the return of these items. Following his intervention some of the items were brought back to Briska but not all found their correct home. If my grandfather needed a gun to shoot a fox, he was able to get a loan of it from the IRA. I believe Mikey Browne acted as the go-between.
> A number of times the IRA billeted some of their troops at our house. They slept on mattresses in the harness room which had a wooden floor. My grandparents were not sympathetic towards the IRA but must have learned fast to protect themselves...On one occasion word came through to our house that a party of twelve IRA men were coming for dinner. As there were already eight to ten people to be fed this was a big order. Somehow with the help of Hannah Coffey, who worked for my grandmother, the men got

---

[74] *Waterford News & Star* 23 April 1920.

fed...[75]

In November 1923 John Hobbs's compensation claim was heard at Waterford court and E A Ryan acted on behalf of the state. The Hobbs family claimed £16.15.0 for teas supplied to republicans and for the use of a horse. Ryan asserted that tea for a half dozen men should have only cost a few pence. Mrs Hobbs said she supplied tea, jams, and meats for dinner. Ryan said a pig's head would have sufficed. She replied that she gave them cold meats and milk pudding. Ryan claimed that they were the only farmers in the county to make such a claim and that many farmers had to feed republicans because they had no choice but did not pursue the matter of compensation. Mrs Hobbs insisted that they had a legitimate claim and the judge awarded £5. It is difficult to know whether Ryan was being particularly hard on the family because they were Protestant and whether he often allowed his Republican sympathies influence his cases.[76]

On 3 July 1920 Emily Ussher noted in her diary that the: 'Volunteers visit Dromana and promise it shall be respected'. Presumably this meant the house would not be burned or damaged.
Mount Congreve house in Kilmeaden was raided on 16 July 1920 and the incident was reported in the *Irish Examiner*:

> In the early hours of this morning a raid for arms occurred at Mount Congreve...Between 50 and 100 men participated...An entrance to the mansion was affected through the windows. The masked men demanded the servants surrender of any arms...Two sporting guns were seized, and a small quantity of ammunition. Motor cars were heard going along the avenue after the raid, during

---

[75] *Decies*, journal of the Waterford Historical & Archaeological Society No 76. 2020, John V. Hobbs, 'The Troubles in Mid-Waterford: A Family Perspective', pp 175- 183.
[76] *Waterford News & Star*, 9 November 1923.

which the mansion was entirely surrounded by the raiders. [77]

William Keane, Vice Commandant of the East Waterford Brigade IRA, recalled a raid on Mount Congreve which took place in August 1920 in his witness statement. It is unclear if this is the same raid which took place on 16 July, and he was confused about the date:

> I went with about 12 of the Dunhill Volunteers under Jimmy Power of Ballycraddock to raid for arms at Major Congreve's house...The raid took place at about 10 or 11p.m. The Dunhill men were armed with shotguns. I carried a revolver. When we knocked at the door of the house, we were answered from the inside by Major Congreve who point blank refused to admit us. We then told him that if he wasn't going to admit us peaceably, we would have to force our way in. He replied that he would shoot without hesitation...On the instructions of the officer in charge, Jimmy Power, four large windows were shattered with shotguns and the boys poured into the house through the broken windows. The O/C held up Mr Congreve while I and four others went upstairs to search for arms which a friendly servant had previously told us were up there. In the wardrobe we discovered the shotguns (silver-mounted) and some cartridges...[78]

While the search was progressing Jimmy Power explained to the major the reason for the raid was to prevent the guns falling into the hands of the British military. The major said that he would not report the raid if they agreed to return the guns 'when all the trouble was over' as they were valuable and of sentimental value him. According to Keane Jimmy Power returned the guns in perfect condition after the Civil War.

---

[77] *Irish Examiner,* 17 July 1920.
[78] BMH WS 1023

39

William Keane,[79] recalled raids on several other houses in August 1920. One of these was at Coolfin House, Portlaw, then occupied by Rev William Westropp Flemyng[80] and his family:

> Each of us was armed with a loaded revolver. Approaching the house, we saw Shanahan standing at a gate in front of the building...we walked up to him and asked if he had any of the calves for sale. As he made to reply, I whipped out my revolver and gave him 'hands up', adding: 'and be quick about it or I'll let you have it'. He immediately raised his hands and I instructed Duignan to tie him up with a rope I had brought with me. I then...went into the house through the open door. There were three ladies inside whom I locked in a dining room. I went upstairs to search for the rifle and, on looking into a wardrobe, I found concealed up the two legs of a trousers two Lee Enfield rifles in perfect condition. I also found two bandoliers loaded with ammunition and a pair of field glasses. I...went outside and warned Shanahan not to leave his position for 20 minutes or I'd shoot him dead from the road. We...got on our bikes and took the back roads to Waterford, where I handed over the capture to...D.J. Walsh.

Some days later Keane and others raided Ballinamona House (about four miles from Waterford), the home of Major Carew.[81] Also in the group was Thomas Brennan,[82] Lieutenant 'D' Company, 4th Battalion, East Waterford Brigade, who recalled the details:

---

[79] BMH WS 1023

[80] He was Canon and Precentor of Waterford Cathedral and rector for 30 years of the united parishes of Clonegam, Guilcagh and Mothel. He was a well-known plant collector. He died in 1921.

[81] Capt. Robert John Henry Carew, M.C., D.L., J.P. (1888-1982) of Ballinamona Park.

[82] BMH WS 1104

The raid took place at night and the party was in charge of Michael O'Neill, captain of D/Company. Others who took part were Wm. Winters, Miles Fanning, Sean Brett, Michael McGrath, Jimmy McGrath and myself. A few of the men were armed with shotguns and revolvers. I did not enter the house that night as I was well known to many of the staff. A few shotguns and a pair of binoculars were taken from Major Carew. He offered no opposition. The same night the same party raided the house of major Carew's uncle, Commander Carew[83] of Ballindud, a few miles away, but we were unsuccessful in obtaining any arms.

In the early part of the War of Independence there was a concerted effort by the IRA to burn RIC barracks throughout the country. In county Waterford most of the RIC barracks were burned or damaged.[84] At Kill the local landlord Colonel Power O'Shee of Gardenmorris was the owner of the building so he had it dismantled before it could be burned, but he obtained permission first from local Sinn Fein leaders.[85]

It was inevitable that Cappagh Barrack would be burned. The sergeant, Richard Johnson, his wife Esther Anne, and their children lived there.[86] The Usshers had offered them accommodation at Cappagh knowing the possibility of an attack on the barrack. However, the inevitable happened and men arrived to do the deed: 'They told Mrs Johnson in answer to her

---

[83] Lieut Commander Richard Clayton Carew (1861-1937), magistrate.
[84] Brendan Byrne, 'Law, Order and the RIC in Waterford 1920-21: A Chronology', pp.117-126.*Decies* 55 1999.
[85] *Waterford News* 1 October 1920.
[86] WCCA WCC/GWA288. 'Waterford County Council, Notices of claims for compensation for criminal injuries, 21/2/1920-18/7/1946'. On 7 January 1920 Sergeant Johnson submitted a claim to Waterford Co Council for the burning of furniture and other items to the value of £190.16.0.

entreaties, that they would spare her things...the raiders did their work quickly and efficiently'. Esther recalled that 'at about half past two in the morning a knock came to the door, and on asking who was there, she was told to get up, as the house was going to be burned. She asked if there was any chance of saving it but was told there was not'. She and her husband claimed £500 for furniture and 'consequential damage'. They were awarded £180.[87]

Mrs Johnson was then forced to accept the Usshers' offer of accommodation. Mrs Johnson decided she would have to pull herself together after the shock of the burning and prepare herself to greet her sympathetic neighbours who were sure to call. However, Emily commented: *'It is incredible that during the three months Mrs Johnson lived with us none of the Protestant neighbours came to see her'.* Beverly Ussher submitted a claim to the Co Council of £1068.19.6 for the burning of the barrack.[88]

Taking in Mrs Johnson was to have serious consequences for the Usshers. Whether they were aware of this at first is unclear. Inevitably the anonymous threatening letter was delivered to Cappagh: *'Unless we got rid of Mrs Johnson within three days, worse would befall. We appealed to Father Gleeson P.P...who assured us he possessed no influence in the matter...I wrote a letter to Brennock the butcher'.*

She was told later that the letter had been intercepted by the Republican censor and he did not actually see it until weeks later. She also wrote a letter to her son Percy informing him of the threat.

---

[87] *Waterford News,* 8 October 1920.
[88] WCCA WCC/GWA288

42

In preparation for the inevitable torching of Cappagh Beverly removed jewelry, silverware, and family papers to the bank in Dungarvan. Emily tried to find a home for her china collection as recalled by her son:

> At the time of which I write, we, in common with all our 'country neighbours' – were awaiting nightly a visit from the gentlemen of the petrol-can and the match box. My mother, wishing to preserve from the flames a collection of Chinese bric-a-brac (some of that 'loot from Pekin during the boxer Rising', which has furnished so many English and Irish country-houses'), sought out...a musty and unvisited museum in our county-town. Having discovered the porter – himself seemingly as old and forgotten as any exhibit in the place – she asked him for the addresses of some of the museum committee members, to whom she could hand over the curios. He replied by four laconic and terrible sentences, delivered in a tone of withering resignation worthy of a Stoic philosopher. 'They are all dead. They have all gone to another world. It may be a better one. *It cannot possibly be any worse'.*[89]

Emily continues the story:

> Mary Gardiner, her nerves already thoroughly upset, was crying gallons...that I shut her up in my bedroom. I took the two big sacred pictures [The Madonna] from Italy (copies after Raphael) to the two Catholic churches at Ballinameela and Modeligo.

---

[89] Arland Ussher, *The Face and Mind of Ireland* (London, 1949), pp 54-55.

Then at 2 a.m. the front doorbell pealed! It is impossible to describe the effect of that sound in the dead stillness of the night...I rushed to the hall door...and opened the bolt. There stood three young men and I could see at once how pleasant were their faces...'We have to apologise for disturbing you at this hour' they said, but we have received a special dispatch from our Minister for Defence to say we must protect you. It is no part of our programme to wage war on women and children, they added proudly. 'And the sergeant is a special friend of mine, so it is a great pleasure,' said the captain.

You had better come in and sit down while I fetch him [husband who was asleep] I suggested. So, they sat down on the old Spanish sofa in the hall, and I prepared to go upstairs to wake Beverly.

Beverly then went down to meet their protectors.

By the time I got to them they were all laughing together, loud enough to wake the whole house, and declaring that they would make Beverly their first High Sheriff in the Sinn Fein Republic!

They informed the Usshers that they intended to send two or three men every night to guard the house. Emily used to leave cigarettes out for them.

How was it that their potential destroyers became their protectors? It was all thanks to their son Percy who tracked down the Waterford representative in the Dáil, Cathal Brugha, appealing to him to intervene and protect the Johnsons and prevent the burning of Cappagh. Brugha was familiar with county Waterford and learned his Munster Irish there. He was elected Sinn Féin MP for Co Waterford in 1918 and was Minister for

Defence from 1919-1922. Percy recalled the circumstances of his meeting with Brugha:

> After the demolition of the R.I.C. barrack in my district, the wife and children of the police-sergeant had been offered by us a refuge in a part of our home...Then, after a few days, came an anonymous letter from some ruffian, giving us notice to eject these 'frinds of the inimy' or be prepared to take the consequences. I immediately sought out our local member of the republican 'Dail'...he was then 'on the run'...so that to find him was no very easy task. At last, however, I got the right directions...having heard my complaint, he at once promised the appropriate orders would be sent to the local volunteer command. From that day for many weeks, an armed guard turned up nightly to protect the wife and children of the R.I.C. sergeant – and ourselves, who were known to be out of sympathy with their movement. They refused all offers of convivial hospitality; they took the most serious view of their duties. Naturally the same men (though personally friendly) would, if commanded, have 'burned us out'; but, up till the Treaty at least, there was very little quite senseless burning.[90]

---

[90] Arland Ussher, *The Face and Mind of Ireland* (London, 1949), pp 40-41.

The Black and Tans

Chapter 6

In the summer of 1920 Emily decided to go to London to give a series of talks drawing attention to the 'atrocities' being committed in Ireland at the time by the Black and Tans. On her way to London, she met Gerald Villiers-Stuart of Richmond House, Cappoquin, who was also on his way there to speak on Irish events. She also met the daughter of the Coolnasmear schoolmaster.

Emily's talks (or drawing room meetings as she called them) were advertised as being by an 'Unknown Lady'. One of her talks was hosted by the Percival family and was attended by Lord Monteagle. However, she felt that her talks had little impact on her upper-class audience and decided to return home.

Gerald Villiers-Stuart (1869-1951) was an author and playwright. He and his American wife Maud Hutcheson lived at Richmond House, Cappoquin. He was a member of Waterford County Council from 1908-1918. During the first world war he served as captain in the Army Service Corps.[91] Villiers-Stuart wrote a letter to a Waterford paper in 1922 in which he made a proposal on how the Pro-Treaty and Anti-Treaty forces could run the country at a local level:

> My intention is to be non-political and entirely uncritical of the men and ideas which are ranged under the Pro-

---

[91] *Thom's Irish Who's Who* (Dublin, 1932), p.253.

Treaty and Anti-Treaty political banners...With the exception of a few areas the existing Government in Dublin and the workaday citizen in the country can only function through the sufferance of an armed force. Old, accumulated wealth is pouring out of Ireland – very little new wealth is being created. Why should not the Central Government through Conference and arrangement with its opposite, return to the County Governments some of the functions which have been centralized in Dublin and there been paralyzed. Their first duty would be a proper policing of the country by a non-political police, who would be responsible to the county and paid by the county.

The editor replied to this letter about decentralization in positive tones and made an interesting observation concerning the unionists of the county:

During the past six months of Ireland's ordeal the Unionists of Waterford have been much on men's thoughts. Many of them when relations between England and Ireland reached breaking point had perceived the uselessness of opposing the national will and abstained from taking any part in public affairs. Others, whilst adopting this attitude superficially, worked vigorously behind the scenes against the cause of Irish freedom...But with a few exceptions, Unionists maintained a pose not without dignity, considering the collapse of the foundations upon which their whole theory of life had been built up. We fancy Mr Gerald Villiers-Stuart would resent being called a Unionist. Yet he is among those who, owing to adherence to a traditional mode of life and allegiance to the Crown, could not take part in the Sinn Fein movement...The letter from him...contains an idea of government...the result of a genuine desire to uplift his native land. As a contribution from an Irish gentleman outside the Sinn Fein movement, evincing a real and sincere love of Ireland, this letter is of great value.[92]

Villiers-Stuart had a summer house at Helvick not far from John Hudson's house. It was situated on the edge of the cliff overlooking Helvick Cove. The house was raided by IRA men from Cork who took alcohol, food, clothes, and cooking utensils. They took over the property while engaged in a fight with Free State troops on 28 July 1922. He made a claim for these items.[93]

The Destruction of Ballycoe House

Ballycoe House was built by Richard Garde Hudson in the early 19th century. It was acquired in the early 1900s by the Dunlea family, who were Catholic and had a bakery business in Grattan Square, Dungarvan. The Dunleas were sympathetic to the republican cause and the house was targeted by British soldiers in an act of revenge for the Burgery Ambush. The ambush occurred on 18 March 1921 not far from Ballycoe House. An auxiliary policeman, Sidney Redman, and Sergeant Michael Hickey of the RIC were killed. The military decided that the Dunlea family had known about the planned ambush but had made no attempt to report it. The incident was reported in many Irish and British newspapers.

The *Freeman's Journal* of 28 March 1921 published a detailed report of what happened to the Dunlea residence:

> A large detachment of Crown forces left Dungarvan for the scene of the ambush, and on reaching Ballycoe House...they informed the occupants, Mrs Dunlea's two daughters that their house was going to be destroyed

---

[92] *Waterford News*, 1 May 1922.
[93] NAI FIN/COMP/2/23/263.

because they had not given notice of the ambush. The slates of the roof were hauled away, and the rafters left bare. The massive furniture of the house broken, including fine mahogany sideboards, pictures, religious and otherwise, silver teapots, silver candlesticks, chairs, mahogany tables, hall tables and chairs, and other valuable property. When the work of destruction was completed, a bomb was exploded in the kitchen. The young ladies were terrified. Mrs Dunlea was not at home at the time. The fine building was left a complete wreck, and was strewn with debris of broken furniture, glass, picture frames and carpets. Much sympathy has been extended to Mrs Dunlea, who has two sons, priests on the mission in Dublin.

Dungarvan photographer Edmond Keohan photographed the house shortly after and one of his pictures was published on the front page of the *Freeman's Journal* on 30 March 1921. He also recorded the damage to the house in his *Illustrated History of Dungarvan* published in 1924. Keohan states that not content with destroying the house and its contents they turned their attention to the exterior and the garden:

> The flowers and shrubs were cut down. Even the creeper on the front of the house they cut away. They smashed the hall door and the windows, and the adjoining conservatory...Then they entered the fruit garden...here they cut down the fruit trees and destroyed everything.

The military also painted slogans on the font of the house: 'Hickey and Redmond – Up the Buffs - Remember - God Save the King'.

Emily Ussher commented on the event in her memoir:

> I have fully described what happened to poor old Mrs Dunlea (her son was a Chaplain at the front), a retired bread merchant (who has been an invalid ever since) in 'The Trail of the Black & Tans' but with a difference. The destruction of Ballycoe House was performed by the

Regiment of the Buffs, whose officer really asked – 'What associations have we with you but those of hatred?'. I went to see the Dunleas directly I heard the news, knowing how fearful most people would be of calling on them for fear of seeming implicated. The old lady of course was not there but the two daughters showed me the roofless house, the wrecked rooms, the mutilated 'sacred pictures'. The whole thing was done on the morning of Good Friday.

I well remember the horror and dismay on every face at the Cappoquin tennis class when counter reprisals began to be undertaken by the IRA and the first country house perished in flames. They had not turned a hair over the fate of the Dunleas and others – but now![94]

In June 1921 the Information Officer of the East Waterford Brigade IRA contacted Michael Collins about the situation in the area. As a footnote to the letter, he noted that 'a Captain Bloomfield, a big Unionist, of this locality has left for S. Africa with his family – he was in mortal dread'. This refers to Captain Godfrey H. Bloomfield of Newpark House. He had been a major in the Bengal Artillery. When Newpark was destroyed by fire in 1932 he moved to Ballymena.[95]

The Trail of the Black and Tans

Emily decided to draw the public's attention to the activities of the Black and Tans in Ireland. She visited Molly Childers (wife of Erskine Childers), who had taken part in the Howth gun running in 1914. After discussing the matter, she suggested Emily write a

---

[94] Emily Ussher memoir, pp 39-40. The Ballycoe incident was used in her book *The Trail of the Black & Tans* and appears in chapter 18. The Rev John Dunlea was appointed chaplain to a Scottish regiment in November 1915. The *Dungarvan Observer* of March 1918 noted that he was home on leave having 'gone through the campaigns in Mesopotamia and Palestine'.

[95] Michael Collins Papers IE/MA/CP/5/2/12/ (xxxiii). *Waterford News*, 27 November 1946.

novel similar to *Uncle Tom's Cabin* [an influential anti-slavery work] and this inspired her to write a novel featuring the Black and Tans and their activities in the Dungarvan area.

One day she was writing the draft of the novel sitting outside Cappagh House when suddenly a party of Black and Tans arrived, so she threw the notebook into the bush next to where she was sitting.

Talbot Press agreed that they would publish her manuscript and she used a pseudonym – 'The Hurler on the Ditch'. Before the publishers could get the book out the Truce was declared on 11 July and the book was put on hold. The preface is dated 5 May 1921 and is signed 'One of Yourselves, Somewhere in Ireland'. The book was not published until October 1921. The dust jacket on the first edition showed the Cromwell sisters hurrying their brother Shaun away from their farmhouse. In the second edition published the following year the cover shows an evil looking group of Black and Tans shooting the tobacconist Mr Connolly. It was designed by Joseph Quin of Dublin.

The book did cause a stir. In November 1921 the RIC in Cork ordered its removal from bookshops. The agent for the Talbot Press submitted a report about the book's suppression: 'About ten days ago...a squad of new R.I.C. entered every shop in Cork displaying the new novel...and, taking offence apparently at some reference to themselves in it, ordered the immediate removal from the windows of all copies...they presented a list of so-called objectionable pages, and used very objectionable language'. Mrs Lenihan of Oliver Plunkett Street refused their request. She had a revolver pointed at her while one of the RIC men grabbed the book from the window display and 'flung it on the floor'.[96]

However, Emily had been given background material from a local RIC man who approved of the book. It received favorable reviews in *Studies*, *Irish Book Lover* and *Banba*. 'An old Nationalist auctioneer called it 'a magnificent production', and a Unionist family near us expressed themselves 'touched and delighted' – so how they are all pleased heaven knows'. Emily wanted the book to be widely available in England, but this did not happen. A publisher could not be found, and newspapers refused to review it. Emily was told that seven copies had been purchased by the Black and Tans at Dungarvan Barracks.

What is the main story of the novel?

It is set during the War of Independence and its theme is the manner in which the Black & Tans operated in Ireland. The principal characters are the Cromwell family: Shaun, Johanna, Nellie, and Mary whose parents are deceased. They live in a small farmhouse overlooking the town of 'Dunloe'. Dunloe is obviously based on Dungarvan: 'Dunloe mainly consisted of its vast central space'. Their house is raided, and Shaun realizes that if a gun hidden in the house is discovered they will be in trouble, so he decides to make a run for it and joins the IRA.

Other key characters include the Powers who live in an old house with a nice garden at Johnstown, not far from Dunloe. This is based on Ballycoe House located off the Waterford road a few miles from Dungarvan. Mrs Power's brother is a cider merchant

---

[96] Emily Ussher, pp. 74-75.

who lives in a house next to the brewery – obviously based on Thomas Power owner of Power's Brewery, Dungarvan.

Early in the novel the Cromwell's uncle, Pat O'Donnell visits the Powers: 'He stepped back to the garden gate and passed between the bright flower beds to where scarlet Japonica sprays hung over a porch...the place seemed an oasis of happy peace'.

These plants were no doubt based on real plants at Ballycoe seen by Emily. She also refers to the porch which did exist at Ballycoe but has been removed in recent renovations. Other real names used by Ussher include Canty Cross, and Mount Melleray Abbey which becomes Stella Montis Abbey.

In the novel the Powers' house at Johnstown is visited by the Black and Tans and destroyed in an orgy of destruction just as at Ballycoe:

> The Powers' gate hung open before him! The elderberry bush, beloved of wood pigeons lay felled to the ground beside it. The roof, with half its slates off, stared from behind the wall. The glass hung out of the windows or was caught in fragments on the blossoming japonica. The garden was trampled, and the fruit trees were snicked. Only the beehives, for obvious reasons, remained unmolested.
>
> Pat walked up the garden path feeling he could not be awake. It was all a terrible nightmare. A stuffed horned owl, which had stood on the piano, lay in the middle of the walk with its feathers pulled out, and the head chopped off. It was difficult to get through the hall, for the front door, the press, and the balustrades lay there in a splintered heap, mixed up with bits of linoleum. The drawing-room where he had chatted with Father Matt was knee-deep in

debris: the face was torn off the piano – the Sheraton desk displayed its internal shelves, but of the armchairs, the table, the pictures, the china, nothing seemed to remain that was distinguishable. Only the square-worked tapestry top of the stool, bereft of its legs, was whole. In the dining-room, too, the solid furniture was reduced to matchwood, and here no piece of it seemed to be more than a few inches in length, and the fragments were mixed up with those of floor coverings, curtains, glass, and with bent and twisted silver. On the walls, however, a fine engraving of the Dublin Parliament in Grattan's time was still to be seen, half-torn out from behind its glass, and Raphael's celebrated fresco representing Constantine's presentation to Pope Sylvestro, still hung there.

In the kitchen five pounds worth of flour, he reckoned, lay bursting out of a slashed sack among the remnants of a dish rack and of a clothes airer. Electro-plated dish covers, still shining, lay dented, with twisted handles, on the polished but doorless range. Upstairs the comfortable bedstead that he had slept upon had been made of such hard- resisting mahogany that some of it yet remained, but nothing else in the room so much as suggested its original shape or use, but for a simple exception! It was the first thing upon which his eyes had lighted that was whole, although the glass indeed was broken – the picture of the Saviour! But he was nevertheless so horrified he could scarce believe his eyes. it was covered with yellow stains, and bits of eggshell stuck in the corners of the frame! Until that moment he had hoped the oratory might have been spared. Alas! It bore the marks of cumulative vengeance. There was a large hole in the roof, and beneath it a deep litter of broken slates, pieces of wood, and purple cloth and white damask, among which lay two bent and broken candlesticks. He knelt on the desecrated spot under the blue sky which shone down on him through the roof and prayed for his friends amongst the ruins of the home into which they had received him only a week ago.

The novel then reveals that the destruction was a reprisal by the Black and Tans for an ambush in which some military had been killed. This echoes the real events of the Burgery Ambush which had taken place nearby in March 1921.

Because Emily did not use her real name on the novel and because of the poor reception it received in England it faded into obscurity and was forgotten about.

Emily Ussher of Cappagh House was also approached in December to lend their house for a dance to celebrate the Treaty:

> But the Dáil has not ratified it yet', I reminded them. 'Perhaps there will be no treaty'. But they would not hear of this at all. They were sure it would be all right! Would I not just lend the rooms for once and leave them to do the inviting? This, I found, was because they dreaded my democratic leanings and they only wanted officers! They also wanted to exclude the Bricky corps. Altogether, the path bristled with pitfalls, and I declined. These same boys who were so anxious to celebrate the Treaty, afterwards became the most determined anti-treatyites of the neighborhood.[97]

---

[97] Emily Ussher, pp 41-42.

'Nothing less than a Communist conspiracy' The Farm Labourers' Strike

Chapter 7

O n 26 August 1920 the ITGWU and the IFU held a conference at the Granville Hotel, Waterford, to fix pay rates for labourers.[98] Until the spring of 1922 employers were still paying this rate. Sir John Keane of Cappoquin was the chairman of the Waterford Farmers' Association. In February 1918 the ITGWU had opened its first county branch in Dungarvan, and others followed throughout the county.[99] By 1921 there was a fall in the price of agricultural produce and farmers wanted to reduce the wages of their labourers. In 1922 they wanted a 30% reduction which led to a strike by farm labourers. In West Waterford the farmers were represented by Sir John Keane, Beverley Ussher, Villiers-Stuart, Richard Musgrave, and the Duke of Devonshire. In January 1922 the Waterford Farmers' Association held their AGM and the chairman, Sir John Keane, called for a united front from farmers. Keane sought protection from the IRA commandant in Dungarvan and from the minister for lands and agriculture. On 20 May 1922 the landowners cut the weekly wages of their labourers from 38 to 30 shillings and several farmers did likewise. The WFA decided that they would not participate in the annual conference to set wage rates and the

[98] Emmet O'Connor, *A Labour History of Waterford* (Kildare, 1989), p.168.
[99] Emmet O'Connor, pp 143-144.

ITGWU response was to call a countrywide strike on 22 May. According to O'Connor 'On 23 May, large bodies of labourers, reinforced by a trainload of pickets from Dungarvan, marched into the west Waterford estates to impose economic blockades'.[100] However, many farmers in east Waterford agreed to pay the existing wage rate for a further year.

In her memoir Emily Ussher recalled in vivid detail how the strike affected their lives and those of their employees at Cappagh. The Usshers were under siege from the local labourers and their representatives, reinforced by trade union activists from Waterford.

The Co-op store at Cappagh had been established by the Usshers and a take-over was planned by local union members. In May 1922 Emily went to visit her mother in England and while there she received a telegraph: 'Return at once. Strike on'. On 27th May she returned to Cappagh and discovered that the Co-op store had been taken over on 23 May:

> That night a mob had assembled in our yard, in front of Clancy's house, and told him to join the Transport Union or clear. 'Shoot me', cried Clancy, throwing up his hands, 'but I won't join'. He cleared with Joe, the groom, and a street of crying children, who carried away the mother's photo, wrapped in newspaper – all that was left of her. He went to his brother's farm in Wexford. Joe, of the Motor Drivers' Union, went to his brother's farm near Cork. The gardener, Sexton, of the Gardeners' Union, refused to deliver up the key of the garden. He was told that if he would come out quietly, he would get strike pay. He came out...and was left to starve with his wife and five children.

---

[100] Emmet O'Connor, p.173.

John Power (ex-soldier and once R.U.U.'s 'man' or more truly friend) trainee under the Ministry of Labour, also left the garden, refusing to join the T.U. Mary Walsh, widow with six children, also refused to 'be made a slave of'. She was threatened with sticks by pickets, dragged from the laundry and promised money she never got.[101]

The remaining staff at Cappagh were Transport Union members: Tom Murray, ploughman, Willie Walsh, Tom Dalton, 'young Murray', Dan Dunne, yard man, John Hayden, Mr Mason, and received fifteen shillings strike pay. Pat Moloney, the carpenter, was not in the union.

Emily's husband, his sister, her son, and others staying at Cappagh tried without success to milk the cows, so they had to pay two of the picketers 35 shillings a week to do the milking. However, they were only given some of the milk and the men kept the rest. Initially two of the pickets, Luke Queally and John Tobin, gave them advice on various tasks. Pickets had been placed at the entrance to Cappagh House to prevent any food getting through.

Percy Arland Ussher later recalled the strike:

> We, the besieged, lived - not happily - for two months on tinned sardines, and other foodstuffs which could be imported by devices known to smugglers; for the pickets were chivalrous and did not press their investigations too far, especially in the case of the ladies. Sometimes friends on motor-bicycles would 'run' the blockade with parcels. In the evening, our bewildered proletariat, more than half full of drink, would gather in dark swarms on the roads, fatuously waving red flags...A sensational news

---

[101] Emily Ussher, p.49.

sheet...was handed round among the demonstrators, in which our funny little strike was represented as a sort of Western Front of the great World Revolution - One week I read the following alarming announcement:

DUKE-AND BARRON-RIDDEN AREA NOW BEING SLAMMED.

...Here therefore is the keystone of the employers' edifice. It should, of course, have been hewn away first, and it would have been if the men had been ready, with a resultant collapse of the whole edifice, but the rest of the structure has now been battered down, and the foundations will speedily be rooted out.[102]

On 5 June Emily and her husband Beverly returned to Cappagh from a meeting in Lismore. At the entrance gate there were thirty men picketing and they searched Beverly's trap and bag. Emily later decided to confront the picketers in the '40 acre' where they had moved:

'Boys', I began. 'You never hear but one side. For your own sakes I want you to hear ours. The life we have always led amongst you, since we came here eight years ago, must tell you what kind of people we are and that we are not your enemies, whatever you are now told. The first thing we did, without being asked, was to raise the wages of our men'.

I was dumfounded by the crass brutality I had encountered. But I still argued on whilst [union] Sec. Landers threw himself on his back on the ground to

---

[102] Arland Ussher, *The Face and Mind of Ireland* (London, 1945), pp 55-56. This refers to the Duke of Devonshire and the Barron family.

wallow more at ease, waggling his fat short legs and flapping his stick airily about...'Look at your substitute for King George! I cried'. 'Your little whiskey king whom you must all obey, and who, I sadly suspect, is drinking your money!'[103]

Landers and his followers moved on and she followed them calling Landers a 'boozing little Black & Tan' and gave him a slap. Before the situation got out of control her son Percy appeared and asked her to return to the house. He told the men that his father was their best employer but that they hadn't got the money to pay the wages which the union demanded. Emily had one last statement: 'We cannot pledge ourselves to give you money for a whole year which we have not got. If you insist, we must give up the place. There will be no more Usshers at Cappagh. You will have driven away your friends'.[104]

Emily was told by one of the IRA who later occupied Cappagh that Landers had drawn up a plan to take over Cappagh and have it divided up which he submitted to the IRA based in Dungarvan barracks. His plan was turned down. Emily's brother-in-law, Charlie Buxton, was staying at Cappagh. He was convinced that the real agenda of Landers and other union members was the acquisition of land and not wage increases. A local farmer's wife told her that the union members 'had all the big demesnes divided up and marked out between them'.[105]

The delivery of food to Cappagh was controlled by the union pickets and Emily recalled that they 'had been looking through the windows to see what we were eating and had sat up all night

---

[103] Emily Ussher, pp 51-52.
[104] Emily Ussher, p.53.
[105] Emily Ussher, p.56.

outside the back door, pelting it with pebbles, asking when we were going, and tried to frighten the little servants with a dummy wooden rifle'. John Power, who had worked for generations of the Ussher family, and lived a few fields away, brought them tinned fruit. One day the strikers warned him not to return. 'John slowly produced a large German jack knife and opened it in a most leisurely way. 'If there's any more about it,' he declared, 'I'll rip ye from the crowns of your heads to the sole of your feet'. The pickets fled!'[106]

At this time the Usshers had agreed to take in Catholic families from Belfast and were preparing the house for their arrival.[107] Emily had visited Mary McSwiney in Cork to discuss the offer of accommodation to the Belfast refugees: 'with her thin lips and peering little eyes – a most uncongenial personality...She gave it not a word of thanks or encouragement'.[108] The refugees never made it to Cappagh.

Mildred Dobbs of Camphire recalled that the strike didn't affect her as much. She states sarcastically that Camphire 'was too far from the public-house for picketing to be popular'. She did have great difficulty getting supplies from the usual shops. One day on her way to Cappoquin she encountered a group of strikers and they asked her if she was Miss Dobbs. They produced a document for her to sign which stated that she agreed to the terms and conditions set out in relation to the worker's pay. She refused and said she was paying fair wages and went to proceed with her bicycle. One of the strikers shouted: 'We'll come and pull you out of your house, you English woman'. She asked why they referred

---

[106] Emily Ussher, p.47.

[107] They were fleeing from a pogrom directed against them by northern unionists.

[108] Emily Ussher, p.59.

to her as an English woman and replied: 'I am not; I'm a descendant of Red Hugh O'Neill and you are not, so I have a much better right here than you'. They again asked her why she would not sign their document and she replied that she was a 'free Irishwoman and will do what I choose'.[109]

Emily visited Mrs Childers in Dublin in June. They discussed the attacks on country houses, but she described the 'uselessness' of these houses and 'would listen to nothing I had to say in their defence'.[110]

Edmund Waldo Becher J.P. of Castlefarm House, Lismore, was agent to the Duke of Devonshire. He had taken over from James Penrose in 1921. 'His residence was entered and people passing in and out were searched, while the water supply was cut off'.[111]

On the 7 June labourers took over Sir John Keane's estate at Cappoquin and declared a 'soviet', milking his prize herd and distributing the income from its sale. 'I heard that pickets had arrived at farm. I went up and found a dozen picket men there including Stapleton and Purcell. Told them that they had no authority to enter my place...They then went and by threats, but no actual violence, got out the garden men. T. Quinlan and J. Boland strongly protested.'[112] The following day he found fifty men, 'unwilling conscripts from Dromana,' at his milking parlour. The following day his tradesmen and sawmill workers were called out by the union. The *Irish Examiner* reported that 'Sir John Keane's pony and cart were commandeered by strikers and then

----

[109] Mildred Dobbs, *Sojourns of a Spinster*, 1933, p.114. Unpublished memoir. Private collection.
[110] Emily Ussher, p.44.
[111] *Freeman's Journal*, 9 June 1923.
[112] Keane Archive, Sir John Keane, diary entry, 7 June 1922.

milk taken and sold to the townspeople...a large force of the pickets marched...to Sir John Keane's sawmills and called out the workmen...proceeding to Tivoli House and ordering out the staff of carpenters and painters etc, employed there in decorating the place, where, it is stated, Sir John intends to take up residence next month'.[113] Fifteen of his cattle were taken and a few days later were found in the Clonmel area. Keane's men returned to work sometime in July 1922.

Emily Ussher noted the shortage of food at Cappagh due to the union picket and how some locals helped them: 'Another young farmer ran the gauntlet successfully with a leg of mutton, which he threw in at our door during the small hours.' On 20 June the commandant of Dungarvan barracks arrived at Cappagh with men and a Thompson machine gun declaring the picket illegal. Their presence did not deter the picketers. Emily noted that the picketers were discouraged by the news that 57 Dromana employees had returned to work: 'The Dromana men had originally been threatened with mob law if they did not come out but after ten days, they seemed to have either acquired arms or to have become conscious of the strength of their own numbers. At any rate, they bid defiance...and returned to work on June 19th'.[114] The Usshers submitted a claim to the council for £140 for damage to the garden, trees cut down and milk commandeered between May and November 1922.[115]

The workers on Sir John Keane's estate returned to work sometime in July.[116] According to O'Connor the strike collapsed

---

[113] *Irish Examiner,* 13 June 1922.
[114] Emily Ussher, p.59.
[115] WCCA WCC/GWA288
[116] Glascott Symes, p.33.

on 5 August and the men returned to work.[117] However, the situation remained unresolved at Curraghmore, the estate of the Marquis of Waterford. Examination of the archives reveals the details of negotiations between the estate workers and the union. It also highlights the seriousness of the situation with statements about closing Curraghmore and letting all employees go. The agent, Major Randolph G Gethin, was in communication with the estate employees and the local union representative. Gethin had arranged a meeting with the employees to explain to them that there was not enough income to pay the full wages demanded by the union. Thomas Foran, General President of the ITGWU, wrote to Gethin expressing his annoyance that the meeting took place without the permission on the union: 'We explained the position fully to the Duke of Devonshire's agent when he called here some weeks ago. The position simply is that the great majority of Labourers...have now signed up until May next at last year's scale of wages...Unless, therefore, the expiring Agreement is renewed there can be no avoidance of immediate trouble.'[118]

Gethin replied to Foran's letter explaining that he did invite the union representative from Waterford to attend but he declined: 'You must admit that the depreciation of Capital and the increase in Rates, Taxes, and Wages, coupled with the fall in prices of farm produce and timber, have hit owners of places like Curraghmore in a way that has not affected the farmers. Lord Waterford's

---

[117] Emmet O'Connor, p.174.
[118] Marquis of Waterford Archive, Thomas Foran, General President, ITGWU, Dublin to Major R G Gethin, Estate Office, 17 Beresford Street, Waterford, 11 July 1922.

income from all sources is not sufficient to meet the outgoings of the Estate'.[119]

Gethin concluded the letter with the hope that the men would accept the offer of 30 shillings a week for a 54-hour week. If they refused, then Lord Waterford would have no choice but to let all the employees go and shut down Curraghmore. Gethin wrote to Lady Osborne at the end of July to inform her that the strike had been postponed, 'for if the men were out now, the whole place would be looted, while as it is they are behaving splendidly in trying to protect Tyrone's property.'[120] Gethin met with the local union representative T. Nagle showing him the financial records and noted that wages would be reduced from 11 August. Nagle replied that most of the farmers had agreed to pay the 35-shilling rate and he saw no reason why Lord Waterford should not do the same and if the men's wages were cut on 11 August it would result in an 'immediate stoppage'. Nagle met with the Curraghmore employees, and they rejected the proposed reduction in their wages.[121] Gethin wrote to the Hon. Claud Anson on the strike day, 11 August, about the grave situation Curraghmore was facing. 'I don't know yet how far they will go in boycotting and acts of sabotage etc, but I cautioned Nagle that if anything illegal was done, it would be taken into account when the strike was over'. He mentioned in particular a 'bad blackguard' named Banks, who had organised the strike at Cleeve's Dairy in Carrick, and who was now in Portlaw and might 'put the men up to all sorts of

---

[119] Marquis of Waterford Archive, Major Gethin, Waterford to Thomas Foran, General President, ITGWU, Dublin, 15 July 1922.

[120] Marquis of Waterford Archive, Randolph Gethin, Estate Office, Beresford Street, Waterford, to Lady Osborne, 29 July 1922.

[121] Marquis of Waterford Archive, Thomas Foran, General President, ITGWU, Dublin to Major R Gethin, 8 August 1922.

devilment'.[122] The following day Gethin had a visit from the parish priest of Portlaw, Father James Walsh. He told Gethin that he was 'fearful of damage to Curraghmore' if the dispute was not resolved quickly. Father Walsh suggested a compromise figure. By 20 September the issue had still not been resolved when Mr Gethin wrote to Lady Osborne.[123] He informed her that Claud Anson had met with the local union secretary and given him an ultimatum – that if the workers did not agree to his suggestion Curraghmore would be closed up by the end of that week. He told her that Harrison and Larkin (Curraghmore employees) were 'fired at', and he could not get the Free State men to protect them, so he sent them away 'on a holiday'. Contact had also been made with the Minister for Labour about the situation. The archive does not reveal the final outcome, but agreement must have been reached and Curraghmore was saved from looting or a much worse fate. The episode could have been used as an excuse to burn Curraghmore in 1923 but it was saved once again.

I.R.A. Levy

The levy was placed on farmers and big house owners and was based on the rateable valuation of their property. Payment of the levy was important as people were threatened with injury, death, or destruction of property if it remained unpaid. Michael Power of the East Waterford Brigade IRA recalled collecting the levy in January 1921:

> I remember collecting a levy on farmers in the locality. This levy was fixed on the valuation of the holding. The

---

122 Marquis of Waterford Archive, Randolph Gethin, Guilcagh House, Portlaw, to Hon. Claud Anson, 11 August 1922.
123 Marquis of Waterford Archive, Randolph Gethin, Estate Office, Waterford, to Lady Osborne, 20 September 1922.

money collected was sent to the Battalion Quartermaster, Martin Cullinane at Dunhill. The levy...was made to provide funds to carry on the fight in the way of buying arms and suchlike. I remember being ordered to threaten any farmer refusing to pay the levy that he would be burned out. There was no necessity to do any burning as everybody paid up.[124]

We know that it was paid by owners of a number of Waterford country houses, Curraghmore, Dromana, Ballynatray, and Cappagh. Emily Ussher described the levy on Cappagh:[125]

I think it was in the Spring of 1921 that the Levy was made...on us on May 10th. For the Levy everybody was assessed according to his rateable value and three neighbouring boys, who we knew well, served an assessment on us for twenty pounds. Beverly (her husband) was away and I refused. Percy (son) ...said if I would not subscribe he'd find the money himself, which he did. He had been saving up to go to France and had got just twenty pounds...He poured it out in a heap which I think touched our visitors...and they handed him a receipt, which would have got us all interned if Black and Tan raiders found it, so I slipped it behind the chimney piece and the wall in my bedroom, where it remains to this day.

In June 1921 Bill Foley was found guilty by an IRA court of taking fish from the weir at Ballynatray and he was ordered to leave Waterford. Mooney believes that this sentence relates to the payment of a £100 levy by the Holroyd-Smyths: 'Mick Mansfield noted in a dispatch to brigade H.Q. that the Holroyd-Smyths had agreed to subscribe to the Arms Fund and that there was to be no

---

[124] BMH WS 1180 pp.8-9.
[125] Emily Ussher, p.35.

interference either with the family or their property.'

On 23 June 1921 the Battalion Adjutant of 2nd battalion IRA and the O.C. visited Dromana and wrote in the visitors' book: 'Both the above had an interesting half hour in Dromana House on the above date'.

Nesta Villiers-Stuart wrote the following note underneath the entry:

> These men took Grattan's Volunteer flags and burned them. They also took all the swords out of the house. The local battalion I.R.A. were furious at this insult to us and traced the men by their handwriting.
> They forced them to give up the swords which are now in Dromana once more.

The O/C was Paddy Morrissey, and the adjutant was Frank Ryan of the 2nd Battalion Lismore. However, the Villiers-Stuarts' reputation as good landlords was insufficient to save the house from possible destruction. Jim Mansfield O/C of 3rd Battalion H.Q. noted the following on 30 June 1921:[126]

> The OC of H Company 3rd Battalion has reported that some persons raided Dromana House for arms and took away swords and coat of mail. One of the party signed himself Commdt 2nd Batt. Send back all the stuff taken from Dromana House to O/C H Company. We have particular reason for not interfering with Dromana, they have promised to pay £100 War Levy. The O/C/ H Company gave his word that nothing would be done to the house pending negotiations for same with the trustees.

---

[126] Military Archives CD274/1 Correspondence Book 28 April-15 May 1921, James Mansfield, Commandant – Record of Activities of 3rd Batt H.Q. West Waterford Brigade 1921.

On 6 July Mansfield reported that he had received an apology for the robbery of the items from Dromana. 'He promised to return all stuff taken from Dromana House. It is for you to see that same is all given back except of course any war material which may be useful to you or me.'[127]

Sir John Keane wrote in his diary in June 1921:

> It is not till the IRA levy is made upon me that there is any real risk of violence – this levy has not been made yet and it is unlikely to be made except on me in person. The longer it can be put off the better and now the Ulster Parliament is in operation and the military measures are to be stronger, bottom may be touched any day. Wood [agent, Lismore Castle] says the risk of burning is just as great, if not greater, when I am at home than away.[128]

Seamus Babington of Carrick-on-Suir, and a member of the 3rd Tipperary Brigade recalled the levy:

> We struck £100 each on Lord Waterford and Colonel Quin of Castletown (which sums were readily paid), £60 on Hayden's estate, £60 on Creggs...John Power refused to pay on the grounds that he was a loyalist and against the IRA activity.[129]

On 14 August 1921 Rivallon de la Poer was asked for £50 'towards the expenses of the I.R.A.' He told the men that he didn't have it and that he needed to find £900 to pay his rates. He was asked for another contribution on 10 February 1922:

---

127 Military Archives CD274/4. Correspondence Book, 2 July-18 July 1921.
128 Keane Archive, Diary of Sir John Keane, 10 June 1921.
129 BMH WS 1595 p.64.

After dinner four men who told me that they belonged to the I.R.A. came to the Hall door. I went out to them, they told me they had come for the levy of £50, which they said was due by me for the upkeep of the Irish Army. This I having not paid, had now been raised to £100. I told them that I had not got £100 to give them, so they then said they would take my cattle. Shortly after this my Steward came to the House to tell me 14 head of cattle had been removed, being taken out by the Clonmel lodge. If this sort of work is allowed to go on, this country will be no place to live in.[130]

His Steward met with Captain McKenna, a representative of the Provisional Government, who assured him the cattle would be returned as soon as the levy was paid. On 16 February ten IRA men arrived at Gurteen and demanded the £100 levy or they would sell the cattle the next day. Rivallon informed them that he had written to the Provisional Government about the matter, but they told him they did not recognise the government. 'It is so very hard to know where one stands with several bodies of men who claim to be the proper government of the country'.

In the Stradbally area it appears that there was unauthorised collecting of money as recalled by Sean Hyde.[131] He was summoned to a meeting with Liam Lynch and was asked to go there and investigate the complaints. Hyde noted that 'the list of robberies was appalling on several private individuals including Widgers, Knockeen; Russells, Seafield; Annestown House; Powers, Kilmeaden etc.' Hyde was told that senior brigade officers were involved, and this turned out to be the case.

---

[130] Diary of Rivallon de la Poer, private collection.
[131] MSP34REF16364

Looting and Wrecking, 1920-1923

Chapter 8

According to Dooley about 275 country houses were burned during the War of Independence and Civil War.[132] During this period houses were damaged by the IRA and Free State troops. Why were these houses targeted for destruction? There are several reasons which varied from one area to the next. Old grudges were acted on, houses which were about to be used as a military base, and reprisals for the shooting of IRA prisoners. Some houses were burned to force owners to move away and sell the estate lands which would then be divided up amongst locals.

Between February 1920 and April 1923 seven country houses were burned in county Waterford: Glenaheiry Lodge, Rockmount, Comeragh, Cappoquin, Gardenmorris, and Tay Lodge. Several others were damaged including the contents. Not all houses burned were large country houses; for instance, Rockmount, the home of the Hunt family, was a modest two-storey three bay house. How did this compare with neighbouring counties? In Tipperary twenty-nine were burned, nineteen in Cork, eleven in Wexford and five in Kilkenny. Some burnings made no sense as

---

[132] Dooley, T. 'The Burning of Irish Country Houses 1920-23', *Atlas of the Irish Revolution* (Cork, 2017), pp 447-453.

the owners such as the Fairholmes at Comeragh had a good reputation as landlords and for their charitable works.

Rumours circulated that the British military were going to use big houses as substitute barracks. Glenaheiry Lodge was the first house to be destroyed in county Waterford during the revolutionary period and had been the subject of a controversial attack in 1907.

Glenaheiry Lodge

Romantic Yarn of the Iron Pot

He tramped from county Galway with a pole around his neck,
(Resembling very closely the famed Adolphus Beck).
He lined the pot with whitewash, as it seemed a little miry,
The man that fired the bomb and cracked the pot at Glenaheiry.

A motor being handy the villain fled away,
And the news was flashed next morning from our county to Cathay,
How some murderous Galwegians had tried to make it hot,
For their landlord by exploding certain mixtures in a pot.[133]

Glenaheiry was a three bay two-storey house with nine rooms built in the 1840s by William Tinsley (1804-1885) for Abraham Coates, agent to the Earl of Stradbroke.[134] There was a projecting pedimented entrance porch of stone. To the right of the entrance was a greenhouse. The house was the hunting lodge of Frederick Oliver Trench (1868-1946), 3rd Baron Ashtown of Woodlawn, Co

---

[133] Private scrapbook, undated news cutting of a poem about the pot used in the Glenaheiry explosion.
[134] J.D. Forbes, *Victorian Architect: the life and works of William Tinsley* (Indiana, 1953), pp 55-56.

Galway, who was married to Grace Cosby of Stradbally Hall. It was purchased by his father from the Earl of Stradbroke in the 1870s. From 1905 to 1910 Trench was the editor of *Grievances from Ireland*, a monthly magazine of the Imperial Protestant Federation which was anti Irish Nationalist and made him a target for the IRA. In 1880 Lord Ashtown inherited the family estate of 22,000 acres in Galway, Waterford and the midlands.[135]

In 1907 a small bomb exploded at Glenaheiry Lodge and Lord Ashtown claimed it had been planted by supporters of a boycott on his Woodlawn estate. Local nationalists and the RIC did not believe this but that it was planned by Lord Ashtown as a publicity-seeking stunt. The bomb had been placed on the drawing room windowsill.[136]

The bomb did cause substantial damage as explained by RIC Sergeant Patrick Reilly:

> The room measures about 18 by 20 feet. It has one door and three plate-glass windows, seven and a half by three and a half feet. The door was completely splintered and blown into the hall. A chair, side table, fender and fire-screen, decanter and siphon were broken. Bookcase was slightly burned. Chair in the hall broken. Dining-room door injured by marks of broken door. Glass in window of dining-room broken. Circular window underneath skylight and over stairs loosened and glass broken. In Lord Ashtown's bedroom the mantle-piece was loosened...[137]

---

[135] Maume, P, *Dictionary of Irish Biography*, Vol 9 (Cambridge, 2009), pp 462-463.

[136] L Perry Curtis, 'The Last Gasp of Southern Unionism', *Eire-Ireland*, Vol.40, 2005, pp.140-188.

[137] www.dipam-ac.uk/eppi/documents/13175/ (Accessed 29/10/2017).

A court case took place in Dungarvan on 2 September 1907. James H. Campbell, K.C., M.P., represented Lord Ashtown with Tim Healy, K.C., M.P., acting for Waterford County Council and the Clonmel Rural District Council to oppose the claim.[138] Sir Neville Chamberlain, Inspector General of Constabulary, was also present. The case was covered extensively in the Irish and British press who sent reporters and artists to Dungarvan to record proceedings. The first witness to be cross-examined by Healy was the author's grandfather, Patrick Fraher. He informed the court that he had worked for nine years at Glenaheiry and left two years previously and was now working in Dungarvan. Patrick was asked specifically about the skillet pots he had seen or used while employed at the lodge. He stated that the under-gamekeeper, Mr Sweeney, had brought him to Mrs Power's public house for some drinks and showed him two pots. He asked Fraher if he had seen them before, and he said no. He then invited him to Dunne's Hotel for further drinks. He was again asked about the pots. He [Sweeney] said, 'That's the pot, and let you swear to it, and it will be allright'. 'I said I could not swear to the pot at all'. Before meeting Sweeney, he met Lizzie Williamson the widow of the former gamekeeper at Glenaheiry at McCarthy's public house. She said – 'You and we are swearing on Lord Ashtown about the pot'. Patrick appears to have a successful day accepting all the free drinks but was not such a fool as to agree to any of the requests made by his benefactors in relation to giving evidence.[139]

Lord Ashtown claimed £200 for damage to his house. He was accused of staging the incident but due to inconclusive evidence he was acquitted and awarded £140. John Roche, M.P. for East

---

[138] *Papers of John Redmond*. National Library of Ireland, Collection List No. 118. p.81.

[139] *Evening Herald*, 23 September 1907.

Galway, wrote to John Redmond saying he had 'not a shadow of a doubt about Lord Ashtown being at the bottom of the plot'.[140]

In March 1908 the Chief Secretary for Ireland, Augustine Birrell, was asked in the House of Commons why Lord Ashtown had been the first and only landlord in Co Waterford to be the subject of a compulsory purchase order under the Evicted Tenants Act 1907. Birrell replied that it was open to every landowner to appeal the decision of the Estates Commissioners.[141]

In early May 1920 Lord Ashtown's agent, James Ormond, who lived near Dungarvan, had shots fired at his house and a gun taken. The previous night Lord Ashtown's gamekeeper, F Adams, had a similar experience.[142]

Glenaheiry Lodge was eventually destroyed in 1920 and while Lord Ashtown was not a popular landlord one reason for the burning of the house is given by one of those involved, Patrick Ryan:[143]

> It was, I think, early in the year 1920 when word reached us that a mansion belonging to Lord Ashtown was about to be occupied by the military. This mansion is about a mile north of Ballymacarbery and would be a big danger to all the I.R.A. units in north west Waterford if used as a military post. One night about 20 or 30 of us from the Nire and Ballymacarbery went out to lord Ashtown's place. We had plenty of straw and paraffin oil. There was a steward in

---

[140] *Papers of John Redmond*, p.285.

[141] Hansard.millbanksystems.com/commons/1908/mar/02/lord-ashtowns-waterford-estate (Accessed 30/10/2017).

[142] *Belfast Newsletter*, 6 May 1920.

[143] BMH WS 1314 Patrick Ryan, Curtiswood, Ballymacarbery. Lieut. 1st Battalion West Waterford Brigade IRA.

charge. We broke our way into the house and set it on fire, making a right good job of it.

A press report detailed what happened on the night:

> At one o'clock on Thursday morning a large party of disguised men, many who them, it is stated, armed, entered the grounds and knocked at a back door of the lodge. It was opened by Porter Adams, a gamekeeper on the estate and who was in charge of the place, and a number of raiders crowded in.
>
> When the scene of the destruction was visited by our representative on Thursday morning woodwork in parts of the building were still alight. Only the walls remained standing, and even these were cracked in places by the heat. The roof had fallen in and from time to time could be herd the crash of falling masonry etc., inside.
>
> About a dozen policemen were on the scene. The door at the back bears the marks of a heavy instrument, such as a crowbar. The gamekeeper says that some shots were fired when the raiders first made their appearance

The lodge was occupied by Mr Adams, gamekeeper, his wife, and Denis O'Brien who were told to get dressed and remove their furniture and belongings. They were then held under guard at nearby Woodbine Cottage until the main house was set on fire. The telegraph lines had been cut from Ballymacarbery to Ballinamult to Kilmanahan.

Denis O'Brien's father had worked on the estate, and Denis had commenced working there as a teenager in the 1890s. 'He evolved into a top class and gifted fisherman'. He was offered the position of gamekeeper and later fishing gilly for the Ashtown fishery. He also looked after the main house, the lodge, Woodbine Cottage and the estate church. His grandson recalled the night of the burning of the main house:

> As the threat to Lord Ashtown's life grew, my grandfather stayed in the lodge with the servants, Mr & Mrs Adams. Personnel from the Ballymacarbery, Nire, Kilbrien, and Touraneena I.R.A. descended on the house in the early hours of the 19 May 1920...they broke in the back door of the mansion...the three occupants were offered the pick of any of the furniture for their troubles which was brought across the field to Woodbine Cottage where they were held under guard...the men had brought paraffin and put straw from the stables in bundles throughout the rooms and set them alight. Afterwards the stables and servant's quarters were also set alight...[and] Woodbine Cottage. It was reported that the main house burned for three days. The action wasn't sanctioned by the I.R.A., the local I.R.A. company heard a rumour that [Lord] Ashtown had offered the lodge...as a barracks. My grandfather received a letter threatening his life [if he attended the court proceedings for compensation].[144]

Because of local ill-feeling Denis had to resign his post and Lord Ashtown paid for him to go to America where he worked picking cotton. He returned after several months and grew potatoes and vegetables on the front lawn and orchard at Glenaheiry. Denis was also a member of the local IRA company which must have made things very awkward for him. When Robert Power Trench (1897-1966) succeeded as 4th Baron Ashtown he handed over the ruined lodge, the estate church, and some land to Denis O'Brien

---

[144] Information from Brendan O'Brien, grandson of Denis O'Brien.

as a thank you for his long years of service to the family. Ashtown continued to fish at Glenaheiry up until his death in 1966.

Lord Ashtown claimed £25,000 for the burning of his house on 20 May 1920, £2,300 for Woodbine Cottage and £200 for a boathouse. The defendants were Waterford County Council and Clonmel No.2 Rural District Council. At the first hearing of the case at the Waterford Quarter Sessions the trustees of the Ashtown estate were represented by Mr Connolly B.L. He informed the court that many of the witnesses had 'been assaulted and prevented, as a result of assaults from attending'. Mary O'Meara, 'a girl of 14 or 15', assistant in Mr Lewis's office, posted the notices to witnesses and she was so intimidated that she said she would rather resign from her post than appear in court to give evidence. Members of the constabulary had to be brought to court under special escort. Connolly noted that threatening notes were sent to witnesses:

NOTICE

If you attend on next Wednesday at Dungarvan, in Ashtown's claims, prepare for eternity -
Blackhand

The case did not proceed on this occasion as the judge ruled that the notices sent to witnesses were incorrectly addressed.[145]

When the case did come to court the evidence indicated that there was a level of vindictiveness in the actions of the attackers which the judge described as 'Bolshevism'. Not only was the house burned but the conservatory was wrecked, and the cottage looted and stripped.

---

[145] *Irish Examiner,* 8 November 1920.

It was claimed in court that the owner had no prior knowledge that the house would be burned. The judge asked why the one eyewitness, a Mr Adams, was not in court. Adams had left the area and they could not ascertain where he was. Sergt Golden, RIC, had arrived at the lodge the morning after the fire and found no evidence of flammable material and it was suggested that the evidence for malicious burning was non-existent. 'If they were going to burden the ratepayers for every house that was burned on evidence of this kind it would only defeat the purpose of the whole Malicious Injury Court'. He found flowerpots on the floor of the conservatory which had been used to smash the glass. He also observed straw at the back of the courtyard stables. There were marks on the exterior of the main door as if it was forced with a crowbar. In the dairy, benches which had been fixed to the wall had been wrenched off and broken. Hay had been set alight in the private rooms under the conservatory. When asked by the judge if he saw any trace of what was used to set fire to the main house, he replied no. On the night of the fire the house was occupied by the porter, Mr Adams, his wife and Denis O'Brien. The morning after the fire Sergt Golden found Adams in the yard with his furniture which had been removed prior to the burning. The furniture had been put in Woodbine Cottage, but this was subsequently destroyed. Adams had left the area at this point. It was stated that Lord Ashtown always had police protection when he was in residence. Golden said that witnesses had been intimidated from appearing in court. The judge asked him to name one of the witnesses. 'James Comwood came to me and said he had been threatened and could not appear as a witness'. Both Comwood and Denis O'Brien had resigned from their posts as a result of threats.

The burning and destruction of Woodbine Cottage was described as 'the worst type of looting'. Constable Finucan visited the cottage on 7 June and found it 'a total wreck'. The doors had been removed, the floorboards, the kitchen range and anything else of value. The boathouse was burned on 18 June according to Constable Sheehan.

The furniture and house contents were valued by auctioneer John D Palmer at £2,207.

Mr Dunlop an architect gave estimates for the rebuilding of the house at £11,322.11.2, the stables and outbuildings £4,343.8.10 and the boathouse £163. The judge awarded £15,000 for the restoration of the main house and stables. Golden stated that before the fire there had been a raid by the IRA searching for arms.

The burning of Glenaheiry was used in a press report as an example of the 'wanton destruction' of property by the IRA:

> His mansion house...was burnt to the ground with all its contents. His fishing lodge and gate lodge were subsequently destroyed by fire. Then followed his keeper's lodge, and the police barracks on his property. The roof was removed from his mill, and the machinery destroyed. The entrance gates, with their massive pillars, and about twenty yards of ornamental railings, were carried off. The fences around the lawn were destroyed, and the steps of the terraces smashed. Some thousands of trees have been cut down and carried away. All the houses in which his Lordship's Protestant employees resided have been burnt to the ground. And to crown this record of wanton destruction, the slates have been removed from

the Protestant church at Kilronan Parish, where his employees worshipped, and the pews carried off.[146]

Lord Ashtown claimed £800 for the entrance gates and £550 for the damage to Kilronan Church.[147]

The *Munster Express* of October 1921 reported on a further claim by Lord Ashtown for destruction of trees at Curraghateskin, parish of Kilronan. The judge awarded £400 for the trees and £600 for 'buildings destroyed' at the same place.[148]

The house was never rebuilt and remained a ruin.

In early July 1920 it was reported that the RIC barrack in Lismore came under attack: 'The soldiers here on Sunday night were fully armed with bombs, hand grenades, rifles, etc. It was learned yesterday that a bullet similar to those used by the military was found embedded in the hall door of the Duke of Devonshire's residence, Lismore Castle. It is probably a result of Sunday night's indiscriminate rifle firing by the military as Lismore Castle is within range of the temporary barracks at Ferry Street corner'.[149]

Cloncoskeran House

This 18th-century house situated outside Dungarvan on the Waterford road was the seat of the Nugent Humble family. According to the 1911 census it was home to Charles Nugent Humble, J.P., D.L., and his four servants. It is described as a first-class house with twenty-five rooms. The family did not have a good reputation as landlords. In the 1860s they evicted many

---

146 *Londonderry Sentinel*, 19 March 1921.
147 WCCA WCC/GWA288
148 *Munster Express*, 8 October 1921.
149 *Irish Examiner*, 3 July 1920.

tenants in order to create parkland around their house. This fact remained in the memory of local people. In 1905 the Dungarvan U.D.C described him as 'a large, landed proprietor and has on his own hands nearly 2,000 acres of land, from most of which we understand tenants have been evicted'.[150]

In February 1920 Charles Nugent Humble submitted a claim for £1000 to Waterford County Council for malicious burning of his hay.[151] A garrison of British soldiers was based at the house from mid-1920 to July 1921.

Patrick Ormond, Dungarvan, in his witness statement,[152] recalled the following details concerning an attack on the house:

> About a mile and a half north east of Dungarvan was the estate of Sir Nugent Humble, the owner of which was in residence all during the period of the struggle for independence. This man was, as can well be imagined, a strong supporter of British Rule. His house and grounds were always at the disposal of the forces of the Crown...A cattle drive, in which I took part was planned. Upwards of 100 men...raided Nugent Humble's estate one night and drove his cattle into Comeragh Mountains and for miles over the countryside.

The *Freeman's Journal* reported that 600 cattle had been driven from Cloncoskeran and that a large number of police and estate workers were trying to recover them.[153]

Another witness, Michael Shalloe[154] of Dungarvan recalled a planned attack on Cloncoskeran:

---

[150] William Fraher, *A Calendar of the Minutes & Records of Dungarvan Town Commissioners & Urban District Council 1855-1950* (Dungarvan,1991), p.146.
[151] WCCA WCC/GWA288
[152] BMH WS 1283
[153] *Freeman's Journal*, 1 May 1920.
[154] BMH WS 1241

In company with about six men from the column, we approached the house of Charles Nugent Humble where the military party were stationed. Sentries could be seen patrolling the grounds. One shot was fired first, in the hope that this would bring out the guard on duty. In fact, the result was that the British opened indiscriminate fire from the sand-bagged windows of the building...They showed no inclination this time to come out and fight.

After about an hour of firing the IRA gave up as the soldiers had no intention of coming out of the house. As they left the scene, they could hear the British still firing at an invisible enemy. Sean Tobin was also present and noted that there were 25 British troops based at Cloncoskeran House. He stated that each of the men fired 25 to 30 rounds through the windows of the house.[155] Emily and Beverly Ussher of Cappagh House visited Cloncoskeran for lunch on 14 June 1921. She described the house as being behind barbed wire entanglements and with a machine gun on the roof of the porch.[156] In 1923 Charles Nugent Humble claimed €400 for his car taken from Cloncoskeran. At the court his solicitor stated that the car was taken on the night of 30 October 1921. It was a 16.18 h.p. Bedford Buick. The judge commented 'You'd get a 6-cylinder car now for £395. They are grand cars. They heat up when you press a button (Laughter). Mr Carroll said 'an ass and cart will do me'. The judge awarded £150.[157]

Charles Nugent Humble also put in a claim for damage to Bayview House, Ballinacourty, near Dungarvan. The claim was for damage to the house and goods taken 'by persons unknown' between 1922 to 31 March 1923.[158] He had purchased the house from Mrs Kate Kennedy of Lacken Lodge who had in turn bought it in March

[155] BMH WS 757

[156] Emily Ussher, p.35.

[157] *Waterford News*, 9 November 1923.

[158] NAI FIN/COMP/2/23/298

1918 for €3,700 from John Hunt. E A Ryan, solicitor for Charles Nugent Humble, stated that the house had been purchased by Mrs Kennedy 'against local wishes' and that the house was looted by locals and not by the IRA. Ryan noted that Nugent Humble 'could not be described as a popular man' and that he was in some kind of partnership with Kate Kennedy but that 'their relations are not easy to define'.[159] The first bidder in the auction for Bayview in 1918 was James Healy of Ballinacourty, who had been farming the 96 acres for forty years. Perhaps this was the reason for the local resentment against Mrs Kennedy.

There was a link between Nugent Humble and Mrs Kennedy. She had begun her working life as a dairy maid at his home, Cloncoskeran House. We know this and more about her life from a court case taken by her estranged husband in 1925. He challenged the content of her will in which she left her fortune to her relatives, insisting that her husband get nothing.[160]

In November 1923 Mrs Kennedy's claim was heard in Waterford. She stated that she owned the house, and it was then occupied by Captain King District Inspector RIC. It was next occupied by the Buffs for about 12 months and when they left it was locked up with its contents. After that many items were taken such as armchairs, sofa, chairs, beds, and mattresses. She said these were taken by 'Irregulars, or whoever they were'. State Solicitor, Arthur Ryan, replied that she knew very well who took the items. Mrs Kennedy said she sent word to George Lennon, vice commandant of the West Waterford IRA brigade, asking him to apprehend the thieves and offered £100 reward. Eight tons of hay were also taken. She had purchased galvanised iron from the British military for £25 which was also stolen. Mr Carroll remarked that Mrs Kennedy 'had fed them regardless of cost. It would make a great novel'. Ryan asked if the people she 'fed on turkey and ham' would then go and steal from her. Mrs Kennedy resented these

---

[159] NAI FIN/COMP/2/23/36

[160] *Dungarvan Observer*, 28 November 1925.

comments and said if she had placed a tenant in Bayview, he would have been shot. John Morrissey of Ballinacourty said that he saw Irregulars loading the lorry with the stolen items. The judge awarded £70 for costs and expenses and £90 for the stolen items.[161]

Nugent Humble also claimed for Duckspool House near Dungarvan for damage to 'premises, lands and goods' between 1922 and 31 March 1923. Historian Matthew Butler stated that Duckspool was used as a 'Republican jail and a place of concealment during the fight for independence'.[162] Duckspool is a tall three-storey house built in the 18th century by the Boate family and later occupied by the Gallweys. Nugent Humble claimed £1,225 which included damage to the house and the removal of furniture and trees in the demesne.[163] In court the engineer, Mr Coughlan, listed damage to floors, doors, locks and shelving. Nugent Humble claimed that the IRA occupied the house on and off and even held a dance there and noted that the place was 'commonage' after that. The judge estimated that the house was probably only worth £100 and recommended an award of £450 for damage to house and fittings. This was accepted by the owner including the condition that all the money was to be expended on repairing the house.[164] It appears however that the final payment was £272-1-0 awarded on 6 November 1923. The Land Commission purchased the house and demesne of twenty acres and sold it to P.J. Moloney who spent £1000 on repairs. Charles Nugent Humble died in 1928 and the compensation money had not been paid to him. Moloney felt that it should come to him which was agreed by all parties. He was awarded £292-12-0 plus costs.

Edward Arthur Ryan the solicitor in this case and many others

---

[161] *Waterford News*, 9 November 1923.
[162] Matthew Butler notebooks. Reference courtesy Julian Walton.
[163] NAI FIN/COMP/2/23/159
[164] *Waterford News*, 9 November 1923.

relating to big houses during the War of Independence and Civil War was a native of Dungarvan. He qualified as a solicitor in 1904 and was called to the bar in 1914, joining the Leinster circuit. In 1910 he contested the parliamentary vacancy for west Waterford, losing to J.J. O'Shee. A publicity postcard issued by him listed his aims which included Home Rule, land purchase, defending the right to freely exercise the franchise, resisting over-taxation, and support for labourers. In 1922 he was appointed state solicitor for Waterford city and county. His obituary noted: 'During the troubled times the late Mr Ryan, who had strong Nationalist principles, appeared for the defence in many of the prosecutions of the Black & Tan era, and his brilliant advocacy gained him the admiration and regard of all who knew him'. District Justice MacCabe commented on his: 'brilliance, his wit, his eloquence...boyish gaiety' which lifted the atmosphere of the 'drab' court proceedings he attended.[165] Indeed reading the newspaper reports of the cases Ryan was involved in it is apparent that he was very fond of witty off-the-cuff remarks. While these are entertaining, they often come across as insensitive towards the person making the claim.

Helvick House

John Thomas Hudson (1850-1930) of Glenbeg House was the owner and builder of Helvick House, a strange and exotic looking house, situated right on the rocks by the sea. The house, consisting of towers, turrets, and latticed windows, was built of stone and concrete in the 1870s on the site of a ruined building owned by the Villiers-Stuarts of Dromana. The house consisted of a drawing room, dining room, writing room, five bedrooms, maid's room, man servant's room, kitchen, storeroom, and tower room entered from an external staircase. His father Richard Garde Hudson was born at Park in Youghal, Co Cork. He was appointed

---

[165] Undated obituary notice, Casey family scrapbook, Waterford County Museum 2019-22-224. *Dungarvan Observer* 1 June 1940. Ryan died on 26 May 1940 at his residence, Ballinacourty House, Dungarvan.

agent to the Duke of Devonshire in Dungarvan in the early 1800s and built a modest country seat, Ballycoe House, just outside the town. In 1885 John Thomas Hudson married Theresa May Gee of Mount Pleasant House, Youghal.[166] He was appointed sub-sheriff of Co Waterford in 1887.[167]

Michael Curran, Ballinagoul, Captain of Ring Company of Volunteers, recalled a raid on the Hudsons' house:

> In the month of May 1919, I received information that guns and ammunition were stored in the residence of the sheriff at Helvick Head (Hudson). At about one o'clock in the morning a party of six of us headed for the sheriff's house. I carried my automatic revolver. The remainder of the men were unarmed. The house was surrounded by a high wall which we scaled. The windows and doors were strongly barricaded. We cut through one of the windows...and gave the place a thorough searching. We found only a small quantity of ammunition lying loose. We ripped the floors and tested the ceilings but, to our dismay, found nothing worthwhile. We took away with us a powerful telescope which proved very useful later on.

There had in fact been five rifles and ammunition hidden in a sofa which were found the following day by the RIC. The house was raided again in 1921. James Mansfield, O/C of 3rd Battalion West Waterford Brigade IRA, noted on 11 May 1921 that there was a rumour that the house was about to be occupied by the marines. He ordered that the house be burned immediately if this was the case.[168] Hudson had appointed a caretaker who left in May 1921 as he was informed that working for the sub-sheriff would not be

---

[166] *Cambridge Independent Press*, 26 February 1887, p.2. He had been appointed in the place of the Nationalist Sub-Sheriff appointed by Sir Thomas Grattan Esmonde M.P. who was himself removed from his post as High Sheriff of Co Waterford by the government.

[167] *Northern Whig*, 9 November 1885.

[168] Military Archives CD274/1 Correspondence Book 28 April- 15 May 1921.

tolerated by the IRA. In early January 1922 Hudson's claim for damages was reported in the press.[169] His clerk, William Brazil, gave evidence that he found partitions, two doors, a plate rack, window, etc., broken, and the furniture destroyed. It was noted that the house was not secured as it had been broken into previously. The judge felt it was 'absurd' that the house was not properly guarded, and that Hudson was now expecting compensation for damage done by trespassers. Laurence Greany estimated the damage at £106.5.0; the judge awarded £75.

John Thomas Hudson put in a claim to the Free State government for damage to his house in Helvick between 1921 and 30 January 1922. This included damage to furniture on 4 August 1921, fittings and doors on 25 November 1921, coach house and goods on 7 January 1922, piping and other fittings on 30 January 1922, and damage to the house on 9 February 1922. He also applied to the Irish Distress Committee in London for compensation.[170]

There is a substantial file relating to the damage to Helvick in the National Archives.[171] It includes correspondence from Thomas J Kelly, State Solicitor, and John J Hudson to the Ministry of Finance. Hudson claimed for furniture which was damaged or stolen. He had appointed a caretaker to look after the house, who left because of threats, and the house was left unguarded. The State Solicitor noted that Hudson couldn't confirm what furniture was looted or destroyed in the house:

> I think the commonsense view is that where you have a large house with the doors and windows broken away and furniture is left unprotected that unfortunately it would be more in keeping with the instincts of human nature to take the furniture away than destroy it on the spot.

---

[169] *Waterford News*, 13 January 1922.
[170] National Archives Kew, No.672. CO 762/43/18
[171] NAI FIN/COMP/2/23/77

He suggested that a lot of the furniture was in houses around Helvick. Kelly noted that the District Circuit judge at Waterford awarded Hudson £400 for furniture and £785 for the house. At the hearing in Waterford Hudson stated that he purchased the fee-simple and acquired the ground rent from Mr Villiers-Stuart for £20 or £30. There had been no tenants for seventy years and only the shell of the buildings stood which he converted into a 'cottage'.[172] Attached to his letter was a confidential report from the Chief Superintendent at Waterford, S O'Duibhir. He concluded that the damage done to Hudson's house was 'malicious'. It was carried out by William Power, Thomas Carey, Nicholas Troy, David Tobin, Richard Tobin, Michael Tobin, Martin Costin, John and Patrick Walsh, all residents of Ring. He stated that the first three were members of the local volunteers at the time and were arrested by the volunteers and 'detained at their camp in Ardmore, the remainder were fined'. O'Duibhir noted that some of the house contents were taken pre-truce, and these were found when the RIC raided their houses after the truce. 'All articles which the raiders could not remove from the house, was broken inside, they even smashed the wainscotting'. He noted that it was difficult to find out more as the local people did not want to talk about it. He concluded that these men had taken advantage of their association with the volunteers, feeling that they were immune from prosecution.

The file includes a list of the furniture and contents stolen or destroyed. Hudson had the list of items complied by William Brazil before the contents were taken or damaged. He explained that he furnished the house 16 years before. He purchased most of the furniture from Goetzman who had a showroom in Dublin at that time. There were exotic items such as a Newfoundland chief's 'staff of office', a model of a Ceylon temple, a copper coffee service presented by an Indian Rajah, Indian snake candlesticks, a Maltese carved stone font with high relief carving, and an Indian bowl on a lion rampant tripod. The staff was valued by Captain

---

[172] *Waterford News,* 2 June 1922.

Carew 'who has lived all his life in New Zealand' at between £30-£35.

Hudson expressed his dismay at the delay in paying him compensation as he had repaired and restored the house but had been waiting two years for recompense.

Hudson's principal residence Glenbeg House was put up for sale in February 1922 and was described as a 'magnificent residence' with 75 acres.[173] It does not appear to have suffered any damage, but it indicates that Hudson was cutting his links with Waterford. Hudson left Helvick in 1914 and went to live permanently at 31 Fitzwilliam Place, Dublin. He sold his Helvick house to Thomas A. Moloney, shipowner and merchant of Dungarvan.

In November 1924 Hudson's compensation case was reviewed in Waterford. The state had decided to contest the decrees made previously by judge O'Brien to investigate whether they were excessive. Previously eight decrees had been made, three of which had come before the Shaw Commission. These related to damage to the house and contents between November 1921 and February 1922. The court heard that Helvick Lodge was 'furnished in keeping with the tastes of the gentleman himself and the position he occupied'. Concerning the question as to why the house was attacked and robbed it was suggested that it was not personal as Hudson got on well with his neighbours. It was because of his job as Sub-Sheriff which he was asked to resign from but refused.

Photographs of the house and plans were shown in court by Mr Connolly. He explained that the house had four sitting rooms, six bedrooms, servants' apartments, conservatory, kitchen, garage, and other out-offices. Hudson told the court that he found bits of garden statues which had been 'tarred and cast on the rocks'. Bedsteads had been thrown through the windows. The judge

---

[173] *Irish Examiner,* 25 February 1922.

awarded £785 for the buildings and reduced the furniture claim from £690 to £400 as he commented that some of it had been looted so it could not be included.[174]

Durrow House

Durrow House was the seat of a branch of the notable Co Waterford Barron family. At the Dungarvan Quarter Sessions in October 1921 Captain R.G. Stoker of 69 Lower Leeson Street, Dublin, claimed £330 for a gent's Rudge bicycle, field boots, haversack, water bottle, two fountain pens, clothing, boxes etc. He also claimed, to the amusement of the court, £220 for a black spaniel and small terrier taken from Durrow House on 15 March 1921.

Mr Wyse Power, B.L., said that Captain Stoker went to the police to report previous raids on his house. He was told that the reason he was targeted was because he was an informer. Stoker told the court that he had retired from the army in 1915. His home had been raided on at least three occasions prior to 17 April 1921.

On 18 March he and his wife were sitting in their room when a group of armed and masked men broke in, calling him an informer. They said they were searching the house for arms and ammunition which he was entitled to hold as a retired army captain. The raiders insisted that they would shoot him if he did not comply with their request. They 'broke open every conceivable place' looking for arms. Stoker stated that 'an alarm was given' and the raiders ran away but said they would be back to kill him. 'Thinking discretion the better part of valour he 'hopped it' (laughter), and did not go to Durrow House afterwards'.

---

[174] *Munster Express*, 29 November 1924.

The judge refused to give compensation for the dogs but gave a decree of £100 for the damaged items.[175] Stoker did return to Waterford if not to Durrow as he is mentioned in a document dated October 1921 from the Waterford Brigade IRA stating that he 'visited occasionally'. 'He is at present engaged in the British Secret Service. Mr Charles Power, B.L., knows this Stoker and can give you fuller details.'[176]

In October 1921 Sir Richard Musgrave of Tourin House was awarded £900 for burning of his hay, houses and farm implements at 4.30 a.m. on 11 July, the morning of the truce.[177] There is no record of the IRA visiting the main residence.

---

[175] *Munster Express,* 8 October 1921.
[176] Michael Collins Papers, IE/MA/CP/5/2/12/ (LXX)
[177] *Munster Express,* 8 October 1921.

'Like Tutankhamun's tomb' -
Looting house contents

Chapter 9

We have already seen in the case of Lord Ashtown's lodge how determined local people could be at removing everything of value, from a set of entrance gates to a garden shrub. Emily Ussher told of rumours about farmhouses 'stuffed with the contents of houses and trains – 'like Tutankhamun's tomb'. However, her son Percy Arland concluded that 'the incendiaries seldom came to steal. They obeyed their mysterious 'orders' – often with very sincere expressions of regret'.[178] There are numerous accounts of the owners of big houses not being given sufficient time to remove papers and valuables from their houses before burning. The Miss Fairholmes of Comeragh House were given ten minutes to grab a few items. On some occasions the incendiaries assisted the owners to remove some artefacts. For instance, at Captain Perry's house, Newcastle, Co Tipperary, the owner was asked what he wanted saved, and he said his library:

> He told us that he had a very valuable library of books and requested permission to save them from the flames. We sent a runner to the Column Commander with this request, and permission to save the books having been given, about ten men were detailed to remove the books from the library...following which straw was spread around the rooms and other men came along to sprinkle this with petrol.[179]

---

[178] Arland Ussher, *The Face and Mind of Ireland*, (London, 1949), pp 52-53.
[179] BMH WS 0783 Lt Col Thomas Ryan, 3rd Tipperary Brigade.

In August 1922 a proclamation was issued concerning stolen property from private houses or government buildings in Waterford. The stolen goods were to be returned to the headquarters of the Waterford Brigade within 48 hours. It noted that 'information has been received that a huge traffic in looted goods is being carried on'.[180]

The Irish Catholic bishops published a statement in November 1922 regarding looting:

> In this lamentable upheaval the moral sense of the people has, we fear, been badly shaken...With feelings of shame we observe that when country houses and public buildings were destroyed the furniture and other fittings were seized and carried away by people in the neighbourhood. We remind them that all such property belongs to the original owners...[181]

Mary De la Poer recalled being at mass in Clonmel in October 1923 at which the priest gave a sermon which included the following warning:

> Father Warren read the Joint Pastoral of the Irish Bishops- warning all those who were in areas against the Government...that telling a lie, looting, destruction of property, harboring rebels, giving information to them etc., etc. that the church no longer would give them absolution.

During a discussion in the Dáil in July 1923 Minister Kevin O'Higgins commented on the looting of country houses:

> I heard one story from Leitrim of a man who went to a

---

[180] *Munster Express,* 5 August 1922.
[181] *Irish Times,* 10 November 1922.

neighbouring mansion and coveted a large gilt-framed mirror and brought it home. He found that it would not go in through his door or window and there did not seem any practical way of getting it into his house short of taking the roof off. He left it lying against the back of the house overnight, and his cow settled the problem next morning by driving his horns through the mirror.[182]

A search through contemporary newspapers shows the scale of theft of house contents and in some cases the materials of the house itself. It is clear from these that not everything perished in the flames and that much was stolen before or after houses were burned. Leap Castle, Co Tipperary, was burned in 1922 but it was reported in the press that 'a great quantity [of the contents] was looted by people from Roscrea and neighbourhood'.[183] At Borodale House, Enniscorthy, a large amount of valuable silver, the contents of the cellar etc. were taken in 1922.[184] In 1923 it was reported that Woodpark House, Co Clare, had been destroyed and that 'everybody in the district went and took anything they fancied'.[185] In 1924 silverware and antiques, many with the crest of the MacKay Wilson family, were discovered in a number farmhouses in Co Longford. These had been stolen from Currygrane House which was looted and burned in 1922.[186] In 1923 it was reported that marble mantlepieces, valuable carpets, pictures, mirrors, etc., had been looted from Ballinahinch House, Co Clare, the seat of the Gore family. Not content with stealing the contents of the house, the very stones were removed, and one Patrick Tuohy was convicted of stealing these and building a new house with them.[187]

---

[182] http://oireachtas.ie/en/debates/debate/seanad/1923-07-31/2/
[183] *Leinster Reporter*, 5 August 1922.
[184] *New Ross Standard*, 12 May 1922.
[185] *Wicklow People*, 10 November 1923.
[186] *Freeman's Journal*, 19 June 1924.
[187] *Freeman's Journal*, 3 November 1923.

Beatrix, Lady Osborne Beauclerk, travelled to Ardmore on 24 August 1923 and stayed with the Keanes in their summer house. They walked to Ardo House which she described as 'a lamentable example of a looted house'.[188] The Anson family of Ballysaggartmore had a summer residence in Ardmore, 'Ardmore House'. The house was broken into on 18 March 1923 and furniture damaged to the value of £200.[189]

Beatrix along with her mother Lady Lansdowne made the journey to see what remained of the family's summer house at Derreen, Co Kerry which had been completely wrecked and looted by local people in September 1922. They stayed at the hotel in Derreen where they received a visit from the local Catholic priest Father S. He was anxious to speak to them before they arrived at the wrecked house:

> He could not bear that we should go to Derreen thinking there was antagonism there against the family...he told us of the widespread plot to get rid of every landlord, so that the land might be free to all, how those who destroyed the house were incited and even paid to do it, how the crowd afterwards went mad, and completely lost their heads; and ever and anon came the earnest refrain *'but 'ou must understand that it was nothing personal to Lord and Lady Lansdoon; noa, it was nothing personal'*.

He informed her that he and the curate had told the locals about the 'wickedness' of what had happened and had preached from the pulpit, refusing absolution to any people who had stolen goods in their houses and urging them to return 'the loot'. Apparently, it worked as he informed Lady Lansdowne that she would see the items which had been returned and that he had opened a bank account in Kenmare into which had been paid

---

[188] Diary of Beatrix, Lady Osborne Beauclerk, 24 August 1923. Private collection.
[189] WCCA WCC/GWA288

'various sums for wine drunk by the raiders'. She asked him to tell her the names of the people who wrecked the house, but he declined. They visited the cottage of Seamus Sullivan (Keeper at Derreen) and his wife Nora. In an untenanted part of the cottage, they found piles of furniture, bedding, crockery etc. which had been looted from Derreen.[190]

While a considerable quantity of contents was taken from country houses, much of the furniture etc. was destroyed in fires. There are also numerous instances where the contents were destroyed or badly damaged while houses were occupied by the IRA and later by Free State troops. This often appears to have been a spiteful act against the owners; perhaps these artefacts represented the enemy for them. Almost every piece of furniture in Mount Congreve was damaged during the occupation by the IRA in 1922. We know this from the detailed inventory carried out by John D Palmer after the house was vacated. The following is an example from the Entrance Hall: '1 mahogany chair broken and 1 scratched, side table scratched, screen torn and scratched, leaves torn out of visitor's book. Cricket bats used, 1 broken...Some books taken from book-case and used, 5 or 6 missing'.

The compensation claim files in the National Archives often have detailed inventories of house contents listed room by room which give an insight into the material possessions of the owners. They also list all the individual rooms by name in a particular house. The list of contents for Lismore Castle names a large variety of reception rooms, agent's living rooms, servants' quarters, and outbuildings. John Hudson's claim for Helvick House includes a detailed list of contents. These included some exotic pieces such as a Newfoundland chief's 'staff of office', a model of a Ceylon temple, a copper coffee service presented by an Indian Rajah, Indian snake candlesticks and an Indian bowl on a lion rampant tripod. It is disappointing that we have no list of the contents of

---

[190] Undated typescript written by Beatrix, Lady Osborne Beauclerk, private collection.

Gardenmorris, which had by all accounts a significant collection. A list existed which was presented to the judge at the compensation court claim at Waterford in 1924.

The emotional strain of the loss of prized family possessions should not be underestimated. In 1923 the *Freeman's Journal* referred to the 'List of Magnificent Irish Mansions given to the flames...with all their artistic treasures and fondly cherished relics of dear ones dead and gone'.[191] Often the estate records were also destroyed, a significant loss to the local history of the particular area. Some of the estate records which survived the burning of Gardenmorris House still bear the scorch marks from the fire.

Leaving Ireland - selling up

An examination of newspapers from this period shows that many country houses in county Waterford were advertised for sale or to let. These included Woodstown, Glenbeg, Ballygally, Old Cappagh House, Belleville Park, Springfield, Ballyin, and Bleach House.

One of the first big house owners to leave Waterford because of intimidation was Alexander J. P. Wise, J.P., D.L., of Belleville Park, Cappoquin. He was a director of the Cappoquin Bacon Factory. In 1921 his house was raided for arms, and he confronted the raiders, refusing to comply with their demands. Emily Ussher recalled that:

> Poor old Mr Wyse [sic] was knocked down and kicked when he resisted the raiders, and he resented the indignity and felt the ingratitude so much that he was the first to uproot and leave the country. The man who treated him so

---

[191] *Freeman's Journal*, 10 February 1923.

badly acted out of pique because Mr Wyse had befriended a boy he disliked. Thus, many of us were victims of jealousies with which we had nothing to do. Mrs Wyse was bitterly missed by the poor around her. One old woman declared she never passed Belleville without leaving a curse on those raiders and many noted the justice of Heaven when they came to a bad end.[192]

She does emphasize that the treatment of Mr Wise was the exception, where local raiders were involved, and that most of the violent acts against landowners were carried out by 'roving bands' who were not from the area. She says that Wise finally decided to sell in October 1921 and move to England after he was asked to accommodate and feed ten volunteers during maneuvers. In November 1921 the sale of Belleville was advertised in the press and referred to the owner 'who is leaving'.[193] The house did not find a buyer and was advertised again in 1925. In January 1922 one newspaper carried a headline: 'Fear of Free State Rule – Irish Peers Abandoning Their Houses'. It noted that Lord Ashtown was following the example of Irish peers such as Lord Portarlington and Lord Gort and was having an auction of his furniture, livestock etc. at his home, Woodlawn, Co Galway.[194]

Ballygally House near Lismore was the home of the Foley Family who were relatives of the writer Arthur Conan Doyle. It was built in the early 1800s, possibly to a design by the architect Sir Richard Morrison. On 18 February 1922 the then owner, William Charles Le Bagge Foley, described as a naval architect of York,

---

192 Emily Ussher, pp 34-35, 45.
193 *Waterford News & Star*, 4 November 1921.
194 *Belfast Newsletter*, 5 January 1922.

Pennsylvania, claimed £120 for the burning of Ballygally. On 13 May he claimed £50 for the 'burning of furniture, goods, chattels'. We do not have any further details about the fire or the extent of the damage, but it was not extensive as the house still stands with much of its period detail intact. On 3 March 1924 the owner made a further claim of £50 for a marble mantlepiece which had been 'destroyed' on the 25 or 26 February 1924.[195]

In April 1922 there was a raid by the IRA on Ardkeen, the residence of Harry de Bromhead. At about 8.45 in the evening the maid answered a knock at the front door and was confronted by eight armed men. They entered the drawing room where Mr de Bromhead and his three daughters were seated. Keeping revolvers levelled at all four of them, the raiders announced that they had come to search for arms. They were informed that there were no arms in the house as they had been handed over to the British long before. The raiders were not happy with this answer and began to ransack the entire house. De Bromhead was threatened if he did not sit still but he insisted on following the men as they searched each room. They left without finding any guns but did take other items.[196]

---

[195] WCCA WCC/GWA 288, Waterford Co Council Notices of Claims for Compensation or Criminal Injuries 1920-1946. Foley (born 1867) was the eldest son of Robert Armstrong Foley (died 1883) and Elizabeth Anne Bagge of Ardmore. In 1898 William married Mary Louise Van Baman of York, Pennsylvania. A York newspaper, *The Gazette*,3 March 1898, described him as an 'expert naval architect...Five years ago he came to this country and at present fills the position of chief draughtsman in the hull department of Newport News Shipbuilding and Dry Dock Company'.
[196] *Waterford News*, 21 April 1922.

Cappagh House occupied

While Cappagh had been put under the protection of Cathal Brugha it did not stop the house being occupied by the IRA. On 17 July 1922 two of them took up residence in one of the workers' houses. Emily's son Percy was back living at Cappagh along with Emily Whitehead[197] and employees John Power and Mary Ahearne. Emily and her husband decided to take a break at a flat they had at Milltown in Dublin. 'We walked to the station carrying two little clocks and other valued trifles – we might never see the place again. And thus, we left the home of so many labours with the labour pickets and the IRA pickets glaring at each other on either side of the lodge gate!' Their journey took them over the viaduct at Ballyvoyle on what was to be one of the last trains to travel over it as it was blown up by the IRA on 8 August.

Beverly Ussher decided he had to get back to Cappagh and managed to get a lift to Waterford from a travelling salesman and from there he hoped to get to Dungarvan on 'Moloney's meal lorry'. He was told that on 11 August thirty men had left Dungarvan for Cappagh House carrying mattresses. On 18 August Emily was informed that the occupation of Cappagh had ended.

In July 1922 'Obby' Beauclerk, 12th Duke of St Albans, wrote from his home at Newtown Anner to his wife Beatrix in London informing her that it was not safe to travel to Ireland and that she should consider going to Bowood or Chatsworth instead. He told her that Clonmel was now the headquarters of the 1st Southern Division IRA, 300 of whom had arrived from Cork some days previously. He stated that the shopkeepers in Clonmel had ceased ordering new stock as it would be requisitioned, resulting in a

---

[197] Emily Whitehead from Nenagh arrived at Cappagh in the Spring of 1918 as a 'Companion-Helper' to Emily Ussher.

shortage of tea, sugar etc. He felt the country would 'lapse into barbarism'; 'the trouble is that many of the youths on the war-path don't care what happens to the country'. Four of the workmen from Knocklofty House were forced to leave work and join the republicans.[198] Some days later he told her the ancient Sir Thomas's Bridge had been destroyed 'in spite of the protests of the priest' whom they told to 'go to blazes and mind his own business'.[199]

Dan Breen in his witness statement commented on the occupation of country houses by the IRA.[200] He refers to an order issued from HQ in Carrick-on-Suir on 24 July 1922 which stated that 'columns on active service were required, as far as possible, to be billeted in mansions, then being presumed to be the property of persons hostile to the Republic'. However, he admits that they were more likely to have taken over farmhouses for the purpose. He does note that some mansions which 'escaped the ravages of fire' continued to be used by the columns until the end of the war. He gives as an example Knocklofty House, near Clonmel, the seat of the Earl of Donoughmore. The latter was described by an IRA officer as 'not a bad skin'. Breen notes that whenever the IRA called to the house there were always six or seven beds ready for them and 'plenty of good food'.

On 2 August Obby Beauclerk wrote to his wife that things were peaceful around Newtown Anner but that they had no post for two weeks and that most of the bridges were destroyed. He was very happy that none of his farm workers had joined the IRA. He

---

[198] Marquis of Waterford Archive, Letter from Obby Beauclerk, Newtown Anner, Clonmel, to 'Bertie', 14 July 1922.
[199] Marquis of Waterford Archive, Letter from Obby Beaulcerk, Newtown Anner, Clonmel, to 'Bertie', 18 July 1922.
[200] BMH WS 1763.

heard that the IRA were at Whitfield and Curraghmore. A week later he wrote to say that some of his workmen who cycled had to walk as their bicycles would have been taken. The Free State soldiers had two field guns 'firing away' between Kilcash and Redmondstown. The previous Sunday he was invited to lunch at Gurteen le Poer Castle. While they were eating, five IRA men came in and demanded lunch and a cart to take them to Rathgormack. 'The leader looked a real bad lot, the remainder of the low, bestial type. They heralded their approach by firing shots...they had one rifle between them, and the rest had revolvers and bombs, and from their accents they hailed from Cork'. On the 17 August he wrote that a shell landed close to the house of 'Old Montgomery'. 'I hear that all sorts of Republican loot has been unearthed in my old friend J. Keefe's farmyard! A few days later he noted that four of his trees had been felled next to the lodge. He was not impressed with the organising abilities of the Free State troops but those he spoke to seemed 'decent fellows'.[201]

On 21 August Emily Whitehead and Percy Ussher described the occupation of Cappagh House to Emily Ussher:

> Five lorry loads of men arrived at Cappagh at 2 a.m. and had every bell ringing, every door banged with every curse, every shout to frighten, as they thought their three comrades were alone there...and pretending they were Free State troops come to destroy them. Then the officer recognised Percy and Em (who had given him tea in the old days when he was 'on the run') and little Mary and John Power, an old friend of his. So, he apologised for the racket and promised to keep his men out of any rooms which they

---

[201] Marquis of Waterford Archive, Obby Beaulcerk, Newtown Anner, to Bertie, 10, 17th and 21 August 1922.

did not wish frequented and gave orders that there should be no thieving nor burning. Thirty men had to be accommodated in the drawing rooms, but these had fortunately been cleared for the refugees, driven out of Belfast, who never came. Four officers slept in the spare rooms. Three orderlies took possession of the kitchen. They flung out of their lorries thirty new mattresses (which they intended to 'burn on the mountain' when they have done with them), bags of sugar, boxes of tea, of bombs, of ammunition and of hand grenades, which were stacked in our hall and on our doorsteps!

John Power who was sleeping in the house removed the stuffed Greenland falcon which had belonged to Beverly's father, the ornithologist Richard J. Ussher. Emily noted that not a thing was taken from the house during the occupation. She does refer to a bullet mark in the wall over the pantry sink. A 'scullery boy' was nearly accidentally shot by a fellow republican, 'the bullet parting the hair' on his friend's head before lodging in the wall'.

Emily finally returned to Cappagh on 22 August and heard about the death of Michael Collins during her journey. She was happy to see the charwoman had cleaned the house, but she did warn her to avoid a certain green velvet armchair as the officers had been 'very fond of it'. Apparently, the IRA left an autograph book behind as a souvenir.

She was told a story that during the occupation of the house by the IRA they pointed to one of their lorries which had the initials IRA painted on its side. According to Emily by this time the ordinary republicans were becoming disillusioned with their leadership and cynically pointed out that the initials on the lorry stood for 'Irish Robbers Association'.

There was a brief period of normality at Cappagh until two IRA men appeared one evening looking for a bed for the night. Emily put them up in the officers' spare room. They left after breakfast 'their machine gun hanging on the hat rack outside the kitchen door'. The Usshers were concerned about their home and Emily noted: 'It was all very well but we were treading on terribly thin ice and never knew the moment when it would break under us, i.e. when the house might be burned down. We buried all the best china in a drain'. They began to pack away other house contents. One day a Christian Brother from Dungarvan called on her and found her in the 'dismantled drawing room'.

> He said later, 'nothing troubled Mrs Ussher except the books'. He persuaded his good old Superior to house them for us. They took five donkey loads and put up shelves at their own expense for them in a room apart (at their monastery in Dungarvan), where they kept them for nearly two years. One loves to remember these gleams of human kindness through the darkness.

Emily recalled that the PP of Modeligo, Father Burke, was very supportive and was always suggesting that she make a record of the conflict. He was not liked by his 'Republican' parishioners because of his fiery sermons and in one of these he condemned the burning of big houses.

Towards the end of August Obby Beauclerk wrote from Newtown Anner to his wife giving her the latest news. A lorry containing the post was seized by the IRA near Montgomery's house and most of the contents burned. 'Old John Wallace...shared in the loot that ensued, returning in triumph with a whole 'Independent' and half an 'Irish Times' rescued from the flames'. Many trees were being felled and a lot of sniping was occurring. Miss Walmsley at

Redmondstown found a bullet lodged in her armchair and had a constant flow of Republicans visiting her looking for food.[202]

Newrath House and the Siege of Waterford, July 1922

Newrath House was situated on the north bank of the River Suir in Waterford city. It was situated next to Waterford golf course. In 1922 the house was occupied by the Penrose family. Elizabeth Graves, who was a guest in the house, wrote a letter to Lady Osborne on 24 July 1922, a few days after the siege of Waterford ended. The letter reveals that they were caught up in the middle of the fighting from both sides. The siege lasted from Tuesday 18 to Friday 21 July. The Free State troops established their base on the north side of the river facing the city. On the evening of the 18th the Penrose family heard gunfire coming from an area called Mount Misery not far from their house. They encountered a group of Free State troops marching up their avenue, but they dispersed to get provisions. Later that night they were having their supper around 9.30 and Elizabeth Graves saw a large group of Free Staters heading for the house:

> This time they had come to stay – one of the officers told me there were about 300 men here that night – fortunately the shed accommodation here is large in comparison to the house...so the men filled up the two large sheds and the workshop, and every available space, including the Drawing Room and Dining Room and other spare rooms. I can't tell you what the house was like next morning...Bread had to be baked till all hours of the night and can fulls of tea made. A girl from the village came up

---

[202] Marquis of Waterford Archive. Osborne Beauclerk, Newtown Anner to his wife Bertie, 28 August 1922.

on Tuesday evening and worked like a black for Mary, the tiny maid here who goes home three nights a week.

That night Mary headed back home into the city but found the bridge up and decided to return to Newrath. However, she found herself in the middle of the firing between both sides and had to take refuge in the golf pavilion near to Newrath. Inside she found the caretaker, a Mr & Mrs McCormac, and two golfers. They had no choice but to spend the night together in the pavilion. The next morning Mary set out again for Newrath but found herself once again dodging bullets and had to run back to the pavilion where she found the two golfers under the bed reciting Hail Marys. The Free State troops had positioned two main gun posts on each side of the golf course.

> On Friday evening came the news of the complete surrender of the enemy and by about 10 pm the whole gang left [Newrath] leaving only the debris of cigarette papers, bully beef cans, socks, and every sort of odd thing! They commandeered three bicycles here, but Colonel Prout told Mr Penrose they would be replaced by new ones.

Elizabeth concludes her letter by telling Lady Osborne that she had been unwell, probably brought on by recent events. She stated that Ireland over the previous six months had been 'more nerve racking' than she had imagined. She felt it would be months before things settled down and wondered how she could be of service in the new Ireland. She had met the Curraghmore agent Major Gethin a few weeks before and thought he was 'very depressed and looked years older'. This was not surprising as the Marquis of Waterford was not in residence at Curraghmore and Gethin was left in charge, facing the possibility that Curraghmore would be wrecked or worse. She ended by saying she thought music would be very beneficial to heal wounds in Ireland and that it would be 'a potent factor in the national development because it seems to me that of all people in the world the Irish must be allowed to give vent to their feelings and express themselves somehow and now is the moment to show them a way'. She was grateful to the Penroses for letting her stay in Newrath with its glorious views, including the Comeraghs and Curraghmore.[203]

Mount Congreve

Mount Congreve was built c.1760 by John Congreve and designed by the Waterford architect John Roberts. The Congreves were Waterford city merchants who acquired the estate from the Christmas family in 1759. They built a Palladian-style house which was reconstructed by Ambrose Congreve between 1965 and 1969. Major John Congreve succeeded his father in 1901. He married Lady Irene Ponsonby, daughter of the Earl of Bessborough.

Mount Congreve was occupied by the IRA on 19 July 1922. During July and August, the staff wrote a series of letters to the Congreves in London informing them about the occupation.

> 27 July 1922
>
> Letter from A. Flynn (Cook) to Lady Congreve, London
>
> My Lady
>
> I expect you have heard by this time that the house was taken over by a garrison of the Republican Army on Wednesday the 19th and kept possession of it until

---

[203] Marquis of Waterford Archive, Elizabeth Graves, Newrath House, Waterford, to Lady Osborne, London, 24 July 1922.

Monday morning. About 12 o'clock on Wednesday a man came and said he was taking over the telephone and that it may be wanted during the night. About 11 o'clock over 70 men all armed came and said they should get beds and they came down to the kitchen and they said they were taking it over...they started to get food ready and we went to the top of the house to get spared mattresses that was in my room. Then they asked rooms for the officers and we showed them up to the top of the house and they took possession of the rooms there.

We thought we might be able to save the good rooms on the corridors and we had to go to the housekeeper's room.

The next night 40 more men came and took possession of their rooms. And on Friday night over 200 men were here and a lot of the Red Cross nurses. After the men coming they expected an attack from the other side of the river and they closed the shutters everywhere.

It was really terrible to hear the roaring of the guns all day. They did not know when they would be shelled as they said they were going to defend the place. On Thursday Annie asked leave if we could take the good china and some things that you asked her to save and we put them in the presses in the housekeeper's room.

There was nothing left in the drawers or wardrobes but was scattered around the place so for some time we cannot give you an idea of what is gone upstairs but all the bacon and ham is gone and all I had in the kitchen. I had to ask them for a bit of food when we wanted it. Since this day week none of us took our clothes off only waiting the word to go.

A few hours after they went on Monday four armed men came and said they wanted to search the house...they came to the front hall to go out they whispered something to one another and ran up the stairs and into the terrace room and took Major Congreve's trench coat...then to Annie's room where we were after putting in our coats...they pulled out everything...and took my purse and every penny I had in it, but what harm we are thankful to God to be alive and have the house over us.

We are still in the basement and will for a few more nights as we heard some of them that crossed the river was at Ardagh's [(Pouldrew House] yesterday and had the bridge blown up there and the Portlaw barracks blown up.

Waterford is peaceful once more...all the fowl are quite alright there are 6 cocks set to sell...I could not send Mrs Congreve's butter last week, Gladys went to town to try and post it and had to bring it back again.[204]

She wrote to Major Congreve the following day, informing him that she was trying to list damage to the house contents. She noted damage to a library chair, and a hall chair was missing. Lady Congreve's violin and gramophone had been moved to the library. Some of his clothes were missing, including his trench coats.[205]On 4 August she told Lady Congreve that Butlerstown Castle had been taken by Free State troops. 'We are very thankful to God for saving us and the house'.

Another servant Annie Doyle wrote to Lady Congreve the following day, updating her on the occupation of the house:

---

[204] Congreve Archive, Letter from A Flynn, cook, to Lady Irene Congreve, London, 27 July 1922.

[205] Congreve Archive, Letter from A Flynn to Major John Congreve, 28 July 1922.

On Wed 19th the sitting room was first taken then they asked for another room off the front hall, so we thought the dining room the best one to give as the carpet was up there,...Next day I asked to get through to the drawing room and we got the china from the big drawing room down to the housekeeper's room...On Sunday 23rd when the men had gone out we went to your Ladyship's bedroom and found it had been taken over the night before by nurses everything from the chests of drawers and some things out of the wardrobe were all scattered about...So we just packed up everything we could and locked them in...Everything was pulled about in Mr Congreve's room and some of the drawers empty. Master Ambrose's was just the same...on Thursday night 20th about 40 extra men came and went...into all the rooms, your Ladyship's bed was used...on Wed last we found the chest of drawers in the Smoking-room had been opened and the uniforms all pulled about, we took them all away...The library was used and everything from the drawers pulled about. A shot went off accidentally and the bullet went through a pane of glass in the front door and through the wall opposite.[206]

Kathleen Hicks, a member of Cuman na mBan, stated that she went to Mount Congreve to warn the IRA that the Free State troops were about to take the place and that she 'got them away in time'.[207]

On 12 August Annie Flynn wrote to Lady Congreve with an update, informing her that the Free State troops visited the house and searched it but found nothing. Mr Palmer the auctioneer had made a list of every damaged item. They had been able to use the upstairs bedrooms for the first time. She lists missing items of bed

---

[206] Congreve Archive, Letter from Annie Doyle to Lady Irene Congreve, 5 August 1922.
[207] MSP34REF57863

linen, field glasses, and two silver cigarette cases and a matchbox which belonged to Mr Congreve.[208]

Thomas S Hearne wrote to Major Congreve on 14 August 1922:

> The house is now unoccupied, and you could return. But the condition of the house is so bad at present and do not think you would live in it...Every room was so occupied and is in a bad state. It will take some time to clean the place...The Republicans broke the door of the stock house and took away the three crosscuts...I am glad to tell you the horses, cattle, sheep, pigs, and the three dogs are alright.[209]

On 21 August it was reported that John Congreve had been awarded £1,400 from the provisional government for 'destruction of property'.[210]

Mr Warde, the gardener at Mount Congreve, wrote to Lady Congreve on 7 September 1922 informing her about the fruit etc. taken by the IRA to the value of £48 and enclosed a list. He noted that Whitfield Court was still occupied by Free State troops.[211]

The person in charge of the IRA at Mount Congreve was George Lennon (1900-1991). At age twenty he was the youngest commander of a flying column during the War of Independence.[212] He wrote an autobiography in which he recalled

---

[208] Congreve Archive, Letter from Annie Flynn to Lady Irene Congreve, 12 August 1922.

[209] Congreve Archive, Letter from Thomas S Hearne to Major John Congreve, 14 August 1922.

[210] *Evening Herald*, 21 August 1922.

[211] Mount Congreve Archive, Letter from R Warde to Lady Irene Congreve, 7 September 1922.

[212] Terence O'Reilly, *Rebel Heart – George Lennon Flying Column Commander* (Cork 2009).

the occupation of Mount Congreve. In July 1922 Waterford city was occupied by the IRA and the Free State troops were attempting to retake the city from across the river. After several days of fighting the Free State army took the city on Friday 21 July and the IRA retreated westwards, taking over a number of houses as bases: Whitfield Court, Mount Congreve, Curraghmore and Butlerstown Castle.

Mount Congreve had been occupied since Wednesday 19 July. Lennon and his men were by now dispirited but nevertheless managed to make the most of their time in the Big House:

> When we got to Mount Congreve the sergeant major begged me to try and get some rest and the quartermaster went off to see the housekeeper about provisions; she assured him there was enough food in the larders to feed eight men for three days, but no longer.
>
> The four junior officers, the Doctor and the local commandant retired with me to the library, and somebody went off to inspect the wine cellar. The cellar was well stocked, mostly with vintage brandy and in a session that lasted three days and three nights we drank it out completely. The library apart from the books was equipped with a gramophone and just one record. Humoresque by Dvorak; we kept playing it until the needle or the record wore out.
>
> The Doctor was something of a demoralizing influence as he kept pacing the floor cursing the Civil War and whoever was responsible for it. From time to time, runners would come in with reports from 'the front' but we immediately chased them out.
>
> The poor Nipper brought me food from the kitchen and begged me to eat or he would help me upstairs, cover me

with blankets and try and get me to sleep. One night of our stay I was shaken awake to consult a pale delicate looking man who said his name was Erskine Childers, in charge of publicity; he wanted an interesting account of the siege for a Republican paper he was printing in the field.

The Doctor (Joe Walsh) suggested a game of golf and one of the buglers offered to caddy for us, but we were interrupted in our play by two stately looking ladies advancing up the avenue.

'My God', said Joe 'It's the Cumann na mBan'.

'What again?'

Half the men were at that moment searching through the strawberry beds and the other half were parading before the front of the mansion dressed in a most extraordinary variety of uniforms and costumes borrowed from the big houses many wardrobes. The house had a tradition of military service going back beyond Waterloo. Some of the men were dressed as admirals, others as generals, and one lad was arrayed in a blazer from Eton or Harrow.

The ladies were very disapproving of all this and informed us they were looking after the welfare of the troops. They said the men should have clean socks every day and should have porridge every morning for breakfast. They caused great hilarity and we returned to our play as the two women stalked off looking very angry. It was a scene of tragic comedy. The hilarity was mostly forced and there was a ground swell of disgust, at times almost despairing.

After all the clothing had been returned ...and everything put back in place we said goodbye to the household staff and left. We were not at all sure where we were going to go next. One thing we agreed on, we were not going to live off the good country people again.[213]

Aspects of Lennon's entertaining account of the occupation of Mount Congreve are corroborated by the letters from the servants there, and the list of damaged items compiled by John D Palmer.[214] The latter lists the damaged record and the 'used' gramophone and a violin. The servants referred to the uniforms which had been pulled out. There is one strange omission from the list of missing/damaged items and that is the wine referred to by Lennon.

On 3 August the Free State Commandant Paddy Paul compiled a report on the strength of the anti-Treaty forces at a number of country houses near Waterford city:
Butlerstown Castle: 1 officer, 15 men. 15 rifles and 1 machine gun.
Mount Congreve House: 2 officers, 40 men, 35 rifles.
Whitfield Court: 30 men, 30 rifles.
Pouldrew House: 25 men, 25 rifles.
Curraghmore House: 100 men, 80 rifles.[215]

By this stage Lennon was disillusioned by events and he resigned soon afterwards. The author Una Troy later used the episode at Mount Congreve in her novel *Dead Star's Light,* published in the 1930s.[216]

> They chose their lodgings well, seeking only the largest and most comfortable houses abandoned by their alarmed

---

[213] George G. Lennon, *Trauma in Time*, 1971. Unpublished memoir, courtesy of Ivan Lennon.

[214] Congreve Archive, List of damaged and missing contents Mount Congreve, pp.10, undated.

[215] Terrence O'Reilly, pp196-197.

[216] Elizabeth Connor, *Dead Star's Light* (London 1938). Una Troy was married to Joseph Walsh who was medical officer to the West Waterford I.R.A.

Anglo-Irish owners, and whiled away the hours by recourse to well-stocked cellars. It seemed ungrateful sometimes to leave behind only a heap of smoking ruins...There seemed little reason why their stay should not be prolonged...Besides the wine and brandy were such that neither John nor Hurley had ever sampled before...And the place held numerous other attractions – wide and glorious parklands, sweeps of sheltering forests, a small rough river...'I wouldn't mind staying here forever', Hurley said. I wonder-when we get our Republic-is there any chance they'd make me a lord'.

Whitfield Court

Not far from Mount Congreve was Whitfield Court, the seat of the Dawnay family. The Italianate house was built c.1841 by Thomas Christmas to replace the 18th-century house situated on a lower site nearby.[217] Major Henry Chavasse leased the house in 1899 until 1913. It was purchased in 1916 by Lady Susan Dawnay, daughter of the 6th Marquis of Waterford. Her husband, Hugh had been killed on 6 November 1914 in France. In 1922 she was in India, leaving the servants in charge. Whitfield was occupied by both the IRA and the Free State Troops. As with Mount Congreve, the servants wrote a series of letters to their employers describing the occupation of the house by the IRA.

The IRA arrived at Whitfield without warning on 21 July 1922 and demanded accommodation. The first letter, dated 25 July 1922, recounts the arrival of the IRA:

> Well, they came on Saturday night late, only gave us about an hour's notice. We prepared as much as we could left all our rooms and Mrs Brown's for them took yours for ourselves and begged the commanders to keep them out

---

[217] Mark Girouard, 'Whitfield Court, Co Waterford', pp 522-526. *Country Life*, 7 September 1967.

of the best rooms, one young man who belongs to Kilmeadan did all he could, but they [are] strangers from Cork, and of course we could not do much. They went all over the house but did not sleep in the best rooms they were searching for men's clothes, and I am afraid they have taken some of Mr Browne's, but we can't tell yet as we don't know what was left...however the house is not damaged at all and can be cleaned up all right – and I am sure you won't mind what is missing if anything.

Towards the end of July Harriet (one of the house servants) updated Lady Susan about the IRA occupation of Whitfield. The house was dirty and untidy. She asked for some wages as the Republicans had stolen any money the servants possessed in the house. The IRA told her that they were tired and knew they were beaten so she felt certain they would surrender. They also indicated that they would leave as soon as the Free State troops approached 'so that there could be no fighting here, they don't want places like this destroyed'.

Harriet wrote to Lady Susan in early August:

Two days after I wrote you, more men came here and are occupying the house still, they have taken any clothes they could make use of. I try to remove any thing I can and lock up, but it is hopeless...the men we have now are rather decent. We have some very fine young men, they are all very polite and kind to us. Now we also have two very nice young girls who are cooking and washing for the men. Your kind letter cheered me and gave me courage. The soldiers are all about Portlaw, and the men here tell me the Free State army is shelling Carrick today. Mount Congreve is in the same state as we are, but I think they found more clothes there, they are all wearing the Major's Kaki shirts and collars, they go from here and get them also.

Harriet sent another letter dated 14 August, informing Lady Susan that the National Troops were now at Whitfield:

About 30 of the National troops are here for more than a week past but expect to move on in a few days. The house is very dirty and will take some time to put right. I think the blankets and matresses ought to be disinfected...Biddy is very anxious to help clean the house. May I have her to do the rough scrubbing...I went to the Rectory last Wednesday evening for the last of the prayer meetings. Mr Ennis said he feels sure they did good as the troubles had passed over us all lightly. Mr Palmer [auctioneer & valuer] came and looked through the house he will come again and examine it properly when the men are all gone...it grieves me to see your house so dirty and things pulled about. I am glad you are all having a good time and I hope these bad times here will soon be over and we have peace again.

While about fifty Free State troops were in occupation, the IRA launched an attack on Whitfield on 19 August led by Tom Keating's column, but they withdrew to Gardenmorris estate as Commandant Paul was leading reinforcements from Waterford. The incident was recorded by Harriet:

We were attacked by the Irregulars on Saturday morning about six o'clock but nothing serious happened only about three or four panes of glass broken, it lasted about an hour...the place was soon crowded with troops from Waterford, but the others had gone when they arrived. We were up all night on the Sunday night expecting another, but only a few shots were fired from towards Powers Knock... We try to keep the place roughly clean and to keep them from spoiling the furniture takes all my time. I have taken things as much as possible out of the bedrooms. We have not had much in the way of food in the shops as we are mostly living on army rashions. However, we can't grumble much these times, the men have to rough it too in war times...It is sad to have them shooting each other. I am sending boots and the picture of Lord Roberts to Hyde Park Gardens.

On 21 September the wife of the gate lodge keeper J Cashin informed her that the Free State troops had left and had not caused too much damage. 'Paddy and the children and myself are fighting away with the grass and weeds'.

Susan's sister Clodagh Anson recalled an event which has been repeated in various publications since:

> It was my sister Susan's gardener who sent the original message to her about the fight which took place at Whitfield when the Sinn Feiners [should read Free Staters] fought the Republicans who were living in the house, and one on each side was killed: "We had a grand funeral for the two soldiers,' he wrote. They were buried together in a corner of the garden, [both sides] walking side by side behind the coffins. I made a wreath for each, knowing it would be your ladyship's wish.' He added as a postscript, 'The antirrhinums growing in the border were greatly admired by all.[218]

The original letter cannot now be found, and the story seems very unlikely.

In March 1922 it was reported that a car stolen from Lady Susan had been returned to Whitfield.[219] On 15 November 1922 Lady Susan's solicitor forwarded a claim on her behalf for damage to the house contents:

> The Irregular forces of the I.R.A., forcibly occupied Whitfield Court...on the 21st day of July 1922 and remained there until the 3rd day of August 1922, on which date it was occupied by the National Troops who remained in occupation thereof till the 19th day of September 1922 and

---

[218] Lady Clodagh Anson, *Victorian Days* (London, 1957), p.252.
[219] *Waterford News & Star*, 13 March 1922.

during the said periods the articles of furniture, clothing, etc., in said house…were damaged, injured, or destroyed or carried away…in the sum of £739.14.2.[220]

A note at the end of the letter records that the case had been adjourned at the Waterford Quarter Sessions of 2 October 'pending consideration of the matter' by the Provisional Government.

Attached to the letter is an inventory of damaged or stolen house contents and their value compiled by John D Palmer, auctioneer, and valuer. Every room in the house is listed including the following: Drawing-Room, Library, White Drawing-Room, Lady Dawnay's Room, Mr. Dawnay's Room, School Room, Day & Night Nurseries, Mrs Burn's Room, Miss Holloway's Room, and the Turret Room.

Claim files which have detailed inventories attached give a good overview of the type of contents which furnished such houses. The Library at Whitfield had damage to a Japanese leather screen, books, a camera, and a writing table were stolen, and the glass had been smashed on a picture of Lord Roberts.

One of the IRA members, Sonny Cullinane, who took part in the retreat from Waterford city, recalled an incident at Whitfield: 'Butlerstown was retaken by the Free State troops. I ran back to Whitfield and found Jim Prendergast, Mick Shalloe, O'Brien and others knocked out drunk on the floor. They had got the wine cellar. We had to move out, so I got the help from the servants to dash the lads with water. We headed across to Mount Congreve'.[221]

The reference to members of the IRA being intoxicated is

---

[220] NAI FIN/COMP/2/23/105.

[221] Seán & Síle Murphy, *The Comeraghs – Gunfire and Civil War* (Middleton 2003), p.143.

120

explained by the list of the contents of the wine cellar: One dozen port 1871, one dozen claret 1868, three dozen port wine seal, four dozen white wine, three dozen madeira, five bottles of whiskey, four bottles of brandy, three dozen of champagne, and six bottles of liqueur.

In November 1922 Lady Susan was awarded £739 in compensation for damage done during the occupation of the house by the IRA.[222] In November 1924 she was given £515 for damage to the house and furniture during the 'Irregular occupation'.[223] Lady Susan and one of her staff Mary Harrington gave evidence. Mary told the court that the IRA opened the wine cellar and took all the wine and used coal and milk and food while in occupation. She said that the furniture had been badly damaged. The judge commented that 'they had all seen houses that had been occupied by troops, and they knew the usage articles got, whether the troops were Irregular, British, or National Army'. Lady Susan claimed £40 for 4 dozen bottles of champagne.[224]

On 30 November 1925 her solicitor submitted a bill to the Ministry of Finance. He explained that Lady Susan did not hire a professional contractor to redecorate the house but used local labour. The total expenditure was £171.10.4. William Foley was employed to do all the painting. In June 1927 the Ministry of Finance informed her solicitor that she would receive increased compensation in accordance with the provisions of the Damage to Property Compensation Amendment Act 1926 which included £21.11.11 for costs and witnesses' expenses.

---

[222] *Irish Examiner*, 29 November 1922.

[223] *Freeman's Journal*, 27 November 1924.

[224] *Munster Express*, November 1924.

Pouldrew House

Pouldrew House was built c.1814 for David Malcomson and had an existing mill nearby. During the Civil War it was occupied by Mrs Mary Ardagh (1868-1945), widow of Robert Michael Ardagh (1852-1921),[225] and her servants. One of the servants at Whitfield Court writing to her employer in early August 1922 noted that Mrs Ardagh had IRA billeted in the house for weeks and was impressed at how well behaved they were.[226] Lady Waterford described the occupation of Pouldrew, referring to the owner as Mrs A.:

> One of our neighbours...fetching a bucket and swab, proceeded under the eye of her visitor, to clean up the horrors (spit). "Excuse me Ma'am", says he "I'll do that for ye", and forthwith wiped the offending traces with the back of his sleeve! This lady objected to her maid-servants being kept up at night, letting in men when the watch was changed in the small hours, and cooking for them; so an 'orderly' of tender age was commandeered from the nearest village, and fried bacon till he dropped with fatigue, while the back stairs were permanently greased by the fat which he spilt from the frying pan as he carried it up to the Mess-room. The lady herself – there being no man in the house – opened the door at 3a.m. each morning to let in the new-comers and having assured herself that all was quiet in the house, again retired to bed. Several batches of Irregulars from different districts came and went in this way...no terribleness was shown by any nor

---

225 The *Dover Express*, 25 May 1902, published notice of their marriage. She was Mary Veteau Cassidy.
226 Letter from Harriet to Lady Susan Dawnay, Whitfield Court, 14 August 1922. Private Collection.

did they meddle with any of her belongings. After the first day, she said she could not possibly supply them with food, so they brought their own supplies...One day some Republican V.A.D.s came asking for food: Mrs A. looked at one of them, and feeling that her face was familiar, said "Surely I have seen you somewhere before? "Ah, Yes", said the girl, "I was in O'Brien's Bakery in Waterford." "Are you Ardagh's flour? "Yes", said Mrs A. "Ah", continued the girl, "We bake you!"[227]

Georgina Gethin noted that Mrs Ardagh was short of decent meat to eat, and the IRA offered some of theirs. 'Mrs Ardagh said don't touch it with the tongs, her cook most indignant said 'But only if she would with her fork'!!

Mary submitted a claim for 58 cans of petrol taken by the IRA on 5 July 1922 and a bicycle taken by armed men on 2 august 1922.[228] Waterford auctioneer John D Palmer sold the contents of Pouldrew for the representatives of the late Robert Ardagh in May 1923.[229] The mill had been purchased the previous month by a Mr O'Brien of Dublin.[230] The mill was burned on 12 September 1923, and he claimed £37,000 damages in 1924.[231]

Annestown House

Annestown House was built in the late 18th century by Major Henry St George Cole (1745-1819), and he is credited with

---

[227] Beatrix, Lady Osborne Beauclerk, unpublished typescript, November 1922. Private Collection.
[228] NAI FIN/COMP/2/23/141
[229] *Waterford News*, 27 April 1923.
[230] *Waterford News*, 20 April 1923.
[231] *Munster Express*, 11 October 1923.

founding the village of Annestown. He was a J.P. and an agent for the Earl of Enniskillen who had 5,000 acres in Co Waterford. Cole was notorious during the 1798 period for hunting down United Irishmen. In the 1830s the house was acquired by the Palliser family. In 1922 the house was owned by Mary Jane Sybil Galloway (1874-1940), daughter of Sir William Palliser C.B. and widow of Major Harold Bessemer Galloway (1868-1915) of Blervie House, Morayshire, who had been killed in action in Flanders in 1915.

Mrs Galloway spent her summers at Annestown and the rest of the year in London or at her husband's estate in Scotland. We know about the fate of the house in 1922 and 1923 through surviving letters written to her by the housemaid Maggie Walker.[232] The following is an extract from a letter written 5 August 1922 in which she says that the IRA had left the house on 3 August:

> They (I.R.A.) came here at eleven at night on July 26th and demanded admittance to the house (about forty armed men). They brought all the mattresses down and laid them on the smoking-room floor, and then some of them slept in the bedrooms on the box mattress of the beds, they used the blankets that were returned last summer and the few that were left after the raids, also curtains, coats, anything they could find for bedding.
>
> One of the men said they would not interfere with anything that was locked up, but then I see that they broke open the linen press and storeroom, used the white quilts, bath towels, the good china etc...

---

[232] According to the 1911 Census Margaret Annie Walker was a housemaid and was born in Co Waterford.

The house is in an awful state, carpets, and everything dirty and spoiled.

While the I.R.A. were there I saw them taking away I think 6 mattresses and a feather bed in different lots to other places.

While they were here, there was nearly 100 more, at Mr Robert Murphy's place near Dunhill in his house and barns, but they left the same day as the lot here went, as the National Troops have come to Tramore.

They are all around the county in everyone's places and some billeted even in small farmhouses and a lot of bridges have been blown up...With the exception of a few local men they were all from Cork. They took away Mr Dobbyn's motor, he had left it here with some part taken...The furniture in your house is not injured in any way except some locks broken and I have two embroidered bedspreads and most of the table linen safe so far.

Two of the I.R.A. went down to the Rockhouse and in through a window on Tuesday and I went after them, and they said they were looking for shirts. I told them that Mr Gubbins had taken all his shirts away. They came away then, but must have gone in again next day and ...broke open a hat box that was locked up with letters and papers, but didn't touch anything else, except to take a pair of boots.

John D Palmer carried out a valuation of the contents on 18 August. He noted that a Persian rug and toys had been stolen, a lavatory door broken and written on, and the window shutters covered with beer stains.[233]

Curraghmore House

In 1897, Henry 6th Marquis of Waterford married Beatrix Frances Petty-FitzMaurice (1877-1953), daughter of the 5th Marquess of Lansdowne. Henry died in 1911 and in 1918 Beatrix married Osborne Beauclerk (1874-1964), 12th Duke of St Albans of Newtown Anner House, Clonmel, Co Tipperary.

To mark the Truce in July 1921 a dance was held at Curraghmore: 'To signalise the return to Co. Waterford of men who had been 'On the run', the Cumann Na mBan organised a ball on Sunday night. It was held in a large room at the courtyard...nearly 200 young men attended'.[234] It was also said that many of the leading IRA members attended.

Beatrix's son by her first marriage John Charles, became the 7th Marquis of Waterford and had his coming-of-age party at Curraghmore on 7 January 1922. It was described as the society event of the year in the south of Ireland. A dance and lunch were organised for 154 tenants and employees in the Riding School. The Marquis was presented with a large ormolu clock and a silver clock and candlesticks from the tenants. He thanked them:

> 'from the bottom of his heart...Many of them were at Curraghmore before he was born. Curraghmore had always prided itself on the happy relations there existed between employer and employee, and since his father's death, ten years ago, the trustees and Major Gethin had maintained that spirit in spite of many difficulties. Many

---

[233] NAI FIN/COMP/2/23/139. Thanks to Cian Flaherty for details from this file.
[234] *Freeman's Journal*, 20 July 1921.

estates in recent years had entirely closed down. In consequence of the rise in wages and the abnormal taxation, it was found very hard to keep up estates like Curraghmore, and they were forced to do things on a greatly reduced scale. With careful management and the co-operation of the employees, he trusted that the old place would long survive. They had been through troublous times, but thank God, the outlook was now brighter, and he hoped that a new Ireland would arise, in which, forgetting all differences of politics and religion, men would have one ideal to work for: viz., the good of their country.[235]

The event was photographed by Waterford photographer A.H. Poole. The marquis was not resident at Curraghmore during the occupation of the Riding House by the IRA in July as he had left for England towards the end of January and did not return during 1922.[236] The estate agent Major Randolph Gethin who lived in Guilcagh House was left in charge.

On the 24 July 1922 at around 8.30am an armoured car and two others arrived at Curraghmore led by Brig Gen [sic] George Lennon.[237] They demanded accommodation for seventy men. Six bedrooms in the house were ordered to be reserved for officers but it is unclear if any were ever occupied. In the afternoon 'dispatch riders arrived in quick succession'. The IRA set fire to the police barrack in Portlaw but by evening the fire had been extinguished and the place boarded up by Major Gethin. Forty IRA arrived at Curraghmore from Carrick in five cars who were

---

[235] *Munster Express*, 14 January 1922. Mark Bence-Jones, *Twilight of the Ascendancy*, (London 1987), p.217.
[236] *Belfast Newsletter*, 23 January 1922.
[237] Marquis of Waterford Archive, Major R Gethin, notes made 22-29 July 1920.

'inclined to be nasty' but left soon after for Waterford. There was a second attempt to burn the barrack and the IRA issued a death threat to the Rector William H. Rennison[238] but instead made him light the match and set fire to the building. Later in the evening twenty more republicans arrived at Curraghmore and they all slept in the Riding House. On the following day the IRA commandeered some Curraghmore estate workers and made them cut down trees in Reynett's Field in order to block the road. They also exploded a mine there.

By Wednesday 26th the IRA were still occupying the Riding School and it was noted that the 'Woods [are] full of them'. They had also placed a signaling post on the top of the round tower at Clonegam and a guard at the Kilbunny Gate. The IRA left Curraghmore the following day.[239]

Major Gethin wrote to Lady Osborne on the 29 July updating her on the situation at Currraghmore:

> I suppose you know all about the occupation of Curraghmore. The Column that was there left us on Thursday and yesterday was absolutely quiet...Clark said...he wanted to bring May in, to cross to England tonight. She will be able to tell you about the damage to Whitfield, which is still occupied by the Republicans, and which is unspeakable!
>
> So far I have managed to keep them out of the house at Curraghmore, but I dread a general falling back from

---

[238] William Henry Rennison (1875-1927), Rector Ardmore from 1914 until 1921 when he was transferred to Portlaw.
[239] Marquis of Waterford Archive, single sheet of notes by Major Gethin, 22 -29 July 1922.

Whitfield, Mount Congreve, and Pouldrew when the National Troops advance from Waterford, for it is when they are on the run they do most damage. They have billeted themselves on nearly everyone in Portlaw, including 'The Industry', and have looted all the shops, and Miss Eva is not so fond of them as she was. There are a lot of them in Bessborough and Belline and I hear they are killing sheep in the former place. I am afraid you must make up your mind to stay in England for some time yet...Thank goodness the strike has been postponed, for if the men were out now the whole place would be looted, while as it is, they are behaving splendidly in trying to protect Tyrone's property.[240]

On 27 July John Russell of the Curraghmore Estate office wrote to Claud Anson about the IRA at Curraghmore. He noted that they brought food and groceries with them but that they had commandeered milk butter and eggs from the farm.[241]

Gethin's wife Georgina also wrote to Lady Osborne informing her of the IRA visits to her house at Guilcagh and to others in the locality:

Much of the day is spent looking on the top of all my cupboards and other places of concealment for the sugar and sardines. The first lot of visitors I thought would upset Mrs Bailiss very much. I found her quite calm making jam, said she had three officers for breakfast. Grace and Eva's guests did not come, their C.O. came inspected their

---

[240] Marquis of Waterford Archive, Major Randolph Gethin, Estate Office, Waterford to Lady Osborne, 29 July 1922.
[241] Marquis of Waterford Archive, John Russell, Estate Office, Waterford to Hon Claud Anson, Royal Automobile Club, Pall Mall, London. 27 July 1922.

arrangement and said his men were all gentlemen and not accustomed to sleeping on the floor! They took up the Dining Room carpet and after lunching at a little table the floor covered with mattresses and cushions; they look rather pathetic but Eva still full of fight. My poor little refugee family is at the Convent of Mercy, Fishguard, but I hope may join some little cousins at Llanfairfechan soon. The accounts of Whitfield are too distressing for words. I suggested Clarke bringing some things here...I suppose no use getting things cleaned.

So far, we have been lucky beyond demanding food and our coats and when refused said they would return and search the house but didn't. It is such a relief knowing the children are not here...It seems strange and depressing the Free Stater's not doing more. The Strangmans, and I believe the Bishop, all have, or had visitors. But we hear very little outside Portlaw. Randolph went to Waterford last Saturday on a bicycle under some trees and over others. [242]

In March 1923 Major Gethin claimed for 'articles seized by armed men' on 2 March 1923, valued at £30.[243]

Doctor David Walker of Springfield House, Portlaw, was the local doctor and was also doctor to the Beresfords at Curraghmore. His wife Caroline wrote to Lady Osborne on 4 August 1922, updating her on what was happening in Portlaw:

---

[242] Marquis of Waterford Archive. Georgina Gethin, Guilcagh House, Portlaw to Lady Osborne, London, July 1922?
[243] WCCA WCC/GWA288

It really is too extraordinary sometimes I feel as if it must be a foolish dream!! Of course, the most serious piece of destruction was the burning of Fiddown Bridge. Yesterday we heard that they completed the destruction of both bridges in Carrick – and Portlaw Bridge is in a very bad way, only enough room to walk over it.

At present they [Republicans] seem inclined to stay – They have left Mount Congreve & Whitfield I believe & Annestown House but are still at Pouldrew, only about ten of them. Last night one of the Milfort visitors with a band of Portlaw 'imps' came and asked him for his bicycle, but they didn't get it. We have only had three here so far, for a meal, and didn't give them a very good one so I hope they thought me a horrid stingy woman. We get our supplies in all sorts of ways, some things are coming by barge to Pouldrew tomorrow. Doc had been using his boat to cross the river, it was down at the stables, and then that was taken, but he got it back…In spite of all these difficulties we had quite a nice tennis party on Tuesday, the Mealys & Mr McC. & family & Mr Gethin and the Rennisons!!

She adds that all the IRA had vacated Milfort [on 4 August] and that her husband had met General Prout and liked him.

Georgina Gethin of Guilcagh House, Portlaw told Lady Osborne that 'Poor Dr W[alker] is cut off from most of his patients, he got so bored with being stopped and questioned going to Carrick he said, 'Can't you see I'm Prout's advance guard'![244]

---

[244] Marquis of Waterford Archive, Georgina Gethin to Lady Osborne July 1922.

131

In October 1922 Beatrix, Lady Osborne, returned to Curraghmore accompanied by her mother Lady Lansdowne and recorded her impressions:

> Three rather disheveled Free State soldiers strolling into town, were the only visible signs of the presence of the National Army, and no incidents marked our drive. There were three or four broken road bridges...one of them near Pouldrew Mills, had only recently been made passable, through the efforts of the Mill Manager...Nearing Portlaw, a lately repaired breach in the road, and several fine trees lying by the side of it, heralded the approach of the Police Barracks, now, alas but a charred skeleton...

> Our friends have many tales of events during the months we were away...and especially of the time when Civil War was first declared, and the Irregulars-or Republicans, occupied nearly all the houses in the neighbourhood. The Free Staters were many miles away...half the country people were more or less in sympathy with the Republicans; so, of what use was it to refuse admittance...when they hammered on the door with their revolvers and demanded bed and board? On the whole if civilly treated, they were courteous enough and behave decently according to their lights. But the lights of labouring men are not our lights, and perhaps it did not occur to them that a lady might object to spitting on the stairs and in the passages of her house...In another house, the Republicans showed great appreciation of the hot baths - an unaccustomed luxury - and could hardly be got out of them.

> At Whitfield, where 30 men took possession of the house, one of them was found by the maid rummaging in the

drawers. When asked what he was doing, he replied that he was looking to see if he could find a photograph of the lady to take away as a souvenir!

Whitfield was also occupied by the Free Staters after the departure of the Republicans...During this time, some of them were caught in an ambush, and two were killed. On the day of the funeral, the finest wreath was the one made by the Whitfield gardener, who, knowing his Lady's kindly disposition - felt it incumbent upon him to show this token of sympathy on her behalf and sent the wreath with her compliments!

Practically every house in the neighbourhood was obliged to put a certain number of men; 70 of them appeared at Curraghmore and demanded accommodation in the house, but after some parleying, they consented to occupy the riding school where...the camp kitchen built for the coming-of-age dinner made the cooking easy...

They did not stay long; there was a rumour that the Free Staters were coming and realising that Curraghmore, commanded by hills on every side, would be a bad place to be caught, the general (a lad of 19 or 20) [George Lennon] proceeded on his way to Dungarvan the same evening, taking two thirds of the men...These were Waterford men; a contingent from Cork demanded admittance the same evening and caused our people grave anxiety, owing to their bad reputation as looters and incendiaries. But the local officer in command of the remaining men...bluffed them into thinking the whole place was already occupied and persuaded them to go straight on...

Further up the river, the billeting of Republicans still continues...and almost every bridge, road or railway is destroyed...the towpath and a cot across the river were the only means of getting to luncheon with our friends (de la Poers of Gurteen) on the other side...We found them strung up in a tense state of nerves from the constant strain of Republican incursions. At luncheon, the maid announced 'Four men for dinner, ma'am and our sorely tried hostess raged in impotent fury. 'Don't give them any meat, don't give them anything good; rabbits, Hegarty, rabbits, on no account give them meat', but our host, seeing a vision of his house in flames, murmured 'Give them enough, Hegarty, give them enough.

She commented on the battered appearance of Clonmel town:

There were many stories of these Free State soldiers in this and other towns; how one, on guard, gave his rifle to a small boy to hold, while he lit a cigarette; how another, anxious to investigate the working of a Thompson gun, fired off a whole belt of cartridges by mistake, killing his Sergeant and wounding several others. In another place a butcher was ordered to kill a bullock for the troops; the bullock ran amok amongst them, so they all fired at it, but only succeeded in killing the butcher.

In November 1922 the Marquis of Waterford received £1500 in compensation for 'damage to property'.

Lady Waterford's parents the Lansdownes of Bowood House owned a huge estate in Co Kerry, with a residence at Derreen. The wrecking of the house during 1922 received widespread coverage in the press. In October 1922 Mr J. Barker of the Irish Compensation Claims Bureau commented on its destruction:

134

The fate of Derreen, though perhaps few mansions have been subjected to precisely the same process of deliberate plunder, is unhappily typical of too many others. The stoppage of the post and telegraph service has made it very difficult for my committee to get in touch with all those who have had their country mansions destroyed...We have, however, obtained sufficient information, for the Irish residents who have been obliged to take refuge in this country, to prove that the process of destruction which has been applied to Lord Lansdowne's residence is only part of a well-organised system which is being applied...all over Ireland for the murder and expulsion of the Irish gentry, their dependents and all those who in the past have shown any British sympathies.[245]

Barker noted that these people had set up a committee in London to campaign for their rights, and their only crime he says was to be loyal to the crown. Those who accepted the Truce and were willing to support the new Free State had been particularly targeted by the 'Republican and Bolshevist party', who now ruled with 'revolver and bomb' in the south of Ireland. He felt that these Irish loyalists had a greater claim on the sympathy of the British people and press than that of the Greek refugees.

In her diary under the date 23 October 1923, Beatrix, Lady Osborne Beauclerk, noted that she and her husband were working in the garden at Curraghmore when four men passed through the grounds. Her husband said he would report them, but they replied that they would shoot him if he did so.[246]

---

[245] *Londonderry Sentinel*, 3 October 1922.
[246] Diary, Tuesday 23 October 1923. Private collection.

Butlerstown Castle

The castle was acquired by Geoffrey le Butiler in the 13th century. In the mid-15th century, it passed by marriage to the Nugents of Cloncoskeran Castle, Dungarvan. In the 16th century it became the residence of a junior branch of the Sherlocks who built a stone house adjoining the castle. In the late 18th century, it was badly damaged by fire and the Sherlocks moved out. It was repaired and occupied by the Backas family. In the 1870s the Ulster nationalist Samuel Ferguson acquired it and restored the castle and house. He left it to his nephew Joseph Bigger.[247] The castle was owned by J Nolan of Butlerstown who had leased it in 1917 along with two acres to a cattle dealer, Michael O'Connor, his wife and ten children. Nolan paid the rates on the building.

When one of the IRA, Sean O'Rourke, was shot he was brought to Butlerstown and looked after by the O'Connors. When the local priest arrived to pray for the wounded man, he warned O'Connor that he was putting himself and his family in danger if he was caught by the British military. When the IRA were on the retreat from Waterford in 1922, they occupied the castle, and this was recalled by O'Connor in a long statement attached to his compensation claim file: 'A great many of the IRA took refuge in the castle for a few weeks. Some of the men advised me to have my family removed someplace for safety, as they were expecting an 18 pounder any minute from the golf links'. He took their advice. For the next couple of weeks three lorry loads of Cork IRA men stayed at the castle on and off. O'Connor states that they left to go the Mount Congreve and Whitfield Court. When they departed, he employed two women to clean the castle for two

---

[247] Julian Walton, 'Butlerstown Castle' in *Unlocking Butlerstown* (Waterford, 2016), pp 60-63.

days. He called his family back but on their first night they were woken from their sleep by loud knocking: 'On asking who was there, was told, Paddy Joe Power from the Glen, and wanted to put up 40 I.R.A. men from Kilmacthomas. They lit some fires, some got food, while others went out on sentry'.

Soon after a shell exploded next to the castle, so O'Connor was once again forced to send his family away. When the Kilmacthomas group left they were replaced by men led by Wyley and O'Donoghue. The castle was taken by Free State troops on 3 August 1922 under the command of Captain Paul. The IRA fired on them, but the Free State men managed to get into the castle led by Commandant Heaslip, Capt Mullany, and Capt Cunningham. The IRA Quartermaster, Capt Wyley, Stephen Ambrose captain of the 'A' company IRA, Commandant Keating, Kilmacthomas and W. O'Donoghue were taken along with sixteen others. Nineteen Mauser rifles, 19 revolvers, one Lewis gun, and a large quantity of ammunition were recovered.[248]

Eighty Free State soldiers then moved into the castle and told the O'Connors to leave. When they left, they were replaced by more soldiers from Tullaroan who stayed for several weeks.

O'Connor's landlord decided he would like the castle back, but O'Connor did not want to vacate it. As a result, Nolan refused to pay the rates. O'Connor claimed £300 for items damaged or taken during the occupation of the castle by the Irregulars and Free State army. In December 1923 he was awarded £150, out of which he had to pay the rates. Over the next few years, he was in financial difficulty and was forced to sell his animals, tools etc. Things came to a head in March 1929 when his landlord Nolan arrived at the castle with the bailiffs and Civic Guards to evict him.

---

[248] *Munster Express*, 5 August 1922.

The family were now homeless, and O'Connor went to Major Congreve to ask for shelter, but he had no house available at the time. Congreve suggested he go to Lady Susan Dawnay at Whitfield Court. She offered him a cottage which she was planning to give to her new gardener.

'Oh! the horror of it all' Gurteen Le Poer Castle

We have an insight into what was happening in the north of the county in the latter part of 1922 from the diary of the Hon. Mary Olivia Augusta De la Poer of Gurteen Le Poer Castle in Kilsheelan. She was the daughter of William Monsell, 1st Baron Emly. In 1881 she married Edmond James De Poher de la Poer (1841-1915), 1st Count de la Poer, Knight of Justice (Devotion) of St John of Jerusalem (Malta), Chamberlain to Pope Pius IX, and Count of the Roman States (created 1864). He was a J.P. and H.M. Lieutenant for Waterford city and county, M.P. for Co Waterford (1866-73) and High Sheriff in 1879. The old house at Gurteen was replaced by the Count who created a much grander Tudor Baronial style castle designed by Samuel Ussher Roberts (1821-1900) and constructed from 1863 to 1866 at a cost of £10,000. He spent much time researching his family history and over the entrance door is carved – 'Poeraig Aboo'. He wanted an imposing house which reflected what he believed to be his ancient family lineage.[249] They had six children: Rivallon, Arnold, Edmond, Elinor, Yseult and Ermyngarde. Edmond died in 1915 and his widow Mary went to live at the dower-house nearby known as Glen Poer.[250]

---

[249] *Burke's Landed Gentry of Ireland*, (London, 1912), pp.572-574.

[250] Now known as Glencomeragh and owned by the Rosminian order. It was a substantial house, built c.1820 which was extended in 1910. In 1912 elaborate water gardens were added.

138

Their son John William Rivallon, (1882-1939) known as 'Riv', inherited the estate and moved into the castle in 1919 with his wife Muriel (or Patricia as she became known after converting to the Catholic faith), and their six children.[251] On the death of his father in 1915 he succeeded as the 2nd Count de la Poer. He was appointed HM Lieutenant of Co Waterford in 1915 and when he left in 1922, he was the last to hold such a post. He had been an officer in the 4th Battalion, Leinster Regiment but had retired on health grounds. Riv decided his mother should move back to the main house while the political situation remained volatile. She began a daily diary at the beginning of 1922 which gives us a first-hand account of the disruption, terror and chaos which occurred. Her son also kept a diary which starts in 1921, but it is not as detailed.

On 19 October 1921 he wrote that he had a visit from five men while he was digging in the water garden. They informed him that a 'General Holiday' had been proclaimed in South Tipperary to commemorate the death of Sean Treacy and that all work and business should cease. He notes in his dairy that the estate workers were not happy with this.

In March 1922 Rivallon travelled to London to attend the Committee of Privileges of the House of Lords. They were considering his claim to the 16th-century Barony of Le Power and Coroghmore. The peerage had been dormant since the senior branch of the family became extinct in the male line in the early 1700s. Rivallon was now claiming it as the senior heirmale. The committee allowed his claim as proved by right of descent (de jure). However, it depended on the outlawry of a Jacobite ancestor which would have to be reversed by an Act of

---

[251] Mark Bence-Jones, *Life in an Irish Country House* (London, 1996), p.143.

Parliament. The British government did not think it appropriate to reverse the outlawry now that Ireland was independent.[252]

On 22 April he had a visit from a group of IRA who wanted to search the house for arms. 'The country is in a very unpleasant state, no one to keep order and being deprived of all our means of defence, the people are at the mercy of any set of unprincipled men who, being armed themselves, can do as they like'. On 4 August two IRA men appeared looking for tea, one from Cork and the other from Clare. One had been wounded in the hand that morning in Carrick on Suir. They complained that they had not been well received by some of the servants. Around 11 pm that night he and his mother had just finished a game of piquet in the smoking room when they heard whistle blasts near the house. 'The shutters of the east window of the smoking room were partly open, as also the window through which the [pet] hare comes in and out. I opened the window and asked what was wanted and was told that 8 men wanted something to eat...We gave them tea and eggs and bread and butter, and they left at about 12.30... They all seemed very tired and glad to have a short rest and something to eat'.

A week later a group of 16 arrived and were put up in the servant's hall. They were given tea and had breakfast, and dinner and tea the following day. 'I must say they have behaved very well and not tried to enter any other part of it, other than the servant's hall'.

His mother's diary is missing the first 15 pages and she begins page 16 on 23 August 1922 by stating that she thought she wouldn't need to continue writing as she felt the 'war' was coming to an end. She refers to the servants who lived in at Gurteen:

---

[252] Mark Bence-Jones, p.144.

Hegarty the housekeeper, Flynn the cook, Annie the dairy maid, and the male servants Goodwin and Moore the chauffeur. Mary de la Poer was a loyal southern unionist and felt Ireland was better under British rule.

She commented that there were not enough Free State troops in the area to drive the IRA out of the surrounding hills. She felt that the situation was getting worse with bridges damaged, trees felled and sniping in Clonmel on a nightly basis. During the day she observed three IRA men near the laundry at Gurteen and one of the maids later told her that they had come looking for food: 'They said that they were starved and that they were up in the hills night and day. One of them said that he was heartily sick of it all but that they had to go on'.[253]

On 1 September she wrote that at 11 p.m. the previous night the front doorbell rang. Her son Riv spoke to the caller who said he wanted accommodation for eight IRA men. They had to call the servants and light the range to prepare food and get mattresses and bedding which she says had been put away after disinfecting [from a previous group]. They were put up in the servants' hall, and two of the live-in staff, Moore and Goodwin, slept in the housekeeper's room. They left the next morning after breakfast and the de la Poers were informed by Miss Danaher that lots of ammunition was found at Cooney's in Clonmel. She also said that one of the Franciscans was caught carrying a carriage load of pigs' heads to the IRA, but he wasn't arrested, and the pigs' heads were confiscated.

Mary was shocked to discover that the Free State soldiers raided the house of a 'respectable' man named Whelan and found a lot of stolen property. Whelan used to cut the corn at Gurteen. She

---

[253] Diary of Mary De la Poer, 23 August 1922.

wasn't impressed with the Free State soldiers: 'I must say all my faith in the latter has disappeared since I was told today that they were a dirty undisciplined lot – They are very numerous in Clonmel lolling about the streets romping with girls driving them about in motors'.

Later in the day the dairy maid informed Mary that a man at her house said the IRA would sleep at Gurteen that night, saying that if they didn't get the best bed clothes he would 'knock someone out'. She was terrified and informed her son Riv. The staff were told to prepare and be on the alert. That night the expected visitors arrived around midnight. There were eight of them and they demanded blankets and one of them insisted he wanted a blanket and not old curtains. Mrs Shannon asked one of the men if he was a Catholic and he replied: 'I am if it is any damned use to me. I believe in nothing and if one is shot after all it is just like a dog's death'. Riv was accustomed to wear a kilt in the evening at Gurteen and the man said: 'By Christ I will plug him through his petticoats'. The next morning the gardener arrived at Gurteen and informed them that the Free State soldiers were nearby in Kilsheelan. 'Our gallant eight were terrified. Two of them (Cooneys from Derrinlaur) bolted instantly...and the others followed soon after'.

On the evening of 5 September Mary had what she described as their 'very worst experience'. There was the usual loud knocking at the front door and a group of republicans led by Frank O'Keefe of the Ormond Hotel, Clonmel, and a Mr Quirke demanded admission for six people. They said the rest of their men were across the river and then would return with them. After three hours they had not returned so the De la Poers went to bed.

Mary continues the story: 'I had only just got to sleep when I heard Riv's voice - Moore had come to tell him the men had arrived, but they wanted more beds – I got ready and followed Riv downstairs. To my horror I heard Riv having an altercation with one of the men. I heard the words 'We are at war' in a bullying and arrogant voice. Riv said 'after all this is my house. I am willing to give food and shelter, but it is unreasonable at this hour of the morning, 3 a.m., to get servants up...' The man was called Lonergan and Riv eventually managed to calm him down. Another man present was a Mr Stokes, one of three brothers, farmers of Priorstown, Clonmel, who was 'very drunk'. They left the following morning at 9 a.m.

Mary reflected on the night: 'It is awful to feel when they enter one's house, every few nights what their power is and what injury they could do us – Oh! the horror of it all. Really as night falls if one hears a sound one shudders'. They decided to have the servants' hall permanently set up for future visits from the IRA.

On the 12 September there was knocking at the front door and Riv asked 'What are you? Regulars or Irregulars'. They replied 'Regulars' and asked if there were any Irregulars or 'Die hards' in the house. There were 35 Free State troops with rifles and machine guns surrounding the house. Riv told them he did have IRA men in the house a few nights previously and they sometimes had about twenty. He opened the front door to find all their rifles trained on him as they were afraid that the Irregulars were inside. The following night four young Irregulars arrived looking for shelter. They said they had lost their leader and had been walking for miles in the rain and were famished and tired. The cook gave them bread, butter and eggs. The next morning, they were late getting up and the cook tried to frighten them by telling them the Free State troops were nearby, but it didn't seem to alarm them at all. The cook informed the de la Poers that many IRA had been arrested including Stokes of Priorstown, the O.C. of the local brigade who had stolen cattle from Gurteen, shot their game and arrived drunk at Gurteen one night looking for shelter.

Mary's friend Margery Bagwell came to visit and told them that they had very little trouble with the IRA at Marlfield House. A few nights later more IRA were put up overnight in Gurteen and Mary says that they would not get out of bed the following morning as they were too comfortable. They said that one night they slept in a haycock and the next in a castle.

On the 19 September she writes that she is feeling depressed. They have had no trains or regular post for two months, no telegrams, and now no post at all, bridges destroyed etc.

A family friend Obby Beauclerk of Newtown Anner House told her that after his last visit to Gurteen, when he returned home, he found nine IRA sleeping in the house and five in the farm. He now understood the de la Poers' anxiety. She also heard that the Franciscan who had given the pigs' heads to the IRA had been dismissed from the order and that four Christian Brothers in Clonmel had left as it was discovered they had been making explosives. The parents had refused to send their children to school while they were still teaching.

In early October she went to Clonmel commenting on how depressing and deserted the town looked. She was unimpressed with the Free State soldiers and noted many of the sentries were 'mere children'. She also commented that they had only visited Gurteen once in three months. Later in the month her son was informed that 1,200 of his demesne trees had been cut down by looters on the other side of the river. Claims for these and other trees were submitted to Waterford County Council. The 1,200 trees were cut between 22 July and 1 December 1922 and a claim of £2,400 was made. 596 trees valued at £1,192 had been cut between 22 December 1922 and 20 March 1923. There were separate claims for three oak and two ash trees and damage to the demesne wall.[254]

On 18 October Rivallon recorded that four IRA came to the house wanting beds for the night. 'I asked if they had not heard the Bishops' Pastoral, and if I let them in, I would not get absolution. They replied that they did care for the Bishops and that if they were there, they, the IRA, would tell them, the Bishops so, also the Bishops had not done what they have now done two years ago'.

One night some of the IRA wishing to be put up for the night at Gurteen climbed up onto a balcony which was outside one of the servants' rooms and asked to be let in. They said they were reluctant to knock on the main door in case they woke the children. On a previous occasion a group of IRA had thrown pebbles at the windows and the cook Mrs Flynn reprimanded them severely for waking the children. Mary reacted to this as follows: 'Really I thought they acted very nicely! Funny to say this when armed men come to one's house at 3 a.m.'. The visitors stayed all next day for breakfast, dinner, and tea and 'walked about as if they had a right to the place'. One of them told her he had been a carpenter earning £7 a week and now he did not have money to buy a stamp.

On 27 October she heard a rumour that Grove House, Co Tipperary, the seat of the Bartons, had been burned. The reason given was that it was about to be occupied by Free State troops. It turned out to be just a rumour.

On 29 October she attended mass in Clonmel, and the priest Father Warren gave a sermon about stealing and looting, telling

---

[254] WCCA WCC/GWA288

his congregation 'that no matter if they went to confession to ten priests, to ten bishops and even to the Pope, they could not get forgiveness until they had repaid what they had stolen. I fancied much coughing accompanied his words. Several I.R.A. were in the church'.

On 4 November Rivallon made the following note of desperation in his diary:

> I hear 200 more Free State troops arrived in Clonmel yesterday. I wish to Heavens all this disturbance would come to an end, and that we could live our lives in peace, but I see no end to it and the country is every day going from bad to worse. It must end in national bankruptcy, already the country owes millions of pounds for damage done, the expense of the army is enormous, and the taxes are already so heavy that they cannot be paid. The end of it will be that, as far as I am concerned, I shall leave the country, much as it would go to my heart to do so.

On 14 November two IRA men arrived at Gurteen around midnight wanting beds for the night. They demanded meat but Moore the servant said there was none. Then they wanted cheese and he told them there was none and gave them bread and milk instead. On 23 December Rivallon noted that since 10 August they had 103 overnight visitors and many more who called for food.

By early December Mary was totally disillusioned and depressed with the situation in Ireland. She visited her former home at Glen Poer and felt she would never get the opportunity to live there again. She was bitter towards the British government, noting that Lord Midleton had spoken in the House of Lords of how the government had 'broken their pledges to the [Irish] loyalists and cast them off – leaving us to the mercy of these high-principled murderers, who hate our class. We who loved the Empire and whose children helped in the time of need. No! but England will pay dearly for her treachery and folly'.

On Christmas Eve four armed republicans arrived at Gurteen demanding a bed for the night. The next morning, they were given breakfast and said they would also like their Christmas dinner, which they received. 'So, so hard on the servants on Christmas day'. Her son commented, 'Such is life in this country. I wonder how much longer I shall be able to stand it.'

'We are no further use to England' 1923 - Gurteen le Poer, Cappagh, Lackendarra and Milfort

Chapter 10

On the 9 January Mary de la Poer wrote that Dr White informed her there was a rumour that Marlfield House, the seat of the Bagwell family near Clonmel, had been burned. It turned out to be true:

> Dear Marlfield, now a mass of ruins. Poor Lulu and her girl and two boys were there when the savages came at 12.30. They wanted to know if Jack [Senator Jack Bagwell] was there. When told he was not – they said they had orders to burn the house and gave them 10 minutes – They forced their way into the house, followed Lulu & ? to their rooms...she put a few jewels and things she valued in a bag, but it was stolen also all their overcoats. She and her children were locked into a stable and only released when their house was ablaze.

She was later told that some of the pictures were saved and that the leader of the gang helped them to save a Gainsborough portrait.

On 11 January she heard a rumour that Cappoquin house was destroyed and also Castleview, Co Cork, the home of the Wyndham Quins. On 30 January she went shopping in Clonmel and was informed by a shopkeeper that 'the extravagance of the army is very great. Huge amounts of meat ordered, far more than the British ever had, and he said that half of the army was republican'.

On the 14th she noted that the railway tracks had been torn up between Kilsheelan and Carrick and the signal box at Kilsheelan station destroyed by fire. By the following day Clonmel was completely cut off, with telegraph wires and poles cut. The IRA still arrived at Gurteen, but only two of them. It was rumoured the IRA intended to burn the courthouse, grammar school, and brewery in Clonmel. A friend of the de la Poers, Mr Scully, architect, of Waterford, spent the night at Gurteen and told them he was very pessimistic about the situation and that there was constant gunfire in Waterford each night.

On 31 January Patrica showed her the newspaper which revealed that Senator Jack Bagwell of Marlfield had been kidnapped by the IRA: 'I can't express what I felt. Jack our great friend whom I had known as a boy, and to think he was in the hands of these fiends – Too, too, awful. Oh! the horror of it all'. The Free State issued a proclamation demanding his release within 48 hours or there would be reprisals against republican prisoners. On 2 February Mary de la Poer heard that Jack was free, but she did not know then that he had escaped.

'Sir Horace Plunkett's home was thoroughly burnt yesterday or the day before. As the wreckers were not satisfied with their previous vandalism, his splendid library etc., are now all gone'.

On the night of 4 February she and Patrica were woken by the parlour maid informing them that Free State soldiers were in the house carrying out a search: 'Patsy and I put on our fur coats and to our surprise three officers came past the door of our room and one would have come in – had I not said 'This is my room' – Such is the 'Savoir Faire' of the Defenders of our country. J Keohan officer! who had been a sorting clerk at the Clonmel Station said: 'We have no need to see the major' and just marched through parts of the house into the pantry and opened the china cupboards. I was amused one of the servants described them as 'humans & insects' – they never went up the tower or to the attics! A very superficial search'.

On 8 February she heard that the home of the Perry family, Woodrooffe House, Co Tipperary was burned along with Castleboro, Lord Carew's seat in Co Wexford. On the 12th she met Mary Perry in Clonmel who was 'resigned' to the fate of their home and informed her that Dollie, Willie and Sylvia had saved a good deal of the furniture. Some days later she heard that Tom Quinlan, the Irregular commander, a farmer from Derrinlaur, had been arrested by the Free State soldiers. 'I am sorry as I feel he did his best to protect us in many ways'. She felt that the local IRA would be more inclined to prevent anything serious happening to the house but now that men such as Quinlan were absent more ruthless IRA men could turn up at Gurteen and not be so sympathetic.

In the days following she was shocked to learn of the destruction of Mullaboden, Co Kildare, Senator Bryan Mahon's house, and Cappoquin, Rockmount, and Comeragh in county Waterford. The de la Poers were getting nervous that their house would be next and on 21 February they were busy all day gathering the family silver for placing in the safe. On 1 March Mary wrote that they placed more valuables in the safe: 'of course we could not put anything big into it such as pictures. We then took as much valuable china as possible and put it into presses near the chapel. R[iv] thinks they would save the chapel'. On the same day Rivallon made the following entry in his diary:

Another month gone and another begun. How they pass as far as I can see little to look forward to in the way of peace in this country. In any case things never can be as they were. We shall have to, if we are able to remain here look forward to quite a different life. Most of the people one knew have left already or will go. Of course, this diary, written as it has been from day to day, only gives just what has happened in our immediate locality and that not at any length. But it may give some idea, if it is ever read in years to come, of what we have gone and are going through and what is put down here applies to the country at large, the same things, and in many cases worse has happened or is happening.

Mary noted on 6 March that Frances de la Poer had left Kilcronagh for good and the contents were being sent to England. She was shocked to hear that Mr O'Reilly's house in Louth was destroyed by fire, including the chapel. He did manage to save a chalice. The servants at Gurteen had all their belongings packed and ready in the event of the house being set alight.

'My maid has packed my dresses, the parlour maid my silver and have left the boxes in a room to near to the door so that they can be easily lifted out'.

At this point she is full of anger and despair:

England may well feel proud of her handy work and of the manner she protects those who were always loyal to her – she has handed us over to Bolshevicks and if a question is asked in Parliament concerning our welfare, she says that it is not polite to answer it -no we may be murdered and robbed – we are no further use to England so it matters not what becomes of us! Ah! I feel bitter, I have not left Ireland for nearly two years – hoping against hope that things would come right – and now at the end of two years all is each day getting worse & worse.

The following day she heard about the burning of Wilton Castle, the seat of Captain Alcock in Wexford. On the 12th she read in the newspaper that Sir Thomas Esmonde's house, Ballynastragh, Co Wexford was destroyed and comments that his nationalist pedigree did not save his house from destruction. 'He was not at home, but they gave his son 10 minutes to clear out – he managed to save the chalice and vestments – I believe he had a valuable library – he had removed pictures & valuables to England'.

The IRA continued to turn up at Gurteen at night looking for food and accommodation. She was particularly annoyed that one night two IRA men turned up, one named Morrissey and the other was the brother of the estate carpenter at Gurteen. Concerning the latter, she wrote: 'Really one's blood boils to think of the cheek of his coming here!!' On 1 April she attended church in Clonmel and commented on the destruction she saw. The railway station was burned but there were forty Free State troops based there who were 'forever getting drunk!' A few days later the de la Poers had to accommodate a group of twenty IRA overnight and feed them. Amongst them were 'Nugent, the Gunner', Hayes the leader, and Quin who helped to burn P. Walsh's house in Clonmel. What shocked her was that one of the group was a brother of a maid at Gurteen. She complained about having to provide mattresses and blankets as she had been told the men suffered from various diseases. After their departure next day, it took sixteen buckets of water to clean the servants' hall.

On 10 April she recorded the visit of a group of Free State soldiers to Gurteen who were searching for IRA men. 'Ten officers came to tea (one had a revolver in his hands when questioning the cook) a gunner and his machinegun was in the kitchen yard. They looked into the dormitory! and saw the beds had not been occupied so were satisfied and left'.

A few days later three Free Staters arrived and said they wanted to search the house for IRA, even though they were told that there were none in the house at that time. The officer in charge asked for Rivallon and informed him that he wished to billet thirty men in the house for three nights. This was agreed but they were only allowed to occupy the servants' wing, or 'dormitory' as it was being jokingly called by the family. However, Rivallon insisted that the officer must have his own room. One of the soldiers who arrived was an ex-service man named Lee who had served with Rivallon in Malta twenty years before. Mary noted that the men were clean, tidy and smart and that many of them were ex-service men. The men were given tea, bread and jam. At this point Mary realised that there could be serious consequences for the family accommodating the Free State soldiers. The surrounding hills were occupied by a large group of IRA. The following morning the men were given a breakfast of eggs, bread and jam. She described the officer as 'a poor sort of youth. Very civil – but thoroughly ignorant of his duties, always referring to his Sergeant for information'. He arrived down for his breakfast at eleven o'clock.

On the 15 April at around 12.30 at night the de la Poers were woken up by tremendous knocking on the front door. They feared the worst. Could it be the IRA arriving to burn Gurteen?

> Patsy and I, we jumped out of bed, told R[iv], got my fur coat on and rushed up to Goodwin's room to tell him to come down. As I went the house literally reverberated from the volume of the battering at the hall door. We all feared that it meant the end of our old home. When Goodwin called out who was there – 'National Troops' was

153

the reply, we did not believe it. But to my joy as they came into the yard, we saw they were in uniform.

Goodwin informed them that there were 47 men who required boiling water to make tea. Mary went to wake the cook, Mrs Flynn, whom she described as 'always so helpful'. The cook and Goodwin gave the men tea, bread, and jam. The officer said that they brought Mr. Halpin from the lodge who directed them to the back door.

The de la Poers were puzzled at the arrival of the Free State soldiers and Mary looked for answers to the mystery. According to her they received a sudden order to travel immediately from Carrick to Clonmel and didn't have time to bring overcoats, rations etc. They were within a mile of Clonmel when a messenger intercepted them and told them to go at once to Gurteen. Her son Riv told her that the officer in charge remarked to him: 'I hope you like the protection we are giving you'. He had posted sentries around the house.

The officer was very pessimistic about the future of Ireland and commented that half the army couldn't be trusted, and he foresaw a 'Workers' Republic and a second Russia'.

> He acknowledges that he was in the war against the British and to my mind sorry he is for it – as he said Ireland was worth fighting for but not the people. He amused Riv by saying: 'I thought I was a brave man to lie in the ditches to shoot soldiers & R.I.C., but I have changed my views. I don't look on it as brave now, 'as that is what is being done to us'. He said a man who had been fighting with him at that time came to his house some time ago looking for him in order to shoot him.

Mary told him that the family were terrified when they heard the loud banging at the front door. He said they looked for a light and could see none and was concerned when they did not open the door, commenting: 'Holy God Almighty they can't be all dead'. They thought the 'Die hards' were occupying the house and preventing the de la Poers from answering.

On 18 April an event occurred at Gurteen which shocked the family. The Free State officer received orders to do a thorough search of the house. They searched the servants' rooms which did not go down well: 'Then the ball began to roll. Infuriated servants came and said they would leave, that they had been insulted etc!!' Letters and despatches from the IRA were found in the bedrooms of two female servants. As a result, none of them were allowed out of the house except with a military escort. The military headquarters in Clonmel had received a tip-off about the girls and about a former nursery maid at Gurteen who left on the morning the troops arrived without informing the family. Mary reacted with the following comment in her diary: 'To think that we have been living in the midst of spying and deception'.

On 20 April Mary was told that two of the soldiers were overheard discussing the reason they were diverted from Clonmel and sent to Gurteen. 'The answer was that the house was to have gone up this week – too, too, ghastly to contemplate. My nerves are fast going – each day brings forth fresh horrors and we know the [IRA] column is not far off and at night one wonders if they will try and surprise the guard – we feel thankful to Almighty God to have so far spared us'.

On 22 April she noted in her diary that 'the kitchen maid had evaded the sentries and was out' but returned later that evening. Her son Rivallon gave the Free State soldiers a football and they were enjoying the distraction of games. The officer in charge of the Free State soldiers was replaced by a Mr Dunne who was described as a former Sergeant Major in the Irish Guards and 'a splendid looking man'. He had been wounded six times in France, and she noted with surprise that he was not allowed to wear his medals.

Over the next few nights there were constant gun exchanges between the IRA and the Free State troops at Gurteen. The children were alarmed by the shooting, but Mary explained that the soldiers were just practising. She felt that the situation could escalate and that they would be safer away from Gurteen.

On 29 April General Prout and Colonel Heslip and Captain Porter paid a visit to Gurteen and were offered tea, which they refused. Prout brought a single barrelled gun and five cartridges for Rivallon, which was all he had available. On the following day Mary was in Clonmel and met Father Warren, who confirmed that Gurteen was to have been set alight by the IRA on the night the Free State troops turned up unexpectedly. What upset her most was the role of the servants. 'It is ghastly to think of, as we have heard some of the servants were implicated and were to have helped in doing the devilish work'. She felt that they were the lucky ones, as three more houses were destroyed, owned by Lord Killanin, Mr Toler and Mr Talbot-Crosbie.

On 2 May she noted that the kitchen maid at Gurteen had resigned. She was under suspicion as an IRA despatch carrier and was not supposed to leave the house. However, she defied the sentries twice, who were forced to fire warning shots over her head. 'Such is our life surrounded by vipers'. It was revealed that certain servants allowed the IRA into Gurteen at night when the family was asleep, where they held strategy meetings in the kitchen.

She noted in her diary that they had been to tea to Newtown Anner on the invitation of Obby and Lady Osborne. She had a chat with Lady Osborne's housemaid, 'dear old Sarah', who told her that the IRA had planned to burn Newtown and Gurteen on the same night. On the night in question, she never went to bed and sat up all night dressed, and her things packed ready for a hasty departure. During the night she said she observed a group of men on the lawn, getting ready she supposed to burn the house, but they left abruptly. Mary and Sarah were upset at the empty appearance of the rooms:

> Pictures gone. That beautiful drawing room; the contents which made it so artistic and so unlike other rooms and without its mistress. I saw a tear in Sarah's eye, and I knew she saw the same in mine. Oh! the changes, the cruel changes. Ones friends gone and their houses either gone or desolate as Newtown now is – Obby feels it so much, he has lost heart – he so hoped that things would improve.

Mary noted that Mr Lonergan, an IRA member who had come to Gurteen one night and had an argument with her son Riv, had been captured. 'By all accounts he is a very bad lot.' She was impressed with the commanding officer of the Free State troops, Mr Dunne, and his ability to ensure his men were well disciplined and behaved well. This was in contrast to the first time she had seen Free State soldiers in Clonmel, who were lacking in discipline and organisation. She noted that Miss Greene, the governess had given in her notice.

Later in May she wrote in her diary that many people were optimistic that the war was coming to an end, but that others felt that the situation was going to get worse as Jim Larkin was going lead a movement for a Workers' Republic.

The quiet interlude at Gurteen came to an abrupt end on the night of 26 May when the de la Poers were awoken from their sleep at 12.40 by loud bangs and continuous gunfire which lasted for about forty minutes. Mary and Patsy shook all over with fear: 'Lewis guns, Thompson guns, rifles, all were going and the bullets whizzing past. The house was hit eight or ten times, but fortunately no windows were broken.' The following day her son Arnold arrived at Gurteen from England with friends, and she noted in her diary that she wished they had been at Gurteen during the gunfight as it would have brought home to them how serious things were in Ireland and how stressful it was for everyone.

Another gunfight occurred at Gurteen on the night of 6 June which lasted for two hours. The IRA were firing at Gurteen from Priorstown, from a waterfall in the demesne and from beneath a large oak tree in the garden. The next morning, they saw evidence of the exchange. A bullet had gone through a bench, the lawn was peppered with bullet holes, a portion of the ornamental parapet had been hit and broken off.

A couple of days later General Prout and Colonel Hurly came to Gurteen to shoot rabbits.

On 13 June she went to Waterford for the first time in a year and a half and was shocked by the destruction she saw at Carrick, where the medieval bridge had been damaged, and the workhouse destroyed. Strangely, she had now come to a consensus with the Republicans about the British government: 'The Fiends were right when they spoke of 'Perfide Albion' – well may Irish loyalists say the same. It matters not if they are murdered or robbed.'

Mary's diary ends on 6 July 1923, noting that a new group of soldiers had arrived at Gurteen, but that they were not as 'soldier-like' as their predecessors.

Cappagh House

In January 1923 the Usshers had visits from both sides in the conflict. One night when they were all in bed a number of Free State soldiers from Dungarvan raided Cappagh and took the fuses used in the old kiln. She was surprised that they did not search the bedrooms in any detail. They then went down the avenue to Old Cappagh House and searched there.

A few nights later they were awakened from their sleep by loud banging on the door. On the landing Emily met one of the workmen, John Power, who was now sleeping in the house. He thought they were Free Staters and was about to let them in, but Emily said no. She wanted to see them first and asked them to light a match so that she could see their faces. They asked her if there were 'any boys hiding' in the house. They refused to show their faces so Emily decided they must be thieves: 'Therewith came a volley of abuse and of shots, accompanied by a crash of glass in the barred window beside the door! Silence. 'You have one of us kill't', said a voice but I heard no groans of wounded or dying. 'Will ye let us in now?' They smashed more windows and demanded £10. Emily offered them ten shillings and she passed it through the broken window. In the process the boy grabbed her hand and she pulled him towards her and was able to see that he was not wearing a uniform, confirming her suspicion that they were thieves. She told them she would inform the authorities about them, which resulted in the smashing of the glass in the dining room windows. Luckily, she had all the shutters closed securely. They submitted a claim to the County Council for £17 for the destruction of nine plate-glass windows between 19 and 23

January.[255] In October 1923 Beverly was paid £100 compensation for his 'Vulcan' car which had been damaged when stolen by the IRA.

Two nights later at two in the morning shots were fired at the house. In the morning they found bullet holes on either side of the balcony window, and another bullet had passed through the glass and made a hole in the wall over a bed. As a result, they decided to sleep on the floor from then on. She and Emily Whitehead decided to take turns to stay awake on watch every night until dawn:

> Oh! the weary horror of those interminable nights! All round us in the woods the Republicans were signaling and whistling to each other...We looked through the window at the moving shadows and the fitful moonbeams outside, careful to show no light ourselves, listening, listening, always listening for steps – whispers – that most awful 2 a.m. bell! How many were doing, or had done, the very same thing in countless lonely homes and how many in vain!

On 5 February the co-op store at Cappagh run by the Finisk Valley Co-operative was destroyed by fire and the letters 'I.R.A.' were daubed on the walls. Emily was devastated by the news as it had been opened by her to benefit local people. She was informed that the local IRA had nothing to with the burning, which was also her belief. Beverly claimed £250 for the burning of the store.[256] He received £216-14-8 in compensation and had rebuilt the store by June 1924.

---

[255] WCCA WCC/GWA288
[256] WCCA WCC/GWA288

The situation was becoming more volatile and the Usshers were glad to receive local support:

> The Hurley twins and Michael Cunningham determined to protect us. These three brave boys, who were working all day, sat up night after night, either in our basement...or patrolling the grounds outside. They had helped us in all our social enterprises and how they stood by us in our hour of bitter need and stood the risk of their lives had they been discovered, or suspected even, by the contending parties. When I think of these boys and what they endured and risked for us and not only for us but for our ungrateful and worthless Protestant tenants in the Giants Rock, I recover faith in human nature, hope for Ireland...

The Giant's Rock was a small house on the Cappagh estate which was being rented by two sisters named Colclough. The Colcloughs' house was attacked again, and this time shots were fired into the house, one of the bullets entering the wall over their bed.

One morning Emily Whitehead told her that three Free State soldiers had been in the basement at Cappagh overnight. They arrived after tea and heavily armed. They told her that Cappagh was going to be burned that night. She was told months later by Mrs Cunningham that the same 'band of Republicans' out of Tipperary (who had according to Emily burned Cappoquin House the following night) had planned to burn Cappagh and Whitechurch.

In the autumn of 1923, the Civic Guards were established and as the barrack had been destroyed at Cappagh four guards and a sergeant moved into Clancy's house in the yard at Cappagh. Emily states that two young IRA men visited her to ask if she could find work for them in Canada. One of them was Jimmy Fraher who she was informed had done 'very cruel things'. 'He had a sensitive, refined face, a face anyone would take to at a glance.' She recalled the farm workers' strike the previous year, telling him how 'sheer heartbreak prevented me from keeping my food down and how I lived in a low fever.' He told her he now felt the same way – 'I thought I was working for Ireland, but the people have turned against us and do not want us anymore.'

Glencorran House, Ardmore

Glencorran House was leased by the Fudge or Fuge family from the Villiers-Stuarts of Dromana. The 1901 census notes that the house had 15 rooms and was occupied by Richard Purcell Fuge, his wife Mary Stewart and their three boys. Richard and Mary were married in 1890 at her family home, Heathfield Towers near Youghal. The main family residence was at Templemary, Buttevant, Co Cork, which was later burnt by the IRA.[257] In 1995 the writer William Trevor described the house he remembered as a boy:

> Its concrete rendering was washed with unobtrusive yellow once, its window frames and hall door were a shade of grey. But now the yellow and the grey have gone, and the window frames have themselves in places. The glass of the fanlight is smashed...The entrance gates have been immoveable for half a century. The smell is of must in one room, of sodden plaster in another. The marble of the mantlepiece has split...the servants' quarters are roofless.

---

[257] Anna- Maria Habja, *Houses of Cork, Vol.I- North*, p.347 (Clare 2002). *Walford's County Families* 1920 p.508.

The now roofless and ruined house is situated on a low cliff at the end of Ballyquin beach. It was a long low single-story four-bay house with tall windows facing toward the sea. On the west side was a projecting entrance porch/hall which had the remains of decorative plasterwork until recently. At the rear of the house was a two-story building which housed the servants. In 1922 it was owned by Henry Fuge who had moved to England as he felt his life was in danger from local IRA. Fuge had also been appointed a resident Magistrate in 1896. The house consisted of a billiard room, dining room, drawing room, study, kitchen, four bedrooms and servant's rooms.

On 5 December 1922 Free State troops searched Glencorran (then empty as Fuge was based in South Abbey, Youghal, and England) and discovered that the IRA were using the house as a billet. 'Nearly all of the furniture had been destroyed or looted', and the damage was estimated at £1,000. On 15 December Captain Foley, Lieutenants Kelly and Brown visited the house again, acting on a tip-off. This time they were looking for cars. 'They found an Overlander car and a motor bike in an outhouse...Both vehicles had been mostly stripped of essential parts. The car belonged to the owner of the house, but they took both machines back to Dungarvan' [barracks].[258]

In May 1923 Free State soldiers found a Ford car at Glencorran. Tommy Mooney notes that the house was often used by the local IRA as a convenient base: 'The house being unoccupied made a ready store, arms dump and billets for the local IRA, and the Mansfields, Prendergasts, Eddys, Cronins, Troys, Currans, and

---

[258] Tommy Mooney, *The Deise Divided-A History of the Waterford Brigade IRA and the Civil War* (Kilkenny, 2014), pp 135, 144.

others from nearby Ardmore and Old Parish had often found it a convenient resting place'.[259]

Fuge applied for compensation of £2000 for the damage to his property. He said that he had been suspected of informing on local IRA members and that he had 'suffered severe harassment on that account ever since. He felt compelled to flee to England for his and his wife's safety'. They had left in January 1921. At the court hearing in 1925 E.A. Ryan appeared for the state and Mr Connolly for the applicant.[260] Ryan stated that there were two claims, one for the furniture and the other for damage to the house. Connolly noted that at a previous hearing the judge had valued the furniture at £750. He informed the judge that: 'a number of armed irregulars took forcible possession of the house and held the house from the 1st November 1922 to 1st April 1923. They did considerable damage to the house and to the furniture during that time'. John Murray, contractor, gave evidence on behalf of Mr Fuge and estimated the costs of repairs and redecoration to be £307. E.A. Ryan pointed out to him that his first estimate was for £500 and appeared to take issue with having to put up new wallpaper in the rooms. Ryan challenged him about this, asserting that the rooms had not been decorated for a long time and that this was the reason the wallpaper was shabby and dirty and not because the irregulars damaged them. Included in Murray's bill was work on whitening a ceiling to which Ryan asked: 'What did the irregulars do to that?

The compensation claim was challenged by Declan Conway, Co Councillor, of Rathlead, Ringville. He wrote to the Waterford County Secretary on the matter:

---

[259] Tommy Mooney, p.199.
[260] *Munster Express*, 13 November 1925.

I beg to submit the following information re R.P. Fuges's claim during the Anglo-Irish war and the Civil War periods, the applicant made no effort whatsoever to protect his house and furniture. As far as I know Mr Fuge was never interfered with or ordered to leave the place. The house being built on the brink of a cliff suffered considerable damage owing to the proximity of the sea. Ther being no caretaker to look after the place...the residence was a regular commonage...the doors and windows being broken down.

Conway's point that most of the damage was caused by proximity to the sea was a feeble assertion. The lack of a caretaker was more likely to do with the fact that whoever was appointed would be threatened by the IRA and forced to give up the post (as was the case at Helvick House). Fuge threatened to sue Conway and the *Waterford News* for publishing the allegations.

The following month State Solicitor E A Ryan wrote to the secretary of the Ministry of Finance about Conway's claims:

The statements made by Mr Conway, whom I understand has a personal grudge in connection with the land against the applicant are so indefinite and vague that it is difficult to make any useful observations on them. Applicant...has challenged him to bring forward any evidence...and it is common knowledge, and it was proved on oath at the hearing of the claim, that the premises were seized and occupied by Irregulars...for a considerable period. Mr Conway himself was known to be associated with them. There was hardly any case which received so much investigation both inside and outside the court as this did...

In the compensation claim file there is a detailed list of the house contents and damage to same. In the hall there was a photo album, framed photographs, croquet and cricket bats, mahogany and oak chairs. In the Drawing room six ornamental jardinieres, 'valuable' Dresden candelabra, statues, pictures and Belleek china. In the Billiard room three rare old bookcases, 'Books piled two feet high and trampled on floor', organ 'destroyed beyond repair', camera, camera stand, photographic material 'smashed or taken'. The books were divided between the study and billiard room and were valued at £200. These consisted of hundreds of books in Morocco bindings 'belonging to Mr Fuge's late uncle', histories of Waterford and Cork, sets of poets, several hundred on French and English literature, novels, and a considerable number on mathematics, mechanical and electrical engineering.

The study also contained an xray screen, ten xray tubes and a large telescope.

Milfort House Portlaw

The house built in the mid-19th century by William Malcomson. At the time of the Civil War it was occupied by the Morley family.[261] Cornelius Morley from Yorkshire was described in the 1901 census as 'shipowner'. He married Susan Penrose Malcomson (1845-1884), and they had six children, one of whom, Violet (1871-1950), had the house in 1923. The house was large and had 36 rooms according to the 1911 census.

Beatrix, Lady Osborne Beauclerk, refers to the occupation of the house:

---

[261] The sale of the house and its contents were advertised in the *Waterford Standard*, 28 April 1951. It was carried out by the trustees of 'the late Miss Violet Morley'.

Milfort, left in charge of two pretty young maids during their mistress's absence in England, was occupied by over two hundred Republicans, many of whom were drunk when they arrived; they did a terrible lot of damage there, burst open drawers, cupboards, and boxes; and helped themselves freely to their contents; but the maids were not molested in any way.

Dr Walker of Portlaw noted that there were 120 IRA sleeping in Milfort. 'Violet does not know this yet, but Miss Grace is going to telegraph her tomorrow. She must be told, but of course <u>no one</u> can put them out of it.   There were a lot of them up on the roof today, I imagine watching the river but what they expect to see there I don't know.[262]

Lackendarra Lodge

This was the hunting lodge of Henry John Chearnley of Salterbridge House near Cappoquin. The Chearnleys were major landowners in the area, with over 15,000 acres. Henry kept a pack of hunting dogs at the lodge which were looked after by James Páidí Whelan. The layout of the lodge was described as 'an oblong around a cobbled courtyard, stable and outhouse on one side, a washhouse opposite and a long hall with six living rooms and a glasshouse at the other side. The house was built of brick with beautifully proportioned rooms with bay windows looking out over the valley'.[263] The Chearnley lands were acquired by the Land Commission in May 1931 for £78,422.[264]

---

[262] Marquis of Waterford Archive, C Walker, Springfield House, Portlaw, to Lady Osborne July 1922.
[263] *Sliabh gCua Annual* 2003, pp 24-25.
[264] *Sliabh gCua Annual* 2001, p.30.

In 1922 the IRA commandeered the building, and it became the headquarters of the 7th Battalion Waterford Brigade IRA. It was the scene of an accidental shooting on 12 May 1922. John Morrissey of Bleantis, Ballinamult, Battalion commander of the 7th Battalion, was shot by his quartermaster, William Queally. Morrissey had just woken up and told Queally to secure a prisoner held in the lodge. Queally replied that no prisoner would escape while he had a gun, which he pointed towards Morrissey. The gun went off accidentally and Morrissey received a fatal wound through the chest. He was 26 years of age. An inquest was held at the lodge by Dr M F Moloney, coroner.[265] It was said that when Morrissey was shot, he jumped up and said: 'I'm done; send for the priest' and he lived for about five minutes. His father, Thomas Morrissey, 'one of the most respectable farmers of the district', applied for a pension as a result of the incident because it was stated that his only son was his 'chief support'.[266] Local tradition states that a certain room in the lodge was haunted thereafter by a ghostly presence. The IRA are said to have partly burned the house when they vacated it.

Chearnley submitted a claim for £1345 for damage to the lodge between June 1922 and May 1923.[267] 'In or about the month of June 1922 the house was commandeered, injured and occupied for a period of twelve months as battalion headquarters of the IRA, during which time the furniture and utensils were destroyed or carried away and the building damaged'. Jeremiah Dempsey, a builder from Cappoquin, provided a detailed estimate for the repairs to the lodge. He lists five bedrooms, dining-room, kitchen, pantry, bathroom, water closet, conservatory, stables, and

265 *Dungarvan Observer,* 20 May 1922.
266 NA/DP8049
267 NAI FIN/COMP/2/23/374

outhouses. He noted that there were six fluted columns under the arches in the entrance hall and a glass door with side lights. The Dining-room had a large double mullioned window 7ft by 7ft. Included in the file is a list of contents dated 24 May 1920. This included an old piano, stove, grandfather clock and a mahogany sideboard in the hall.

He was awarded £1075 plus £29.2.7 costs and expenses on condition that the money be spent on erecting a new dwelling or towards repairing the ruined building. In September 1924 the Commissioners of Public Works suggested that Chearnley be offered £300 free of conditions to rebuild as it appeared unlikely that he would restore or build a new house on the site as it was 'remote and inaccessible' and there would be no demand from a purchaser for a dwelling in the area. In December 1924 Chearnley's solicitor contacted the Ministry of Finance stating that he would accept £475 free of any re-instatement clause with an additional £29.2.7 for costs. Chearnley received £275 for damage to the contents.

In 1923 it was purchased by a retired RIC man, Martin Power, who restored it. It fell into dereliction in the late 1950s and is now a ruin.

'Soon no country house will be left'
1923 – The campaign of fire

Chapter 11

On 30 November 1922 Liam Lynch issued an order to burn the houses of senators. Thirty- seven houses were destroyed by the end of March 1923. Kevin O'Higgins noted in 1923 that over the previous twelve months houses had been burned for no other reason than that of

> driving the occupiers out of the area, with a view to the forcible seizure and illegal occupation of their lands. Every citizen in Ireland is entitled to look to the Government to maintain his legal rights, and to protect his property...it is the intention of the Government...to protect to the full extent of its resources the rights of all citizens be they landlords or tenants, farmers or labourers.

Sir Horace Plunkett was away when his house, Kilteragh, was destroyed in January 1923. He moved to London and his diary[268] records visits from Irish people who had similar experiences, such as Sir John Keane of Cappoquin. On 10 April 1923 he had a visit from Keane who told him that he was going to resign his post as senator in protest at the 'ill treatment of the class he is

---

268

www.nli.ie/pdfs/diaries_of_sir_horace_curzon_plunkett/1923_diary_of_sir_ho race_curzon_plunkett.pdf (Accessed 12/12/2017).

supposed to represent' (in relation to compensation). 'His account of the state of public life in Ireland is very depressing'. Keane paid a further visit in October that year and Plunkett described him as 'another exile from Erin'.

In the 1890s Ballynatray House on the River Blackwater was inherited by the eldest daughter of Earl Mount Cashell, Lady Harriette Gertrude Isabella Smyth. In 1868 she attempted to elope with the brother of the gamekeeper, Patrick Fleming, but the attempt was blocked by the family. In 1872 she married Col. John Henry Graham Holroyd. Their eldest son was Captain Rowland Henry Tyssen Holroyd-Smyth, who was known as 'Rowley' or 'The Captain' to locals. In 1902 he married Alice Ponsonby. Rowley was only interested in horses and hunting and neglected the estate. In early April 1923 Mrs Arbuthnot, daughter of Sir Henry and Lady Blake of Myrtle Grove, Youghal, called on Horace Plunkett. She spoke to him concerning the Holroyd-Smyths:

> Rowley has deserted Alice and is hunting in Leicestershire, probably on the ground that he would be shot (no great calamity) if he remained at Ballynatray, whereas Alice could "carry on" somehow. Dastardly and heartless cowardice. I was glad to hear that Alice thinks of trying to get a cottage and 10 acres or so of land in Devonshire, leaving Ballynatray to be let on the 11 months system, the house doubtless being burned. I hope she will get out of the country at any cost.

Frida Keane recalled the revolutionary period at Ballynatray:

> When Troubles and Civil War came to Ireland, Roly left Ballynatray and went to England, taking his foxhounds with him, for he was never without hounds even after he

had given up the Mastership of the old Coshmore and Coshbride Hunt. He visited friends for some months accompanied by five couple of hungry hounds. When one household could stand no more, he moved on to another one. We heard that his pack left him and made their way to Fishguard, where they were found sitting on the pier gazing out to sea and waiting for the Rosslare boat, but I do not vouch for the veracity of the story. Alice was left alone to tend Ballynatray and to cope unaided with bands of Irregular troops, who wandered in and out and expected to be fed. Neither Alice nor Roly were interested in politics and both were much loved by the country people; it was known that before the British Army left Ireland they were not infrequently entertained by Roly in the drawing room of Ballynatray, whilst Alice was, at the same time, entertaining the I.R.A. in the kitchens.[269]

The Holroyd-Smyths did submit claims for damage to gates, fences and trees at Newtown on 13 August 1922 and on 24 April, 13 August and 14 September 1922 due to a 'dispute with the transport union'.[270] According to Tommy Mooney four cars were taken from Ballynatray and burned in December 1922.[271]

Pax Whelan recalled that there had been a robbery at Ballynatray before the Civil War. He and other IRA members sorted it out, for which Mrs Holroyd-Smyth was grateful and told Whelan:

---

[269] Frida Keane, *The Valley is too Lush, A memoir of country house life in the Blackwater Valley* (Dublin 2015), pp 47-48.
[270] NAI FIN/COMP/2/23/210, FIN/COMP/2/23/187
[271] Tommy Mooney, *The Deise Divided: A History of the Waterford Brigade I.R.A. and the Civil War* (Dungarvan, 2012), p.151.

if I can do anything for you...please let me know'. Two republicans, Mike Fitzgerald and Pat O'Reilly were arrested and taken to Waterford where it was believed they would be shot. 'We went to her; she was in the horsey set and we knew that she was friendly with W.T. Cosgrave. She travelled to Dublin and met Cosgrave. He told her he could do nothing as the British Government was insisting on their execution. They had taken part in an ambush in Youghal in 1921, when the road was mined and a lorry containing band-boys was blown up.

Both men were executed on 25 January 1923[272] The *Irish Times* carried a report on the circumstances:

> Michael Fitzgerald, South Main Street, Youghal, and Patrick O'Reilly Coastguard Station, Youghal, were tried by a military court on the charge of having possession without proper authority, of arms and ammunition at Ballinaclash, Clashmore, on December 4th 1922. Both accused were found guilty and sentenced to death. The execution took place this morning at Waterford at 8 o'clock. Our correspondent adds that the two men appeared to be quite cheerful. When passing through Barrack Street they shouted – 'Up Cork', and 'Long live the Republic'.[273]

In 2019 Whytes auctioneers sold a collection of papers relating to this event which belonged to Alice Holroyd-Smyth.[274] It included a letter from John Prout, Commandant General, GOC 2nd Southern

---

[272] Uinseann MacEoin, *Survivors* (Dublin, 1980). Interview with Pax Whelan pp 144-145.

[273] *Irish Times*, 26 January 1923.

[274] Whyte's Auctioneers, 'Eclectic Collector', 6 April 2019, Lot 203.

Command, acknowledging her letter appealing for the lives of Michael Fitzgerald and Patrick O'Reilly. O'Reilly wrote her a letter on 25 January 1923 'an hour before my doom'. The correspondence also included letters from IRA prisoners, George C Kiely, Dan O'Brien, Patrick Hogan and Pat Fitzgerald. Michael Cashman, O.C., Glendine Company IRA wrote her a letter on 18 January 1922 requesting a loan of her horse and car. Other items included photographs of the coffins of Fitzgerald and O'Reilly and several issues of An t-Oglach. Few other Anglo-Irish ladies must have possessed such a collection.

Ballynatray was not burned, probably because of the goodwill of the local IRA towards Mrs Holroyd- Smyth.

The *Wicklow People* criticised the burning of Palmerstown House, the seat of the Earl of Mayo, and the home of Sir Horace Plunkett who 'took a practical interest in the betterment of Ireland'. 'The burning of the mansions as part of a campaign against the Free State Government makes Ireland distinctly poorer. Very often the mansions burned are the property of people of Liberal views who could not be regarded as enemies of their country, even if they did not agree in all respects with the opinions held by the majority in the days of constitutional agitation'.[275]

Frida Keane recalled visits to her family home, Fortwilliam House, by IRA and Free State troops:

> Raiders came sometimes at night to Fortwilliam, but they did not come to burn or terrorise. We would stand at the bedroom window, shivering a little in the cold as we heard the tramp of soldiers' boots on the avenue and the click of the gate. In the moon light we could see the raiders, usually

---

[275] *Wicklow People*, 10 February 1923.

masked, come to the door and we heard the long peal of the front doorbell. Harry would always go; he would not let any other member of the household answer that call, and the raiders were civil and a little sheepish. When asked not to go into little Diana's nursery they did not go. Bicycles belonging to us children and the maids were hidden between ceiling and roof, and they did not find them, and our horses had been ridden secretly by night to Grallagh, where our friend Michael O'Brien, who had helped my father start his pack of hounds, grazed them for us until better times came. Only once did our hearts leap into our mouths, for when our frightened dog barked on and on and would not be silenced, we heard a rough voice say, 'Yerrah boy. Shoot the sod.[276]

Cappoquin House

John Keane, a lawyer, is believed to be the founder of the Cappoquin Keanes. In 1738 he and John Hales acquired the Cappoquin estate of 7,213 acres on a 999-year lease from the Earl of Cork and Burlington. The family appears to have lived in the old castle with 17th century additions right up to the 1770s when a new house was built on the site. His son Richard died in 1769 and the estate passed to his son, Sir John Keane (1757-1829). He is credited with building the present house in 1779 and called it Belmont. Around 1913/14 the architect L. Page Dickinson (1881-1958) of Orpen & Dickinson, Dublin, was employed to improve aspects of the house. This work included a new portico on the west side to replace an ironwork Regency veranda and a decorative plasterwork scheme for the walls and ceiling of the drawing room. Some photographs exist in the archive showing

---

[276] Frida Keane, p.90.

the moulded designs for the plasterwork, which was carried out by Michael Creedon of Clare Lane, Dublin.

In his claim for compensation Keane recalled the circumstances of the burning of Cappoquin:

> My family and I were away at the time. The house was unoccupied. I had to reside temporarily in Dublin in my capacity as Senator. Early in the morning of the 20th February 1923 the attention of one of my employees was directed to the fire. He saw Cappoquin House blazing furiously. He obtained assistance and prevented the fire from spreading to the servant's wing. The fire was undoubtedly malicious as the floor of one of the rooms in the servant's wing was partly burned away, showed that an attempt had been made to set the house on fire there also.[277]

One of the estate employees, Edward Brady, was an eyewitness to the destruction:

I was called by one of my children at 3 o'clock, he told me Sir John Keane's house was on fire...I then went up and when I arrived there the principal part of the front and back block was a blazing furnace, the roof gone and all the lofts and windows, with the exception of two at the west end over the portico...From what I hear an entrance was made through the study window also Master Richard's workshop window was raised up and a hole burned in the floor...There was two chairs put under the stairs going up to the nursery and set on fire but the stairs did not take fire...one of the soldiers told me the lower part of house

---

[277] NAI FIN/COMP/2/23/228.

was not on fire but the top was all in one blaze when he arrived there...we are getting everything that is loose away.[278]

Keane's secretary, Miss Bell, informed him that the roof was completely destroyed by 4 a.m. along with the interior, but the servants' wing survived and the conservatory. The surviving wing was occupied next day by Free State soldiers who did further damage.[279]

Who was responsible for the burning of Cappoquin? According to Frida Keane writing in the 1970s, the Keanes were reassured that it was not locals but a Flying Column from outside the area who had been put up at Mount Melleray Abbey.[280] Emily Ussher was sure that it was 'a roving band out of Tipperary' who burned Cappoquin.[281] Recent research by the author appears to indicate that local people assisted the IRA who carried out the burning. Two members of the Donoghue family of Lismore worked for Sir John Keane: James, who was the weighmaster at the Market House, and his son James Ernest who worked as a gardener. Another son, Michael Vincent O'Donoghue, was a member of the Cappoquin Volunteers in 1918 and later that year won a scholarship to U.C.C. At the start of the Civil War, he was appointed Brigade Engineer to the Cork no.3 Brigade.[282] Michael compiled a substantial witness statement detailing his activities

---

[278] Keane Archive, MS report by Edward Brady, undated.
[279] Keane Archive, John D.Palmer to Sir John Keane, 22 February 1923.
[280] Frida Keane, *The Valley is too Lush- A memoir of country house life in the Blackwater Valley*, (Dublin 2015) p.86.
[281] Emily Ussher, p.73.
[282] Donald Brady, 'Michael Vincent O'Donoghue', *Essays from Lismore* (Dungarvan, 2014), pp.211-225.

during the revolutionary period.[283] What does come across in reading this is a resentment towards the Keanes in Cappoquin.

Another participant in the burning of Cappoquin was Nora O'Keefe who had a public house, The Cats Bar, near Mount Melleray Abbey. Nora was a member of Cumann Na mBan and was active in supporting the Republican cause throughout the War of Independence and Civil War. When she applied for a pension in 1934, she detailed her activities during this period. In one document she states that she 'gave important information re the burning of Sir John Keane's house which was burned in November'. In another she said that: 'When Cappoquin Mansion was burned I supplied oil etc as can be proved by Capt S. O'Meara'.[284] This evidence clearly indicates local involvement in the burning. One source indicated to the author that Michael Vincent Donoghue planned the burning and used the Tipperary Brigade to carry out the deed, which shifted suspicion from local people.[285] There is a document in the Moss Twomey Papers stating the reason why Cappoquin, Mr Kenny's house near Waterford, and Mr White's in Waterford were burned: 'The owners of the above houses will be verbally informed that their houses are being destroyed as a reprisal for the executions which have taken place in Kilkenny, Waterford and Roscrea'. This order was issued by the 2nd Southern Division IRA, order No.2, 7 February 1923.[286] Patrick Williams Kenny, J.P., lived at Kingsmeadow House and was a member of Waterford Corporation. Dr Vincent White was a supporter of the Treaty and lived in Broad Street, Waterford city. When the IRA burnt

[283] BMH WS 1741.
[284] WMSP34REF5678NORAOKEEFE.pdf
[285] Interview with the late Joe Conway, Dungarvan, on 23/1/2017.
[286] UCDA, Moss Twomey Papers, P69/92/135. Thanks to Cian Flaherty for drawing this to my attention.

Rockmount, the residence of Arthur Hunt, they gave the same reason.[287]

On the return journey from Derreen in February 1923, Beatrix, Dowager Marchioness of Waterford and her mother stopped at Cappoquin to visit Sir John and Lady Keane at Tivoli. They went to see the nearby ruin of Cappoquin house:

> It had been a fine house, well proportioned, with decorations of the Adams period; now it was but a shell. One's heart ached for the owners – and I was thankful that Tyrone's [Her son the 7th Marquis of Waterford] age had debarred him from being appointed a Senator in the early days of the Free State.[288]

In early March 1923 it was reported in the press that Sir John Keane had submitted a claim to the Lismore Rural Council of £30,000 for the burning of his house.[289] The actual claim was for £24,613 which consisted of £23,400 for the house and £1,213 for the furniture.

On 13 March 1923 Cork auctioneer, J.F. Wood, held an auction at Cappoquin to sell off dairy cows, farm implements and 'useful Furniture, Pictures, etc, saved from the recent fire'. An advertisement for the sale listed some of the contents, such as an oil painting with a 'massive gilt frame', and twenty other pictures which consisted of oil paintings and etchings. Also included in the sale were bedroom furniture, chairs, and tables.[290]

---

[287] *Munster Express*, 7 June 1923.
[288] Typescript of the recollections of Beatrix, Lady Waterford, p.27. Private Collection.
[289] *Nottingham Journal*, 7 March 1923.
[290] *Irish Examiner*, 10 March 1923.

After the fire Sir John Keane and his wife rented a house in England. Their gamekeeper, John Hurley, was threatened at gunpoint by the IRA and had left Ireland and settled in Stratford-on-Avon.[291]

The Keanes were determined to rebuild Cappoquin and had advice from the architect Page L Dickenson but as he was not available to oversee the work this position went to Richard Caulfield Orpen R.H.A. (1863-1938). Dickenson explained the architectural importance of the house and what its interior had been like before the fire:

> The house is one of the best known among Southern Irish Mansions. It was built during the last quarter of the 18th century, and besides being planned on a generous scale, it contained many features of architectural beauty and importance. Among these were handsome richly carved joinery to the principal rooms, and some very good 'Adams' plaster work, most difficult and costly to reproduce. The house had recently, in 1913, had certain structural alterations carried out, and had been fully decorated throughout at a cost of £5,000...It contained up to date acetylene gas and central heating plants. The external walls are of stone with brick lining in most instances, and the external treatment is in the best eighteenth manner...I am familiar with the house having stayed there while carrying out work for Sir John Keane. I have also illustrated certain details of the plaster work in my book 'Georgian Mansions'. The house contained some excellent mantlepieces which would be likely to fetch high

---

[291] NAI FIN 1/2391.

prices if sold in London or America, and these are not included in this valuation.[292]

He estimated the restoration and reconstruction would cost £23,400.

John D Palmer, auctioneer, compiled a list of the damaged and destroyed items on 23 July 1923. The damaged items included three swords and seven mahogany doors. The total valuation was £372, minus £239 the cost of salvage. The valuation of contents burned in the fire came to £974. These included a grand piano, engravings, large mirrors, dolls' house, two mahogany bookcases with open fronts, books in the library, drawing room etc., 'including first editions, rare volumes, military, historical etc'. The most expensive items were the books valued at £300.

The Keanes went to great lengths to reproduce the character of the house, with the acquisition of original doors, fireplaces etc., and the reinstatement of decorative plasterwork. The latter supplied by G Jackson & Sons, London. Sections of the original decorative plasterwork were rescued from the ruins, and it was intended to reproduce as much of this as possible. However, this proved too expensive, and it was decided to use standard fibrous moulds, but of a high quality and level of detail. The present main entrance was very plain before the fire. It was rendered with plaster coign stones and no decorative details. After the fire a classical doorcase and window surrounds were added in reconstituted stone and made by estate workers. The render was removed exposing the rubble stone. A detailed archive relating to

---

[292] NAI FIN/COMP/2/23/228.

the reconstruction survives which was examined in detail by Glascott Symes in his book on Cappoquin House.[293]

In a Senate discussion about the Land Bill in 1923 Keane accepted that it marked the final stage of the land question in Ireland. He felt that this was the correct way forward but qualified this by adding: 'and yet there was a feeling of regret in the country at the passing of the landlord classes, because after all, that class had been the expression of culture in the country'.[294] Did the general population really express regret at the demise of landlords or was the regret mainly felt by the landlord class?

In January 1924 Keane wrote to the Ministry of Finance explaining that he needed to get a new roof on the house by summer, but this would not be possible as his compensation case would not be heard until May. In order to proceed with the work immediately he required an advance of £500. In November 1924 the architect Richard Caulfield Orpen wrote to the Ministry of Finance enclosing an itemised list of expenditure from 1 April to 31 October 1924. 'Sir John Keane is now carrying out his restoration by direct labour and without a contractor'.

An English newspaper noted the unusual roof finish of Cappoquin with the heading 'Ancestral Home in Concrete'. It described the novelty of a flat concrete roof.[295] In late December 1929 a progress report was published in the local press:

> The work of rebuilding which started in 1924 is now rapidly nearing completion...its wanton destruction over

---

[293] Glascott Symes, *Sir John Keane and Cappoquin House in time of war and revolution* (Dublin, 2016).
[294] *Weekly Freeman's Journal*, 4 August 1923.
[295] *Portsmouth Evening News*, 8 October 1925.

seven years ago caused general regret at the time. Now, however, it has risen Phoenix-like from its ashes...The architect for the work was Mr Orpen...while the roof was specially designed by Mr Delap. Dublin. The heaviest and most intricate portion of the work was entrusted to Mr. E Brady, Cappoquin, and the excellent manner in which he has executed everything in his line is a marvel of perfection and artistic taste...[It] required 150 tons of cement to make concrete blocks for the roof, and adding more than 500 tons of gravel...The huge concrete blocks weighing over a ton each, were made on the ground, and lifted into position on the roof by a powerful steam crane...three extra chimney stacks have been added...The woodwork portion of the contract was carried out by Mr James Hackett, Cappoquin, assisted by Messrs Garret and Frank Dalton, Ballingown, and the beautiful bookcases made for the spacious library by Mr Hackett as well as artistic shelves and window frames, show wonderful perfection of workmanship. The large dining-room and ballroom...are beautifully laid with new floors of stained and polished teak wood, while the floor of the hall is laid in large diamond-shaped tiles...carried out by Mr Brady. The entire house is brilliantly lighted with electricity, which is supplied by a private dynamo worked by turbine from the Cappoquin Sawmills. Several of the principal rooms on the ground floor are already completed.[296]

The *Dungarvan Observer* reported on the coming-of-age party at Cappoquin for Sir John's son, Richard, in 1930: 'There was an enormous gathering [of] over 200 people. Except the ornamentation, all the reconstruction work was done by local

---

[296] *Dungarvan Observer*, 28 December 1929.

labour, and the new house is a replica in every detail of the original'.[297]

On 29 December 1932 Sir John wrote to the Department of Finance informing them that work on the house was nearing completion and asking for the balance of his compensation.

The total award was £12,894 plus £66.9.3. for expenses. He was granted an additional 10% which came to £1289.8.0 making a total of £14,249.17.3.

Comeragh House

The house was owned by the Palliser family who were descended from William Palliser, Archbishop of Cashel (1694-1727), a native of Yorkshire. John Bury (d.1769) assumed the surname Palliser from his uncle William whom he succeeded. He had a son Col Wray Palliser of Derryluskan Co Tipperary and Comeragh Co Waterford who married a Miss Chaloner. They had John Palliser of Derryluskan who married Grace Barton in 1784. They had Wray Bury (1788-1863) of Derryluskan and Comeragh. In 1814 he married Anne Gledstanes of Annesgift, Co Tipperary. Their son, John (1817-1887) was the noted explorer. In order to pay for his extensive travels, he mortgaged Comeragh to his sister Grace Fairholme in 1884. After his death in 1887 Comeragh was transferred from Grace to her daughter Caroline.

In 1853 Grace, daughter of Col Wray Palliser, married William Fairholme of Chapel-On-Leader, Lauderdale, Scotland.[298] They had five daughters: Anne (d.1869); Caroline (who sold Chapel-On-Leader and settled at Comeragh); Mary, who died unmarried

---

[297] *Dungarvan Observer*, 1 January 1930.
[298] The Fairholmes were of Craigiehall, West Lothian, Scotland.

on 15 December 1932; Louisa, who died unmarried 2 September 1933; and Katherine who died unmarried 5 October 1934.

Mary [Minnie] Fairholme was a friend of the widowed Lady Kingston of Mitchelstown Castle and was described as an 'assistant' to her second husband, William Downes Webber, in 1900.[299] According to the *Primose League Gazette* for 1895 she was the secretary of the Mitchelstown branch of the Primose League [Founded in 1883 to spread Conservative principles]. Mary has been immortalised by Elizabeth Bowen in the often-quoted section of her book *Bowen's Court*[300]. This passage summed up the beginning of the end to a whole way of life for the Anglo-Irish:

> That afternoon we walked up the Castle avenue, greeted by the gusty sound of a band. The hosts of the party were the late Lady Kingston's second husband Mr. Willie Webber and his companion Miss Minnie Fairholme. They were not young, and, owing to the extreme draughtiness everywhere, they received their guests indoors, at the far end of Big George's gallery.

> It was an afternoon when the simplest person begins to anticipate memory – this Mitchelstown garden party, it was agreed, would remain in everyone's memory as historic. Many of those guests, those vehement talkers, would be scattered, houseless, sonless, or themselves dead.

---

[299] Bill Power, *White Knights, Dark Earls – The Rise and Fall of an Anglo-Irish Dynasty* (Cork, 2002), p.201.
[300] Elizabeth Bowen, *Bowen's Court* (London, 1942), pp 323-324.

After the burning of Mitchelstown Castle Mary Fairholme claimed for the destruction of her Stradivarius violin and other personal belongings to the value of £300.[301] It has been suggested that the violin did not perish in the fire but was among the many items looted from the castle.[302]

Grace Fairholme was interested in local history: she was a member of John O'Daly's Ossianic Society from 1859-1861 and was elected a member of the Royal Society of Antiquaries of Ireland in 1889. Her sister Caroline became a member in 1912. Grace was a friend of the Irish scholar Patrick Carmody who lived near Comeragh.[303]

In the 1911 census Comeragh House was occupied by Caroline and Louisa Fairholme and their servants: Johanna Butler, cook, Mary Fitzgerald, parlour maid and Kate Hogan, dairymaid, both born in Co Waterford. There was a forester, Hugh Barclay, a Presbyterian. The house contained 21 rooms.

The IRA decided to burn Comeragh on 18 February 1923. It is difficult to know why as the Fairholmes appear to have been good landlords and did much charitable work. A local newspaper carried a report on the burning of Comeragh:

> Armed men appeared at Miss Fairholme's and ordered those in the house out, giving them ten minutes to do so. Miss Fairholme, an elderly lady, tried to save some papers, but only managed to get a small lot, when the dwelling was set on fire and completely burned.

---

[301] Bill Power, p.234.

[302] Information from Bill Power, Mitchelstown.

[303] Padraig Ó Macháin, 'Patrick Carmody, Irish Scholar' in *Decies* 53, 1997. pp 132-135.

In her application for compensation Caroline Fairholme stated that the IRA burned her home because her family had 'by tradition and practice...been avowed and consistent supporters of the British Crown'.[304] Her solicitor commented that: 'As a result of violent political and ancestral enmity it is notorious that during the trouble in Ireland the masses of the people were extremely hostile to members of claimant's class.'

Caroline had given a plot of land at Mahon Bridge on which was built the Catholic curate's house, but this and other charitable works did not save Comeragh from destruction.[305]

Emily Ussher[306] was puzzled as to why Comeragh was burned:

> In the case of the Miss Fairholmes, it excited the utmost indignation among all sorts and conditions of people who knew them to be the souls of goodness and benevolence. One of them was sitting in her evening dress at her fireside when the raiders appeared on Sunday evening and was not given time even to put a shawl over her shoulders or allowed to carry out a clock, she particularly valued. They had seen their cherished home burn before their eyes. But even so, they would not leave the ruins but lived for weeks in the dairy. A legend (they deny the truth of it) spread far and near that Miss C. Fairholme had said to one of the men she knew to be a son of a neighbouring farmer, 'I am sorry to see you here, Keating. But there is a verse in the bible 'Vengeance is mine, saith the Lord'. Afterwards, when

[304] TNA CO 762/94/3: Fairholme, Waterford.
[305] Patrick Power, *Waterford & Lismore A Compendious History of the United Diocese* (Cork, 1937), p.203.
[306] Emily Ussher, pp 73-74.

Keating died a painful and horrible death, this story was told again'.

Miss Fairholme noted that it was impossible to rebuild the house with the amount of money allowed in compensation, and the house when it was rebuilt was 'vastly inferior' to the original. Louisa put in a claim of £200 for her stamp collection. The Fairholmes' solicitor asked that their friends Lady Frances Alice Anderson and Mary Carew be asked to attend the compensation hearing to support them.

State Solicitor E. A. Ryan wrote to the Ministry of Finance in 1924 concerning the house contents. He noted that the furniture claim had been investigated by J.H. Avery of the Board of Works who valued the contents destroyed at £5000. Avery claimed that this was underestimated as 'the house was sumptuously furnished and contained a very rare collection of valuable pictures and antiques.' Regarding the house, R Donnelly of the Board of Works assessed its value. The Fairholmes claimed £25,000, but this was later reduced by the Ministry of Finance to £11,124 for partial restoration. Donnelly suggested the Fairholmes be given £6,000 for 'bare restoration without any ornamentation'. The Fairholmes were unhappy with this, saying that they could not restore and rebuild the house to any decent standard of finish for that figure. The judge suggested they build a modern house on the site and accept compensation of £8000. Ryan states that Miss Fairholme agreed with this 'only under protest'.[307]

In November 1923 Charles Langley put in a claim on behalf of Caroline Fairholme for £94.17.0 for repairs to a pony and trap stolen by 'armed men' and for two heifers valued at £17 each. He

---

[307] NAI FIN/COMP/2/23/37 E A Ryan, State Solicitor, Dungarvan, to the Secretary, Ministry of Finance, 18 June 1924.

188

was awarded £65.[308] In late May 1924 Grace Fairholme was awarded £13,000 at Waterford Quarter Sessions for the burning of the house and contents.[309]

We don't know what contents survived the fire apart from one picture and some photograph albums. After Miss Caroline Grace Fairholme's death her executors held an auction of the remaining contents in November 1941. The auction was organised by John D Palmer, Waterford. A news report described it as 'the most successful auction to be held for some years in Co. Waterford. There was a very large attendance of buyers from all over Ireland and splendid prices were realised'. One item of particular interest was a painting which sold for £3-10-0. This painting featured in the press the following year where it was described as 'the only picture saved from the disastrous fire...and sold in 1941...to Mr W. Reilly, Dublin, is now causing widespread interest, and is likely to be profitable to its new owner, who had an offer for it of over £200'. The article stated that the painting was being restored in Dublin and this had resulted in it being attributed to Frans Francken (1581-1642) of Antwerp. It was believed to be a work titled: 'Joseph's coffin and the destruction of the Egyptians'. There is a painting with this theme by Francken at Tyntesfield House, near Bristol, which is titled: 'The Israelites gathering around Joseph's Sarcophagus after crossing of the Sea'. The Comeragh painting could be a version of this subject, but whether or not it was a good copy or by Francken himself is now difficult to prove. The story notes that the painting had been rescued from the fire at Comeragh House by auctioneer John D Palmer. However, when

---

[308] *Waterford News,* 9 November 1923.
[309] *Sunday Independent,* 1 June 1924.

it was sold in 1941 several dealers felt it was a copy by an amateur.[310]

In January 1942 the contents of Caroline's will were published.[311] It showed that in spite of the house being burned in 1923 she had a close relationship with the people she knew in the area. The press singled out her bequests of £1,000 to 'her servants', Mary and Alice Fitzgerald. She also included other estate workers such as Edward Fitzgerald who received £50, and £15 to each workman who had been employed for a period of five years. She left £1,000 to her agent Charles Langley, £500 to the parish of Kilrossanty, £500 to Mrs W P Carmody, and £200 upon trust for the purchase of an annuity for James Carmody.

When Mary died in December 1932 her obituary[312] described her as a person 'whose popularity and charity were well-known throughout the County Waterford'. The article continued:

> The family has always been very popular in the County Waterford, and their departure from Ireland when their residence, Comeragh House, was burnt in 1922, was much regretted. Such, however, was their love of this country that they had the property completely rebuilt and returned to live at Comeragh in 1926 since when they have added to their reputation for charity and consideration towards their tenants. The late Miss Mary Fairholme, on her return to Ireland took over the management of the estate. She carried out a drainage scheme at Comeragh for the sole purpose of giving much-needed employment in the district. Miss Fairholme was of a very active

---

[310] *Munster Express*, 4 September 1942.

[311] *The Nationalist*, 7 January 1942.

[312] *Waterford Standard*, 24 December 1932.

disposition and drove her own motor car until quite recently.

Gardenmorris House, Kill

The house is noted in the Civil Survey of 1654 and was extended in the 18th and 19th centuries in a French chateau style. Bence-Jones states that the 17th-century house was of red brick. There is a date stone inset on one of the outside walls inscribed RP 1631, but it is not clear if this is original or a 19th century addition. The core of the house was of three stories, and it had a large roof lantern which appears in a photograph of c. 1910.

Gardenmorris was the home of the Power O'Shee family who were Catholics.[313] Lt Col Richard Alfred Power O'Shee had a distinguished career in the Royal Engineers and in colonial administration. In 1920 he married a Frenchwoman, Bernadette de Francqueville of Chateau d'Yzeux near Amiens. His brother John Marcus (1869-1944) was County Inspector of the RIC. His other brother George Ivor (1873-1939) was a Colonel in the British army. Richard and Bernadette had no children.

In the summer of 1920, the house was raided for arms, as recalled by Michael Power, one of the IRA who took part:

> I remember raiding the house of a Colonel O'Shea at Gardenmorris...where we had been told by some of his servants (girls) that there were guns and a quantity of .303 ammunition. We were successful in getting the guns, some of which were heavy type used by Col. O'Shea for big game hunting in Africa. We learned, however, that the Colonel had dumped a large quantity of .303 ammunition in a large

---

[313] Ivan Fitzgerald, 'The Power O'Shee Family, Gardenmorris, County Waterford', *Irish Genealogist*, XIV,1 (2014) pp 14-22.

pond near his house, and I remember well being held by the legs by some of our lads as I 'fished' the stuff from the bottom of the pond.[314]

During the War of Independence, the IRA attempted to burn the barrack in Kill owned by the Power O'Shees but did not succeed. In early October 1920 the *Waterford News* reported that Colonel Power O'Shee had dismantled the building, having first asked the permission of the 'Sinn Feiners of the district before doing so'.[315] Power O'Shee was asked by Archdeacon Burkitt of Stradbally if he would like him to store valuables in case Gardenmorris would be burned. The Colonel is said to have remarked: 'They'll never burn us out, we're Irish and we're Catholic.'[316]

The Gardenmorris estate was run by trustees – John Power O'Shee, of Marchings, Chigwell, Essex, and Henry E King Tennison, Earl of Kingston, Kilronan Castle, Carrick-on-Shannon.

The house was burned while the family were away. At the court hearing in Dungarvan to adjudicate on the level of compensation, an account of the burning was presented:

> On the night of Thursday 22 February 1923 at about 10 o'clock p.m. a number of armed men called at Gardenmorris and broke into the house. They then saturated the premises with petrol and oil and continuing at the upper stories set the place on fire working down to the ground floor. They placed a guard over the claimant's steward, R. Robinson and threatened to shoot him if he stirred out. The gardener, John Barrett and his wife were

---

[314] BMH WS 1180
[315] *Waterford News*, 1 October 1920.
[316] Information from Julian Walton.

also held up and no one was permitted to move about until the armed men had left. After these men went away the steward and gardener, with the help of people from the neighbourhood and some soldiers who came about midnight tried to extinguish the fire and managed to save the servant's wing – the main house however was burned to the ground and all the furniture with some trifling exceptions destroyed.[317]

This account clearly states that people from around tried to save the house, but another view is given by Emily Ussher of Cappagh House:

Poor Miss O'Shee arrived on the scene as soon as she could to find crowds of 'respectable' looters, on foot and driving, coming to see what they could pick up. The O'Shees too had served their neighbourhood well and had built School and Chapel. They are a very old Catholic family and have suffered in bygone generations for their faith.

Mary De la Poer of Gurteen le Poer, Kilsheelan, recorded the event in her diary:

24 February 1923

The sad news today Desart Court and Gardenmorris have gone. The Desarts who spent their lives doing good for the people and this their reward, and the Poer O'Shees who were such good friends of the family one can't bear to think that their dear old house is gone. Soon no country house

---

[317] NAI FIN/COMP/2/23/37

193

will be left, and Ireland will be famous for nothing but savagery, brutality and ruins.[318]

'My brother will rebuild a storey higher than before', declared Miss O'Shee to sympathisers; and the Major, after surveying the wreck, waved away condolence with a gesture of his hand. That was the proud old spirit'.[319]

The trustees along with Col Power O'Shee claimed £49,900 for the burning of the house and £7590 for contents. On 13 May 1924 the case was heard at the Waterford Quarter Sessions. E.A. Ryan, State Solicitor, 'laughingly remarked' to the judge before proceedings commenced that he hoped that the judge knew something about antiques, as there were many to consider in the claim. It was explained to the court that Col Power O'Shee was a tenant for life which had been arranged by the trustees in 1899. The judge was told that there would be a claim of £15,563 for the house and he remarked that this was a lot of money. Mr Connolly for the applicant explained that Gardenmorris was 'a beautiful mansion and was the ancestral home of this family for generations'. E.A. Ryan wanted 'proof of malice'. The lodge-keeper, Mr Robinson said the raiders demanded paraffin oil, which he did not have. After about an hour he went to see the burning house and smelt paraffin and petrol.

The court awarded £15,563 plus costs of £46.9.6. A claim for £7,590 was also submitted for the furniture and other contents destroyed in the fire. The court awarded £7,000.[320]

---

318 Thanks to Anthony de la Poer for access to this diary.
319 Emily Ussher, p.74.
320 *Munster Express*, 7 June 1924.

What is not mentioned is the family papers which were rescued. These were kept in iron boxes which appears to have protected them. However, a number were damaged by the fire. Major Patrick Power O'Shee donated them to the Public Record Office and most of them are now in the National Library of Ireland.[321]

Col Power O'Shee employed the architect Thomas Scully (1869-1946) of Waterford to rebuild the house. Scully had worked as an engineer on the Waterford & Limerick Railway Co. In 1898 he set up his own business as an engineer/architect and designed many churches and bank buildings in Munster. He was assisted by P. Costen & Son of Waterford. While the house was being rebuilt Power O'Shee moved to France where his address was Murier, Paramé, Ille et Vilaine, Brittany.

The State Solicitor, E A Ryan wrote to the Ministry of Finance in June 1924 and discussed the furniture claim:

> As regards the furniture claim the Board of Works was represented by Mr J.H. Avery. His original estimate of the value of the furniture destroyed was £5,739, but after the claim had been fully gone into by the judge, he admitted that a great number of the articles claimed for had been undervalued...He stated in his report to me that Col Poer O'Shee was a collector of antiques, both china and furniture, and that Gardenmorris was more in the nature of a museum than a residence, and that local gentlemen of standing and repute in the district assured him of this. The judge came to the conclusion...that £7000 would represent fair and reasonable compensation.

---

[321] Papers of the families of Shee of Sheestown, Co Kilkenny, and Power of Gardenmorris etc. NLI.Ms18,482.

There is no list of items destroyed included in the compensation claim file in the National Archive. However, when Col Power O'Shee gave evidence at the Waterford court hearing a list of furniture and other contents was produced. 'There was an allowance of £328 for salvage'.[322] Included in the furnishings were several family portraits of the O'Shees, one dated 1645.[323]

Power O'Shee wrote to the secretary of the Ministry of Finance in September 1924 informing him that work had commenced on the rebuilding of Gardenmorris at the end of June. In the course of the work an internal wall collapsed, and he requested additional funds to cover this unexpected event.

In November O'Shee commented that work on the house was progressing well and he had begun to collect furniture. In May 1925 he wrote to the Ministry of Finance enquiring about import duty on furniture. 'I have at present bought a certain quantity of furniture, some of it is in my house here, some stored, and some is stored in London. Some is new and some second hand.' He felt that people in his situation should not have to pay duty on furniture which was meant to replace that destroyed by the IRA.

The house was rebuilt much as it was before but without the third story and the roof lantern. A claim for £23-10-0 was also submitted by Nellie Roche of Tinteskin, Kilmuckridge, Co Wexford for 'burning of clothing' and 'personal goods' destroyed in the fire. She was probably a servant at Gardenmorris.[324]

---

[322] *Munster Express*, 7 June 1924.
[323] *Wexford People*, 19 October 1872.
[324] NAI FIN/COMP/2/23/182.
    WCCA WCC/GWA288, Waterford Co Council Notices of claims for compensation for criminal injuries.

While the family were Catholic and charitable to locals, the fact that they all had careers in the British army and administration would have been sufficient excuse for a disgruntled band of IRA to burn the house. It is not clear if the raiders were assisted by any of the estate staff to gain entry to the house. We don't know why the family were absent, and where they were staying.

Patrick Iver Power O'Shee was the last of the line. He moved to England and put the estate up for sale. He died on 19 April 1985.

Rockmount

Rockmount was the seat of the Hunt family. It was a small two story over basement house built in the mid-19th century. According to the 1911 census it contained 22 rooms and was occupied by Arthur Hunt and two servants: Annie Walsh, housekeeper, and Bridget Harney, general servant.

In 1921 Arthur Hunt was awarded £400 for the burning of a large quantity of hay on his farm at Newtown.[325] Rockmount was burned by the IRA on 18 February 1923, the same night as Comeragh House. Arthur's son Thomas was aged five at the time and vividly recalled the event in correspondence with the author in 2017:[326]

> My mother was over in England with her parents, so my father sent her a telegram with the 'sad news about our house' followed by a letter:
>
> Dungarvan 16 February 1923
>
> My dearest Old Girl,

---

[325] *Irish Examiner,* 7 June 1921.
[326] Letters from Tom Hunt to the author, 6/3/2017, 31/3/2017.

You will have had my wire with sad news about our house being burnt. Could not save anything scarcely. I got my desk and papers out and your desk and just a few odds and ends. Nurse got the two kids away to John's room and I hope they have gone to Seafield by now. I sent Monahan (groom) this morn fearing they might also be burnt – as Comeragh House also gone. I went up last night to see them [Fairholmes of Comeragh House]. The fellows came at 9 o'clock and only gave us five minutes. All your things are gone – You better get measured for a habit T Perkins. Such luck Grace had gone as it would have been very bad for her. I came to see Jack Williams (solicitor Dungarvan) but he cannot take up claim so will go to Chapman. I cannot write more – I will sleep in room next to John's for a night or two. I am bewildered but hope to hunt tomorrow, it will do me good'.

Best love Yr loving Arthur.

Although I was only 5½ years old at the time, I still have a few vivid memories of the event. Earlier that day a delivery of some 50 gallons of paraffin had been delivered to the house and stored in the basement for use in the lamps...the fire was started in the sitting-room which had been drenched in paraffin. Although I can't be sure, I believe that the gang who burned the house were not the same men who were based on Rockmount. I was told they were on their way home west to Cork & Kerry and decided as a last act to burn several houses in County Waterford whose owners were believed to be unionists.

John the groom who looked after the trap horse and pony, came into my little bedroom, picked me out of bed and carried me over to a cottage in the farm-yard, about 100 yards away. The cottage had not been used for some months, so Robin [his brother] and I had to bed down in filthy bed clothes. We were almost bitten to death by swarms of hungry fleas.

Next morning my father took me over to see the smoke still rising from our home. Only the four outer walls remained standing, the centre of the house was a heap of rubble. Only two things remained intact – the iron safe built into an outside wall and just above it, a wooden cupboard...inside of which was a collection of old cylindrical phonograph records some of which had partly melted...Perhaps the most valuable item to be lost was the very first Waterloo cup for hare coursing by greyhounds.

Later in the day Robin and I were taken in the trap to stay with my aunt Grace Russell at Seafield.

My father was totally unprepared for this calamity because the IRA had promised that they would not burn the house -and for good reason. For some time during the Civil War, the IRA had a tented camp in a field behind Comeragh Lodge and each evening the company officers came into the Rockmount kitchen and were given a main meal.

Rockmount was rebuilt by 1925. The British government paid for the rebuilding on the old site, but my father took the humane decision to extend the house to the east by adding a new wing. This contained on the ground floor, a new kitchen, pantry, scullery and larder, and above a nursery (for me and my brother) and bedrooms for the cook and housemaid. My father (quite properly) paid for the new extension. The building contractor was Hearne of Waterford.

Even though his father was only given a short time to remove personal belongings from the house, his son recalled that the neighbours arrived and managed to rescue 'many pieces of furniture and other portable objects which they stacked up on the lawn'.[327] It is unusual that the arsonists allowed this to happen but perhaps they were in a hurry and left soon after setting the house on fire, or the neighbours arrived while Arthur was still removing items. The Hunts were able to move to Comeragh Lodge, situated nearby and owned by the family. Tom Hunt, who died aged 100 in 2019, still felt the hurt and trauma of his home being consumed by flames on that February day in 1923.

Arthur Hunt knew that there was a good chance his car would be taken, and he immobilised it my removing the wheels and burying them in the wood. At the Waterford Quarter Sessions in late May 1924, he claimed £9,611 for the destruction of his property.[328] Arthur asked the men who came to burn the house why they were taking such action and they replied that it was 'as a reprisal for the recent executions in Waterford and Kilkenny'.[329]

According to the compensation claim files, Arthur submitted a claim for the destruction of his dwelling house and goods by armed men.[330] He claimed £11,200 and was awarded £5,250. Hunt hired the Waterford architect Thomas Scully and a Mr Hearne as contractor. Their estimate for the restoration came to £6,805. At the court hearing the architect and contractor 'put up a strenuous fight for this sum'. W Gleeson assessed the claim for the furniture and recommended a sum of £2,200 which was

---

[327] Robin Bury, *Buried Lives, The Protestants of Southern Ireland* (Dublin, 2017), p.91.
[328] *Sunday Independent*, 1 June 1924.
[329] *Munster Express*, 7 June 1924.
[330] NAI FIN/COMP/2/23/212

granted. However, the judge awarded £3,050 for the rebuilding of the house.

Arthur Hunt told the Irish Grants Committee that 'in his district practically all Protestant houses were burnt in a similar way'.[331]

Annestown House was damaged and looted again on 27 February 1923. On 8 March Miss Walker wrote to Mrs Galloway with the details:

> The drawing floor and carpets are burnt through in several places. The flames went up around the archway and windows, a lot of the curtains are burned. The piano is standing but the top is burned and in pieces, the big mirror over the mantel is all cracked. Some pictures are burned, but not many, as the people pulled them down first.
>
> Two large velvet armchairs are burned...I can't tell how many of the small chairs. The writing table in the drawing-room...the top of it is all smashed, like with a sledge and the table with the brass rim is scorched and blistered. Palmer [auctioneer] took all that fitted in the van, cases of china, pictures, small tables, chairs, bureau, writing tables etc.

She also mentioned that Arthur Hunt of Rockmount had visited and noted that he was 'very broken down' after the destruction of his house. 'It is an awful loss to them and the Miss Fairholmes, [Comeragh] all their things are gone'.

The compensation claim file described the damage:

[331] TNA, CO762/85/7:HUNT WATERFORD

Windows smashed to give vent to fire. The furniture was piled up on the Drawing Room floor and a considerable fire was started, taking complete hold of the flooring and the joists under. 230 sq. feet is completely burned, the whole of one window, shutters and trimmings and much of the surrounding woodwork is scorched. The papering & painting in those rooms is destroyed and but for the timely assistance rendered, the whole of the house would have been burned.

The IRA were not finished with Annestown House, and two further raids took place in March. On the 25th Miss Walker wrote that: 'your House was raided and robbed late last night, and a considerable amount of damage done. Everything was pulled about and scattered round the floors and passages.'

The raiders smashed some of the contents and stole blankets, clocks and the silver communion service belonging to the church. They also took the hunting clothes, livery coat and a red evening coat. They also took the farm-yard door and removed saddles and harnesses. She concluded her letter by saying that all the telephone wires were cut. 'It is dreadful the state the country is in, but it was very quiet around here till now'. There was a further raid on 30 March in which all the linen was taken. Miss Walker ends the letter with a note of despair: 'I don't know what can be done there is no safety anywhere. Robbers have walked into several farmer's houses in the district and demanded and taken clothes, bedclothes, money, etc. If it goes on much longer I expect they will come round to all our houses'.

The owner of Annestown House, Mrs Mary Jane Sybil Galloway, claimed for damage due to 'occupation by Irregular forces' on 26 July, and 3 August 1922 and by 'armed men' on 27 February 1923. She also claimed for damage to nearby Rock House on 27

February 1923.[332] The file notes that the house was attacked by armed men who 'broke up and smashed the doors, windows, and furniture and other contents thereof and set same on fire'. Another claim was submitted for Rock House by the tenant, Marcus Stamer Beresford Gubbins of 31 Thurloe Square, London.[333] In November 1924 details of the court case for damages was reported in the local press. Mr Connolly solicitor for Mrs Galloway, stated that the two houses were set on fire by Irregulars on the night of 27 February 1923. Mary Walker of The Lodge, Annestown was called as a witness. She recalled that armed men called to the house demanding keys and said they would 'make short work of the houses'. They then left but at around 12.20 she saw that Annestown House, and Rock House had been set alight. Some of the furniture, wardrobes and panels were smashed and burned.

The damage was inspected by John Palmer, auctioneer, and valuer. John Hearne, building contractor, estimated the damage at £175. E. A. Ryan, State Solicitor, presented a figure of £36.10.0. The judge awarded £108. Mr Gleeson, Board of Works valuer, estimated the damage to Annestown as a result of occupation by Irregulars and the fire to be £530. Mrs Galloway had claimed £170 for her Bechstein piano, but he said it only had minor da mage and the award of £60 was very generous. E. A Ryan asked him if he had seen the cuckoo clock. 'I did and all that was missing was the bird' (laughter). Hearne estimated the fire damage to the drawing room at £340 but Ryan suggested that £94 was more realistic. Ryan asked for an explanation in relation to a claim for £20 for 'temporary protection' and asked Mrs Galloway if she would need armoured cars, which drew laughter from the court.

---

[332] NAI FIN/COMP/2/23/139
[333] NAI FIN/COMP/2/23/219

She replied that she couldn't just leave the house unattended for everyone to wander through it.

The judge awarded £1,060 to Mrs Galloway for damage to the houses and contents and £60 to Mr Gubbins for damage to furniture.[334]

The Lismore artist Fanny Currey leased a shooting Lodge at The Vee which was originally built as a barrack. She often stayed there with her friend and fellow artist Helen O'Hara and used it as a base for painting expeditions. It was burnt by the IRA probably because of its past association as a barrack.[335]

'The wind whistled through broken window- panes'

Lismore Castle

One of the most spectacular country houses in Ireland, Lismore is the seat of the Cavendish family, dukes of Devonshire. At this period, it was owned by Victor Cavendish, 9th Duke of Devonshire (1868-1938) who had inherited on the death of his uncle in 1908. He was Secretary of State for the Colonies from 1922-1924. The family were generally regarded as good landlords and employed many local people on the estate.

However, taking the castle would be a symbolic action and the IRA proceeded to do so in June 1922. James Ormond, Captain of the Lismore Company IRA recalled the event:[336]

> When the Civil War broke out in 1922 Jack Cody took over command of the Battalion and with about sixteen men and

---

[334] *Freeman's Journal*, 27 November 1924. *Waterford News*, 28 November 1924.
[335] Mildred Dobbs memoir, p.116.
[336] BMH WS 1289

myself, occupied Lismore Castle. We held it for two months until the order came to evacuate the castle. When the Free State troops arrived in Lismore we went 'on the run' but kept sniping at the castle...

Mildred Dobbs recalled the occupation in her memoir:

The republicans had seized Lismore Castle and quartered themselves there in numbers, wrecking the place completely. The first day they discovered some champagne in the cellars and some of them in their ensuing exuberance danced on the roof of the tall tower from which one fell and was killed.[337]

The door of the wine cellar had been broken open and the contents which included champagne claret, whiskey, and 1870 port consumed. The duke later claimed £200 in compensation. The wine book had gone missing, so this was an estimate of the value of its contents.

The IRA had planned to burn the castle but were surprised by the arrival of the Free State troops. General Liam Tobin, Deputy Director of Intelligence to Michael Collins, heard about the planned destruction of the castle and sent troops to prevent it. The IRA evacuated the castle on 10 August on the orders of Liam Lynch.[338] Alice Keane of Fortwilliam House and her daughter Frida[339] arrived in Lismore as the Free State troops left the castle:

The army was evacuating, and lorry loads of troops were coming out and passing over the bridge on their way north,

---

[337] Mildred Dobbs memoir, p.116

[338] Tommy Mooney, *The Deise Divided: A History of the Waterford Brigade I.R.A. and the Civil War* (Kilkenny, 2014), p.96.

[339] Frida Keane, pp 92-93.

but there was still a sentry on the battlements. 'Hello dearies!' he shouted as we looked up and he fired his rifle in the air. Mother did not think this the way to behave 'What monstrous cheek!' she said and slapped the pony with the reins...Mr Penrose, who was land agent for the Duke of Devonshire, joined us...he told us to return in half an hour so that we could go with him over the castle. There were some battle-scarred vehicles that had refused to leave with their owners and a tangle of barbed wire round the great beech tree in the centre, on which all the wastepaper in the world seemed to be speared. We knew the castle well in childhood...To see it now was a vision of desolation that made us silent, but Mr Penrose was pleased to find that the damage was superficial. The republican army had been the first to occupy the castle and had intended to set it on fire before they left. A surprise attack from the Free Staters...had caught them unawares and they had no time to light their fires. In many of the rooms there were still piles of straw, and petrol cans ready for the burning. The Free State troops had quickly found their way to the magnificent cellar...Every drop of that priceless wine...had been enjoyed by the military, and there were empty bottles in every room of the castle. When the soldiers had needed fire- wood they had broken the legs off the furniture, the dining room chairs were squatting on the floor like hatching hens. There was a panel burned out of a tapestry in the sitting room and some bullet holes in the passage from a machine gun that must have been fired from inside the house. 'Nothing of any consequence' said Mr Penrose, as we looked appalled at the dirt and disorder and a squalor that we had never imagined could exist. The wind whistled through broken window- panes...

The *Londonderry Sentinel* of 22 August 1922 carried a headline: 'Lismore Castle saved'. The article noted that a national column operating from Fermoy had captured Tallow and Lismore. They found no opposition in Lismore and on entering the castle they found the rooms 'saturated in oil and was prepared for destruction'. Apparently, the IRA did not have time to set fire to the castle, having left in a hurry. One newspaper account noted that the IRA were leaving the castle just as the Free State troops were entering by the front entrance:

> The main body proceeded to Lismore, where they found that the irregulars had beaten a very hasty retreat. One of the first places seen to was the famed Lismore Castle...and it was soon discovered that though the entire building had been liberally sprinkled with oil the retreat was so hasty that the Irregulars had not time to set it afire. Indeed, on close inquiry into the affair it was ascertained that they only made their exit through the back entrance as the National troops entered at the front. The news of the safety of this historic castle will be received with joy...[340]

It appears that Michael Collins had concerns about the destruction of the castle. In an article on Collins in the *Daily Express* Tim Healy noted that 'the saving of this glorious edifice with its priceless Gaelic manuscripts and ecclesiastical relics, daily occupied his thoughts, and his final day on earth was cheered by the news of the successful operations in Lismore. This dashing soldier was at heart a student and interested in every phase of history and art'.[341]

---

[340] *Irish Examiner*, 22 August 1922.
[341] *Sunday Independent*, 27 August 1922.

In early September it was reported that the staff at Lismore Castle had returned to work after their 'enforced idleness' due to the occupation of the castle by the IRA.[342]

On 22 September 1922 Sergeant Major Thomas Murray, Dublin Guards, and a member of the Free State troops died at the castle as a result of an accident involving a Thompson machine gun. He was 20 years old and had been a member of the IRA during the War of Independence.[343] A similar accident happened to a Private Myles Broughton some days later.[344] A native of Wicklow, he was reading a letter from his mother, when a comrade's rifle went off, fatally wounding him.[345]

There were eighty-five Free State troops based in Lismore Castle in early November 1922.[346]

Beatrix, Lady Osborne Beauclerk and her mother the Marchioness of Lansdowne passed through Lismore in 1922 and she made the following observations about the castle: 'Lismore Castle...at first sight as beautiful as ever, but on closer inspection showing many broken windows, filled up with sandbags and deal boards. The Free State troops were still in possession, and we heard sad tales of the damage done both by them and their predecessors, the Republicans, but no doubt the presence of the 'Staters' had prevented more fatal disaster'.[347]

---

[342] *Evening Echo*, 8 September 1922.
[343] www.Irishmedals.ie/National-Army-Killed.php [Accessed 31/10/2017]
[344] Tommy Mooney, p.116.
[345] *Southern Star*, 14 October 1922.
[346] Tommy Mooney, p.129.
[347] Beatrix, Lady Osborne Beauclerk, unpublished memoir of a journey to Derreen Co Kerry, typescript, p.2.Private collection.

Mary de la Poer noted in her diary on 11 January 1923:

> I was told the Free State troops in Lismore Castle have destroyed and looted the contents of the house and that the Lismore girls are well set up in Mrs and Miss Penrose's blouses and clothes![348]

In early February the *Irish Examiner* reported on a gun attack on the castle:

> Residents of Lismore were kept awake from 1 to 3 p.m. on Sunday morning last when it was stated that an attack on the posts stationed at Lismore Castle took place. Machine-gun and rifle fire resounded fiercely on that calm moonlight night...and rumours of the very wildest nature were afloat on Sunday morning. Blood was observed on the Green Road area leading to the western side of the castle- but it transpired that a donkey had been shot there in crossfire.[349]

A few days previously a sentry on duty at the bridge was fired at and had a 'marvellous escape, the bullet piercing his cap and a second bullet it is stated, piercing his coat'.[350]

In August a few papers carried the story 'Hay cut on the 'Flower Garden' at Lismore Castle'. It noted that for the first time ever a crop of hay had been cut on the site of the garden and that the

---

[348] Unpublished diary of Mary Olivia de la Poer of Gurteen le Poer, Kilsheelan, private collection.

[349] *Irish Examiner*, 8 February 1923.

[350] *Irish Examiner*, 1 February 1923.

castle was still occupied by National troops. There were a number of broken windows to be seen and 'other damage'.[351]

The National troops also held republican prisoners in the castle. In October a Mr Morrissey of Coolbagh, Clashmore, managed to make a successful escape.[352]

In early November 1923 the duke was awarded £2,500 by the Compensation Committee.[353]It was reported on 19 November that the duke had claimed £124.10.0 for saddles, bridles and harnesses and other items damaged during the occupation of the castle by republicans. At the court in Dungarvan the judge awarded £100.[354]

On 23 November 1923 a message was sent to Lismore from headquarters in Cork ordering the Free State troops to vacate the castle. This had still not been done by 10 January 1924 and a further order was sent to vacate the castle immediately and hand it over to the agent.[355]

In November 1924 the duke was awarded £170 in compensation for maps and documents taken from the castle and £50 for the destruction of the Police barrack in Lismore.[356]

The damage to the castle was significant and took a number of years to repair. In April 1925 it was reported in the press[357] that the Duke and Duchess of Devonshire with two of their children

---

351 *Freeman's Journal*, 16 August 1923.
352 *Freeman's Journal*, 19 October 1923.
353 *Waterford News & Star*, 9 November 1923.
354 *Sheffield Daily Telegraph*, 19 November 1923.
355 Tommy Mooney, p.228.
356 *Freeman's Journal*, 27 November 1924.
357 *Dungarvan Observer*, 11 April 1925.

had arrived in Lismore and were staying in the Devonshire Arms hotel. He visited the castle with his agent Mr Becher and his architect Lawrence McOboy Fitzgerald to assess the damage. The newspaper noted that 'it is the intention of their Graces to have the castle repaired and made habitable as their summer residence, and this news was received with feelings of gratification by the Lismore public. A few extra men have during the week been given employment at the castle...'

The *Derbyshire Advertiser* expressed surprise that the duke was still closely attached to his Lismore residence:

> Only a year or two ago it would have been unthinkable for one in so peculiar a sense an hereditary leader of English Unionism, to have set foot in Southern Ireland. We all know the Duke has to stay at an hotel because his house was practically destroyed and has not yet been rebuilt, but the wonderful thing is that he should be there at all. The Duke of Devonshire has loyally accepted the...Treaty. Indeed, during his time in the Colonial Office, he showed sympathetic insight into the difficulties confronting the Southern Irish Government that won him the regard alike of Mr Tim Healy and of Mr Cosgrave.[358]

The following month it was reported that 'extra tradesmen and labourers are employed in repair and renovation work...which will this summer be more or less occupied'.[359] The duke moved back to the castle on 8 May.[360] In 1925 during a budget debate in the Dáil, it was pointed out that wages in Ireland were too high. An example was the fact that the Duke of Devonshire was

---

[358] *Derbyshire Advertiser & Journal*, 17 April 1925.
[359] *Dungarvan Observer*, 2 May 1925.
[360] *Dungarvan Observer*, 16 May 1925.

expending £5,000 on Lismore Castle but 'the cost of local labour was too high, and labour had to be imported'.[361] Two compensation claims were submitted in relation to the occupation of Lismore Castle. One was from the duke's agent Edmund W Becher, of Castlefarm House, Lismore, who was claiming on behalf of the duke. The claim of £1666.12.6 was for damage to the castle and items taken by Irregulars between 3 and 21 August and for maps taken or damaged by Irregulars on 19 July 1922.[362] £1264 of this sum was to be expended on repairs and redecoration. The maps were important as a record of the estate as they contained details of tenants' holdings, boundaries, tree planting, and drainage over a thirty-year period. They also included a set of leather-bound copies of the six-inch maps for Waterford, Tipperary and Cork. The IRA did give a receipt for the maps, which were never recovered.

How bad was the damage to the interior of the castle? The claim submitted on behalf of the duke contains a room by room listing of damage and the repairs required. The entire castle was to be scoured and fumigated before redecoration could commence. Every room required repainting or papering along with the ceilings. In a number of cases doors were damaged and needed replacing. Many of the principal rooms had 'gothic furniture' which had been destroyed or damaged. Many of the plate glass windows of the castle were broken and needed replacing. In the Ballroom the heraldic stained-glass window had been damaged in two sections and a new thirty-feet length of oak cresting was required to replace that damaged along with eleven glass globes. The drawing room walls were to be re-covered in brocade.

---

[361] *Irish Times*, 24 April 1925.
[362] NAI FIN/COMP/2/23/76

The other claim was from James Edward Penrose, Branksome, Milford on Sea, Hampshire, who had been agent at the castle during the take-over by the IRA. His claim was for personal property and furniture in the castle damaged by National Army forces between 28 July and 30 November 1922.[363]

Mildred Dobbs observed that in spite of the presence of the Free State troops things did not change all that much. She says that small groups of IRA were moving around the county insisting on lodgings and food. 'Most people gave hospitality to any bands of armed men, whether Free State or Republican, whatever their sympathies; indeed, it was the only thing to do. As a rule, they behaved well, accepted what they were given and left, but sometimes, as in the case of Mrs Forsayeth at Whitechurch House, they took possession of the greater part of the house and, living in it, quickly reduced the rooms to a fearful state of dirt and destruction'.[364] It is unclear whether this refers to IRA or Free State troops. Emily Ussher recalled that in February 1923 Cappagh and Whitechurch were about to be burned by 'some roving band of republicans out of Tipperary, (who burned Cappoquin the following night). However, they heard that Whitechurch was occupied by Free State troops and decided to pass it by. Ussher notes that the Forsayeths had left Whitechurch the previous autumn fearing the house would be attacked.[365]

Whitechurch was originally built by the Power family of Clashmore. In 1838 Francis Theophilus Henry Hastings, 13th Earl of Huntingdon (1808-1875), married Anne, daughter and heiress of Richard Power of Clashmore House. Through this marriage the Power lands passed to the Earl of Huntingdon. By the 1870s the

---

[363] NAI FIN/COMP/2/23/73
[364] Mildred Dobbs memoir, p.117.
[365] Emily Ussher, p.73.

family held over 6,000 acres in County Waterford. Hastings rebuilt or embellished an existing house on the site at Whitechurch which is referred to in 1837 as the seat of R. Power.

Lieut Col. Richard William Forsayeth retired in 1885 from his position as military surgeon in India and acquired Whitechurch House. According to the 1911 census he lived there with his wife Margaret (a native of Antrim) and his two sons, Gordon William (a Law student at Trinity) and Francis Noel, and a daughter Amy Kate. The house had 18 rooms according to the census record. In 1906 the Forsayeths discovered a cave on their property which is known as the Brothers' Cave which they began to investigate and record the finds. Col Forsayeth kept a series of notebooks and detailed drawings of the excavations and finds. There were so many finds from the cave and others nearby that they filled two rooms at Whitechurch. The damage caused to this collection by the IRA is one of the most serious losses to the archaeological heritage of Co Waterford and Ireland. Marion Dowd in her recent book on the archaeology of Irish caves points out the significance of the Forsayeth collection.[366]

Col Forsayeth died in 1919 just as the War of Independence was beginning. According to Dowd and Corlett the house was taken over by the IRA in 1920 and the collection was damaged and disturbed. From a date point of view this does not match with Mildred Dobbs's account which was gives the date 1922 but perhaps the IRA occupied the house on both occasions. The historian Canon Patrick Power noted:

> The collection in Whitechurch House was left in utter confusion by uninvited guests...It is an irreparable misfortune that the collections, so carefully labelled and

---

[366] Marion Dowd, *The Archaeology of Caves in Ireland* (Oxford, 2021), p.36.

arranged in innumerable boxes, filling two great rooms at Whitechuch...should have fallen into the hands of vandals. A somewhat redeeming feature of the situation is a partial salvage of the scattered and broken materials and transference to U.C.C. by kind permission of Miss Forsayeth and her brother.[367]

In April 1923 Mrs Forsayeth sold the entire contents of Whitechurch.[368] In August 1923 she submitted a claim to the County Council for £244.19.2 for damage to her dwelling house and clothing carried out between 22 April and 6 June 1923.[369] In November 1923 Margaret Forsayeth, Ardmore, was awarded £600 by the Compensation Committee.[370] Mildred Dobbs commented in 1933: 'The Forsayeths are all gone...and are very much missed by those they employed and befriended'.[371]

During the Civil War the Keanes' house at Fortwilliam was occupied by Free State troops:

> The raids on Fortwilliam did not continue, because we had Free Staters (Irish Government troops) billeted on us. The kitchen wing was cleared for their use and all the servants were brought into our part of the house and slept in the spare bedrooms; they, and we children as well, were sternly forbidden by my father to go near the soldiers; these were not much in evidence, for they slept in the day time and went about their business at night, but there

---

[367] Rev. P Power, 'Exploration of Bone Caves Co Waterford', *Irish Naturalist's Journal*, Vol.2, No.6, Nov. 1928, pp 122-123.
[368] *Waterford News,* 13 April 1923.
[369] WCCA WCC/GWA288
[370] *Waterford News & Star*, 9 November 1923.
[371] Mildred Dobbs memoir, p.20.

were a great many of them, and my father had to go to Dublin to see their Chief of Staff before they would go away.[372]

Tay Lodge

This house was owned by the Langley family. It was built in the late 18th century when it was known as Rockbrook. Around 1803 a new front was added. In 1813 it was the home of Phineas Hunt, who married Elizabeth Langley of Fethard in 1814. In the 1850s Charles Langley leased the house when he became agent to the Palliser family of Comeragh.[373] In 1890 Langley came in for criticism from the Rathgormack branch of the Tenants National League describing the 'tyrannical and vindictive conduct of Mr Langley of Comeragh in not coming to terms with the Foy tenantry'.[374] In the same year the Mothel branch of the Land League passed a resolution: 'That we, the members of this branch, condemn the action of Charles Langley, of Tay Lodge, Comeragh, for being grassing Edmond Fitzgerald's evicted farm at Kilnasbeg, and that we look upon him as an evictor and grass-grabber, and that we look on those who buy and sell to him being just as bad'.[375]

According to the 1911 census it was a first-class house with fifteen rooms. The owner Charles Langley belonged to the Church of Ireland and was employed as a land agent to the Fairholmes of Comeragh, a magistrate, and farmer. His wife Edith Ardagh was born in Canada. There were three children, Eileen, Charles and Arthur. There were three servants: a governess, Agnes Patterson,

---

[372] Frida Keane, p.90.
[373] Email from Peter Langley 5/11/2001.
[374] Waterford County Museum, *Minute Book of the Rathgormack Branch of the Tenants National League*, 26 October 1890.
[375] *Munster Express*, 17 May 1890.

216

Kate Doyle, cook, and Elizabeth Quin, housemaid. When Charles died in 1930 his obituary noted that 'he was well-known as a land valuer in cases under various Land Acts where questions of rent were being fixed between landlords and tenants'.[376]

In August 1922 an IRA man named Dobbyn of Butlerstown was accidentally shot by a comrade while they were billeted at Tay Lodge.[377]

The house was attacked on 20 March 1923 by the IRA, as recalled by Peter Langley:

> I believe he had been warned that something like this might happen, so the previous Sunday, while everyone was at mass, he had buried the drum in the garden and planted cabbages on top. Unable to get the fire going properly, the groom who lived in the yard rounded up a lot of the locals. The IRA departed eventually, and the fire was put out without too much damage being done. I still have a dressing table one of the drawers of which is charred. [378]

The compensation claim file in the National Archives shows that the house suffered extensive damage and the incident is described:

> On the 20th day of March 1923, a number of armed men came to Tay Lodge and set it on fire and endeavoured to destroy the house and its contents. The furniture was smashed up by them, and fires were lighted in several rooms. The attempt to completely destroy the building

---

[376] *Munster Express*, 27 June 1930.
[377] *Munster Express*, 12 August 1922.
[378] Robin Bury, p.91.

failed but substantial damage to the house and the contents...was caused.

John Hearne the builder and contactor produced a schedule of repairs, and the following extract refers to the Dining Room which was 19 X 16 feet and 12 feet high:

The window glass was completely smashed; the furniture was piled high in the centre of the room and then set on fire. The centre of the floor is burned, and the architrave and portion of the skirting to recess is charred. The painting of all woodwork, ceiling of room and papering of walls is destroyed and must be renewed.

Over the years the Langley family have jokingly said that the reason the house didn't burn to the ground was that it was so damp. However, a comment in the compensation claim file gives a more plausible explanation:

The attempt to burn the house failed through the kindly help of good neighbours and to the fact that a copious supply of water was at hand to save the property. With great presence of mind Mr Langley started the ram to work and kept the supply of water coming into the reserve tanks, and but for his prompt action, and the kindly help of his neighbours the whole residence would have been burned out.

Charles Langley claimed £1298.8.11 in damages for furniture, books, pictures, carpets, bedding and other effects. He received £861.8.11 which included costs. He employed William Barr as contractor to carry out the repairs and redecoration of the interiors. On the 9 October 1924 Langley notified the Ministry of Finance that the repairs had been completed and carried out in accordance with the 'reinstatement condition' for a sum of £255.

218

His solicitor requested that the compensation money for this amount be paid as soon as possible as he wished to pay the contactor.

Emily Ussher stated that the Langleys had removed most of their furniture and the petrol the previous night.[379] Included in the claim file is a separate list of clothing destroyed. Mrs Langley's clothing included: one fur muff, an afternoon dress, a tea gown, a summer dress, a long-knitted coat, a foot muff, gloves, veils, shoes, and hats. The son Arthur claimed for two suits, two pairs of boots, and a cricket bat. A bullock and two lambs taken in 1922 were also claimed for.[380] The Langleys left Tay Lodge in 1961.

Camphire House

Camphire was originally a seat of the Ussher family. In 1902 it was purchased from Arthur Ussher by Robert Conway Dobbs (1842-1915), a retired solicitor. In 1869 he married Edith, daughter of Henry Fowler Broadwood of Lyne, Horsham, Sussex.[381] They had three sons and three daughters. The remains of the medieval tower house were still preserved to the rear of the 19th-century house which had been rebuilt to an Italianate design by Charles Lanyon.

In 1933 Mildred Dobbs (1878-1965) wrote a memoir of life at Camphire which includes a chapter on the revolutionary period.[382] The family had previously lived in a shooting lodge in Co Kerry. Mildred described the contrast between their wild Kerry home and Camphire, which was 'more like England with its

---

[379] Emily Ussher, p.73.

[380] NAI FIN/COMP/2/23/207

[381] *Irish Times*, Obituary of Robert Conway Dobbs, 5 January 1915.

[382] Mildred Dobbs, *Sojourns of a Spinster*, 1933. Unpublished memoir, private collection.

big beeches and oaks'. According to her its chief glory was the walled garden where with a 'first-rate' gardener they grew fruit, flowers, and vegetables. There was a dairy farm of 200 acres. Mildred's brothers were away so she lived at Camphire with her parents and sister Edith Sybil (1877-1961). She was a Unionist and was not in favour of Home Rule. She commented that 'there were few in Ireland who did not look on Home Rule as anything but a step to complete severance from the Empire'.[383]

Mildred's Ford car had been sabotaged to prevent her using it and she decided to sell it and use her bicycle instead. Clark notes that the seizure of cars was particularly prevalent in Co Waterford.[384] Andrew Kirwan described how cars were acquired in the Kilmacthomas area:

> My main source of supply was the people of the so-called 'gentry' class. These persons, being in general pro-British...had no trouble obtaining permits to use their cars. Whenever, therefore, the old Model T Ford refused to function, I visited the house of one of these gentry, who I knew had a car, and commandeered it for the job in hands at the time. I had, of course one or two of the boys with me...and we were all armed with revolvers, but it was never necessary to use guns. Indeed, we rarely had to produce them. We requested use of the cars 'for the I.R.A.' and we got them. In every case, we returned the cars when their purpose was secured except where exceptional circumstances prevented us.[385]

---

[383] Mildred Dobbs memoir, p.94.
[384] Gemma Clark, p.21.
[385] BMH WS 1179.

Mildred commented: 'The war of the I.R.A. against the British intensified as the year 1921 wore on, and the policy of seizing cycles to mount the growing numbers of their recruits was adopted by the Sinn Feiners. We were all advised to send our cycles to the Royal Irish Constabulary barracks for safe-keeping, but I was loath to send mine because it was so useful to me'. She decided to hide the groom's bicycle which she put in the vinery in the walled garden and put her own in the tool shed. She was confident the bikes would not be found as they had no gardener at the time. The IRA also carried out searches for bicycles and called to Camphire one night. She informed them that she had removed the bikes and they demanded to know where she had placed them:

> The leader hushed the others and asked me to send someone to let them in. I objected, as I did not wish my mother, who was old, to be molested. However, he told me that they did not want to go upstairs...The leader was a weather-beaten man with a bronzed face, aged about 36, he was followed by one who wore a piece of calico over his face which was tucked in under the turned-up collar of his oilskin coat and had two round holes for eyes; he had a sou'wester on his head so nothing was visible except his hands and his boots. The next man wore motor goggles, and the remainder were undistinguished and were all young men, but only seven or eight of them came inside the gate. The leader...began to shout: 'What have you done with the bicycles, you will have to tell me?...At that moment a man behind me made some exclamation and I turned quickly to see what he was at; as I turned my shoulder bumped against some hard object and, glancing down, I saw that it was a small automatic in the leader's hand. I then heard my voice say: 'Oh, I beg your pardon' and the

part of me which was looking on was so amused at the idea of begging pardon for bumping into a revolver that I burst out laughing; he got very red and put the thing in his pocket.

We next adjourned to the house, which was searched for field-glasses or other things likely to be useful. They found a small pair of ivory and gilt opera glasses and a broken flash-lamp, which they took. We then exchanged polite 'Goodnights'…and I went on to report to my mother, whom I found sitting up in bed wearing her best nightcap and bed jacket…and was quite disappointed not to have received a visit from them.

She later realised that the man with his head covered who knew the layout of the house in detail was not in fact a man but the former cook who had left to get married.

The following day she went to her brother's house at Kilmorna, near Lismore, where his wife Lady Dobbs was in occupation as he was still in India. She removed their bicycle and brought it back to Camphire. She decided to wrap the three bicycles and bury them in the melon pits which were full of sand. Mildred repeated the process during the Civil War, burying the family bible and 'other irreplaceable things'.

When the Black and Tans were introduced to the area, she said they behaved well because they were effectively controlled by District Inspector Captain Robinson who was a nephew of Lord Carson. Her comments are not supported by people like Emily Ussher of Cappagh and Frida Keane of Cappoquin who were not impressed with the behaviour of the Black and Tans in west Waterford.

A group of IRA broke into Bleach House at Villierstown on 30 October 1922. The owner Mr Hall was absent. According to Mildred they spent the night 'looting, breaking the plate across to see if it were real silver or not, and removing all valuables and wearing apparel they could lay hands on'. She was concerned that Camphire would suffer the same fate.

Camphire was raided on 31 October 1922 and Mildred has left a detailed account of the event which is worth quoting. It gives a vivid insight into what the experience was like. Mildred promised to spend the winter with her mother in Painswick and leave the groom as caretaker at Camphire. She had been to Lismore to obtain money from the bank to pay wages and to purchase her ticket. Arriving home, she settled down to eat her supper in the study:

> I was half-way through when I noticed that the wires of the hall-door bell which crossed the ceiling [at one of the rooms] were moving, though not enough to ring the bell in the passage beyond. I jumped up, ran upstairs to a bedroom with a window overlooking the front doorsteps, and thought I saw only one man waiting there. Several men had been coming to settle up accounts with me at about that hour and it was my habit to inspect them first from the window and then let them in.
>
> I threw up the window and put out my head, and there was just enough moonlight for me to distinguish four men carrying rifles. I called out, "Good evening, boys, what do you want?"
>
> "Are you Miss Dobbs?"
>
> "I am."

"Well, I'm a Republican Officer, with three men, quartered on you for the night." This was exactly the tale told to Mrs Hall two nights before, so I knew that the expected robbers had arrived. I explained that I was leaving, so that all beds, except mine and those belonging to the two maids, were dismantled and told them that they would be much better off in the farmhouse where there were four beds ready, and that I would get the key for them.

I went off to get it and incidentally to warn the maids to get out at the back of the house and away through the garden to their homes. I returned to the window upstairs and heard the men grumbling at being kept waiting in the rain, and at last they began to kick the door, so I put my head out and told them I had the key and would throw it down. The leader called up that he was an officer and must obey orders and occupy the house. I remarked that for all I could see of them they might be the robbers who had robbed Mr Hall's house, so I would not let them in.

He replied, "It's a leaden message you'd get for that, if you were a man."

An answer which I had heard was once used by another woman flashed into my mind; I leant well out and said, "If I were a man none of you would be here," at which there was a prolonged silence.

At last, they announced their intention of breaking in; I called out that if they did, I would do my best against them and I shut the window. I suddenly remembered the £30 which I had turned out of my pockets on to the study table when I came in, so I rushed downstairs and into the study to find that they had already broken the window of the lobby beyond the study, had got in and were hammering at the door leading from it to the study. Luckily, I had just had two good bolts fixed on the inside and had shot them before sitting down to supper.

I gathered up the notes on the writing-table, stuffed them into the pocket of my skirt and, seizing the duplex lamp, left the room, turning the key in the lock to delay their progress should they succeed in breaking in. I thought of the valuable china and the clock on the drawing-room mantelpiece, and hurriedly hid them under the sofa, where they were completely hidden by the valence. Next, I returned to the hall and placed the lamp, which was too heavy to carry with comfort, on to a table, where it gave sufficient light through the dining-room door for me to see what I was doing, and with both hands free it took next to no time to pull out the plate-drawer, take it over to the big bookcase and empty it behind some large volumes in the bottom shelf. The salt-cellars and various bits on the sideboard, all old Irish silver, found a place behind other books. I had barely finished before I heard the men in the kitchen; I fled into the hall, snapped out the Duplex lamp, seized the hand-lamp, ran upstairs and into my bedroom which was in the back wing. I put the lighted lamp inside a wardrobe, then tip-toed back to the gallery, surrounding the hall, to see what was happening.

The hall is a double one, the front part used as a sitting-room, but only a couple of pillars mark the division between it and the back where the broad staircase leads down from above. The wing-door leading to the kitchen passage opened and two men striking matches came through; their eyes fell with delight upon the lamp I had left; they lit it and returned to the kitchen premises. I went to my room and looking out along the side of the house I could see the light appear in the kitchen, then in the larder and finally in the servants' hall, the only place where there was a fire.

I sat down and came to the conclusion that the situation could not well be much worse; the men were despicable, so I had better get out and try to obtain help. The carpets were all up, so I put on very thin walking-shoes to avoid making a noise on the bare boards of the passages and staircase and, throwing on a coat and tweed hat, I stole downstairs intending to get my bicycle from the porch, lock the door behind me and get off to Lismore. I stupidly did not keep my ears open as I started down the staircase, as I imagined the men to be warming themselves at the fire in the servants' hall. I had just reached the bottom step when – like in a nightmare – the swing-door under the stairs opened and a man carrying the lamp came through, followed by the other three. I tore across the hall to the study door hoping to escape that way, found it locked and could not get the key, which was still in my pocket, so I stood back in the deep doorway wondering what was going to happen.

The hall clock began to strike eight as the men came through, and its tones must have kept them from hearing my flying steps. The lamp held in front of them dazzled their eyes so that they did not see me. I felt a fool wearing a coat and hat, while if I had carried them I could have got rid of the evidence that I was about to go for help, but fortunately I was dressed in dark brown tweed and the doorway in which I stood was also dark brown which all conduced to my safety.

The men came up the hall; I recognised the leader and knowing there is nothing like facing an Irishman I lifted one foot to step out and do so, when he put the lamp down on the writing-table at the other side of the hall and they all trooped into the drawing-room, the door of which I had left open. During the moment they remained there I succeeded in fitting the key into the lock of the door behind me and got inside. I heard them go into the dining-room and the rattle of the sideboard drawer as they pulled it out. I slipped the key out of the door and locked it on the inside. There I was, unable to get at either bicycle, mackintosh or umbrella, so there was nothing for it but to start off on foot in the rain.

I passed out through the lobby from which the men had tried to get into the study, as there was a door leading on to the drive and started through the fields. It was still raining hard, and I was soaked up to the knees by the long grass before I reached the high road. I felt sure that I should meet no one as it was All Hallows Eve, so I pegged away in the dark, finding my thin shoes a great disadvantage. I hid the cash I had on me where I could pick it up again and went on. I reached Lismore about 9.30pm and, hurrying through the Main Street, turned down towards the Castle. I had heard the Free State troops were very nervous, so when I had passed through the riding-gate and a sentry shouted "Halt, who goes there?" I stopped instantly and called out, "Friend; can I see an officer?" my voice sounding very thin and feeble in contrast to his robust tones.

She met Captain Blake who was in charge and eventually he agreed to go to Camphire. Mildred was in an armoured car with eight men and another armoured car with about a dozen men followed.

'with two officers and four men, [I] tip-toed across the gravel drive, slipped the key into the side-door and got into the study. We paused there to listen, and I heard a chair scrape on the tiles of the kitchen. The lamp the men had taken from the hall was the only one not put away in the house, so I knew that all the men must be together in the kitchen, that kind being always terrified of the dark - evil consciences, I expect. At any rate, counting on that, I led the way across the hall, striking matches for light, all walking on tiptoe and trying to make no sound on the bare boards. I pegged back the swing doors and led down the passage to the corner, from which I could see the light coming under the closed kitchen door.

I pointed, "Run quickly and you'll catch them." Before the first man had reached the door, I had got back round the corner, suddenly terrified out of my wits. My one idea was to run. Suddenly I felt gravel under my feet and realised I was outside the side door, running straight towards the men on the tennis lawn who had been told to shoot. I had just sense enough to turn and go in again.

I was like a rabbit trying to get down a hole. The next thing I knew I was crouched under the lavatory basin in the lobby, with the hard pipes pressing into my back, and with my hands over my ears to keep out the sound of the shots I expected to hear. After a little I felt better and cautiously removed my hands. I only heard a shouting and rough-and-tumble going on, so I ventured back into the study where, developing a fit of shivering, I attempted in a feeble way to try and make a fire, in the cold fireplace, with paper and a few sticks and logs.

My half-finished supper was there on the table, and with the help of a candle I found on the mantelpiece, and lighted, I saw that the clock gave the hour as 1.30 a.m. A moment later one of the men came through the door, very cock-a-hoop, and rattled off the names of the four men, whom he said they had caught before they could get to their feet, as they were sitting round the kitchen table, their rifles stacked in a corner where they could not get at them. I only know the name Ormund, the former I.R.A. commander in charge of Lismore Castle.

The man asked for lights, as they were going to bring the prisoners through. I ran upstairs, fetched a collection of candle-ends, and lighting them, placed them about so that there should be no hitch. I opened the double doors into the porch and the wide front door beyond and, not wishing to see the prisoners, or to be seen by them, I retired to the study. I heard them led across the hall; there was a pause as they reached the end and a murmur of voices; then they went through the porch and I heard their feet on the gravel.

I moved out to the hall, expecting at least to take leave of Captain Blake, but I only found Agnes and Minnie, each clinging to a curtain at either side of the porch doorway. "I am glad to see you are all right, Agnes, but where are the officers?"

"They are all gone, miss, they are all gone," she said in a kind of wail. I rushed out of the hall-door and into the moonlight, which was now quite strong, and saw the little troop of men going in a bunch up the drive, and that is the last I saw or heard of them from that day to this. They had gone off without even waiting to find out if we were afraid to be left without protection.

I was much concerned at the prisoners having seen them, so instead of saying nothing about my adventures, I spread the news broadcast next day that I alone was responsible in going for help. The girls belonged to the neighbourhood, so they and their families might have suffered considerably if it was thought they had helped in the capture. It was now 2 o'clock and there was nothing to do but go to bed with hot bottles.

The next morning, we surveyed the ruin in all the downstairs rooms. Every drawer in cupboard, desk and cabinet had their contents pulled out on the floor in the search for valuables. The storeroom had been broken open and one of the large jorums of old rum, which had come from the cellar of a great-great-aunt, which we used on occasion as liqueur, was on the kitchen table half empty. They had used some large goblets of Waterford glass to drink it out of, and one lay, unbroken, on the bricks of the kitchen floor, having survived the turmoil of the capture, which had left most of the chairs in ruins.

A book with the Halls' name in it and a couple of hats which had also come from Bleach, showed that they were the same band which had looted that house. I collected a few souvenirs: a rifle cartridge and two rosaries, and a button or two. On the table were tins of brown polish and boot brushes; the robbers had evidently been polishing up their Sam Brown belts and generally making themselves presentable for Mass in the morning.

Mildred left Camphire on 3 November 1922. In Lismore she waited for the Cappoquin Bacon Factory lorry which was to bring her to Cork. She says that many of her neighbours 'rich and poor' met her to congratulate her on her escape. However, not all the locals agreed, and she recalled that 'two old crones' walked up and down to one side of the fountain cursing her.

According to Lady Waterford, Mildred Dobbs had to leave after the IRA raid on the house; she noted that 'on the very next night the Irregulars attacked her house and wreaked their vengeance on it'.[386] The remaining contents of the house were sold over two days in July 1923 by John D Palmer of Waterford.[387] Frank Wood, Mildred's agent, submitted a claim for a silver watch, five Italian cameos, and an antique Japanese ivory fan. The looters broke ornaments, tore books, ripped her clothing and put candle grease on them.[388] According to the claim submitted by Mr Wood, the damage took place on 15 January 1923, and it was suggested that this was done by Free State troops and not IRA. The court case concerning compensation for damage was held in November 1924. Miss Dobbs was claiming £60 on behalf of her mother. She stated that 'considerable damage' had been done, and bottles of port (dated 1860) and sherry removed from the cellars. E. Arthur Ryan, State Solicitor, referred to Miss Dobbs's list of stolen items which she headed 'Articles taken during a raid by national troops'. The thieves had also written 'Diehard Reprisal' on a wall. The caretaker at Camphire was Michael Hickey who corroborated Miss Dobbs's account. The judge concluded that it was probable

---

[386] Beatrix Lady Osborne Beauclerk, unpublished typescript, p.11. Private collection.
[387] *Waterford News*, 6 July 1923.
[388] NAI FIN/COMP/2/23/395. Thanks to Cian Flaherty for details from this file.

that the men who broke into the house and stole items were national troops and he awarded Miss Dobbs £7.10.0.[389]

Camphire was subsequently occupied by her brother Henry Robert Conway Dobbs (1871-1934) who was married to Agnes Esme Rivaz; they had four children, Mary, Robert, Henry and Susan. The latter lived at Camphire until her death in 2009.

---

[389] *Munster Express*, 29 November 1924.

Aftermath
Compensation - Abandon - Rebuild?

Chapter 12

T he Damage to Property (Compensation) Act 1923 was passed in the Oireachtas on 12 May 1923. This act dealt with claims which occurred after the Truce of 11 July 1921 and up to 20 March 1923. It superseded the Compensation (Ireland) Commission set up by the British for damage to property between 21 January 1919 and 11 July 1921. The scheme was administered by the County Courts throughout the Free State.

In March 1923 *The Times* of London, commenting on the Compensation Bill, noted that 'hundreds of houses throughout Southern Ireland have been burnt to the ground, the incendiaries caring nothing whether the owners were some irreconcilable Unionist, such a devoted servant of his country as Sir Horace Plunkett, or the President of the Free State'. The paper felt that the bill required drastic revision so that the victims of 'anarchy' be attended to as a priority.[390] In the same month, in reply to questions from Sir John Keane, President Cosgrave explained the way loans would be distributed:

---

[390] *Dublin Evening Telegraph*, 31 March 1923.

Where a house was worth £20,000 with furniture worth £10,000 was destroyed, the money would not be paid in respect of the £20,000 until work was begun, and then the instalments would commence. Directly the award was made for the £10,000 worth of furniture the applicant would receive £2000 in cash and £8,000 in securities.[391]

The question of compensation for the burning of houses was discussed in Seanad Éireann on 13 April 1923. A number of Senators wanted clarification on a section of the Bill.[392] There was an interpretation that judges could award a figure to the owner of a destroyed house and suggest that the owner purchase a similar house elsewhere and not rebuild if the house was very old and large. It was stated that many owners no longer wanted to live in these large houses as they were unsuitable for living in the early 20th century.

The Chairman explained the thinking behind the Bill's approach to compensating owners to rebuild their houses:

> The standard we arrived at was, having regard to modern requirements in regard to building, what sum would enable the owner to acquire a house that would be equally good in point of substance, dignity and style, but which would not, of course, cost anything like the amount that would be required to reinstate and restore the old building. It seems to me that the Government have followed those decisions of ours, and have endeavoured to adopt them in this clause, because they say where the Judge thinks that to restore the original building would be

---

[391] *Northern Whig*, 29 March 1923.
[392] https://beta.oireacthas.ie/en/debates/debate/dail/1923_08_01/27/ [Accessed 12/12/2017].

either economically absurd or impracticable, he should, as an alternative, award the owner such an amount as will get him accommodation such as he had in the other house. Those are the words used in effect - accommodation elsewhere equivalent in value and comfort to what he had in other premises.

Sir John Keane emphasised that these houses were more than just bricks and mortar:

> With all due respects to what you said, I do not think that the method of acquiring a value by comparison with another house in the district is satisfactory, because we know from practical experience that it is not fair to ask a person whose house has been burned to go into another house even if it is similar, because the very site of his own house is hallowed in the memory of the sufferer. The whole surroundings are there, and although he may acquire another building elsewhere that is not the point. He wants the money, not to enable him to replace a white elephant, but to replace the injured building by another building which will provide suitable accommodation of the standard appropriate for the persons resident before the injury. Replacements are far higher now, and houses have gone up in value.

Mr Ernest Blythe, Minister for Finance, noted that the government was anxious that people should rebuild, and that people who occupied houses should remain in the country:

> This clause really deals with a large class of cases where we think there is no practical hope that they will be rebuilt, and it is to give people something for their "white elephant." Where people want to rebuild a house in its old

form, and perhaps in a less pretentious style, that would probably be a reasonable case for asking full reinstatement conditions. That would come in in 3 (b), where people could show reasonable cause for full reinstatement conditions, and though they do not want to erect as big a house, they might erect a suitable one.

By July 1924 the Free State government had paid out £300,000 in payments relating to post-truce damage. In November 1924 the committee of the Irish Claims Compensation Association issued a statement relating to the claims of southern Irish loyalists. They described the Damage to Property Act (1923) as 'a travesty of justice and a distinct breach of the pledges given previously'. It noted that in nearly every case the amount awarded for the destruction of buildings was inadequate. If the owners did rebuild, they were threatened under the provisions of the Land Act 1923 that 'compulsory expropriation of their demesnes and untenanted lands will take place'.[393] In March 1924 Lord Muskerry spoke in the House of Lords in relation to the difficulties experienced by Irish loyalists in obtaining compensation for injury to themselves and their property. He recalled that in 1921 his house was raided, and contents taken which he was unable to claim for under the Malicious Injuries Act as this was considered an act of stealing or looting. He felt that the compensation committee went out of their way to reduce the amount being claimed for by loyalists. A friend of his felt that 'it is a well-known fact that no loyalist would be fairly dealt with. On the other hand, those whose property was destroyed by the British were more than pleased, for they say England has dealt with them by paying more in compensation than the destroyed property was valued for'. Muskerry felt that the disbandment of the RIC was a big

---

[393] *The Scotsman*, 24 November 1924.

mistake as they were replaced by the unarmed Civic Guards. He concluded ironically that 'the only protection that has ever been afforded in Ireland, the only attempt ever made to stop looting, was when the Republicans were in force in a district. They did try to stop looting and give protection, but they were well-armed men'. He believed the final blow to Irish loyalists was when the King approved of the Destruction of Property (Compensation) Act 1923, which dismissed all claims for injuries committed prior to 11 July 1921. Lord Arnold, the Under-Secretary of State for the Colonies, replied on behalf of the government. He noted that early on claims were processed in the courts 'in the absence of any defence', and the full amount awarded. This was an unsustainable situation as 40,000 claims had been submitted in relation to damage and destruction to property in Ireland between 21 January 1919 and 11 July 1921. He concluded by stating that no government (British or Free State) had made as much effort 'in the course of history' to assist those who had suffered in 'internal strife'.[394]

On 13 April 1925 Percy Arland Ussher, Cappagh House, married Emily Whitehead, daughter of Christopher Whitehead of Nenagh, Co Tipperary. The wedding took place at Whitechurch and was performed by Rev. J. Going. Percy's mother recalled that those who had picketed Cappagh during the strike in 1922 gave them presents and the IRA quartermaster, Jim Power, drove them to the church.

By 1925 a number of country houses were being rebuilt or restored. Some owners were unable to rebuild their houses which had been totally destroyed by fire as the compensation offered

---

[394] http://hansard.millbanksystems.com/lords/1924/mar/05/claims-of-Irish-loyalists

was insufficient. In county Waterford all of the houses destroyed by fire were rebuilt to something like their former appearance, at least on the exterior. The section of Comeragh House which survived the fire was restored but was only about half the size of the original house. Cappoquin was restored in great detail and new architectural embellishments added such as new interior stucco work, front door surround and roof balustrades. The *Irish Times* of 16 June 1925 published the following report:

County Families Returning - Welcome Prospects In The Free State - Southern Mansions Restored.

> The work of re-building a number of the country residences in the South of Ireland, destroyed during the troubles...is now in progress, and it is expected that the reconstruction of a number of others will be expected at an early date.

> The property destroyed belonged to gentlemen who were large employers of labour in nearly every instance, and people in the different districts interested are glad that prospects are now held out of a return to the former level of prosperity.

> Many property owners who were driven from the country are undoubtedly anxious to return; and their old neighbours - and indeed, the people generally - are equally anxious to welcome them back.

> The Marquis of Landowne's seat at Derreen...which had been looted and burned, has been re-built by a Cork firm...and a considerable portion of the furniture has been returned...

Lismore castle, the Irish seat of the Duke of Devonshire, though not burned, was very badly damaged; and one of the first orders given by the Duke on recovery from his recent illness was for its complete restoration. A very large amount of work is given in different departments of the estate, and very little unemployment now exists in Lismore or the surrounding districts.

However, not everyone was happy with the compensation paid out to property owners. The *Dungarvan Observer* published a report of a council meeting during which there was a heated debate in relation to the issue:

Mr Conway…knew certain people who got compensation in this county who in the trouble of 1918 cleared out and left no one to mind their property, and then when the ceasefire came, they returned to the people they despised and disowned. Mr O'Ryan said his view was that a certain class had applied for compensation for destruction of property should not have got 1d. In other countries such people who sided with the enemy had their property taken from them. These men helped English against Ireland, and if his party won the war they would get no compensation. They should get no compensation, but they should be driven out of the country. The chairman asked if any councilor had information in relation to compensation cases, they should contact the Minister for Finance directly. Councillor O'Ryan replied, 'You might as well be idle.[395]

---

[395] *Dungarvan Observer*, 28 February 1925.

This report shows the level of bitterness which still existed towards the owners of Big Houses. Even though many families remained and rebuilt their houses where possible, they realised life would never be the same again. This feeling of loss is summed up by Harriet Bagwell, writing in 1924:

> The old life is passing away never to return. At Marlfield, old family portraits looked down on us from the walls...The life that separated those people from our day was a gradual and natural evolution, but with us there has been a violent revolution and...old Family Homes have perished, leaving nothing but ruins. Some of those we had known, met with violent deaths. Homes came to an end and Families were scattered. Many have died heartbroken, who had lived in, and loved Ireland and tried to make things better here.[396]

What was the situation in county Waterford? Many of the principal families remained, such as Villiers-Stuarts, Beresfords, Keanes, Duke of Devonshire, Musgraves, de la Poers and Congreves. Life did return to a kind of normality. It is clear from the letters and diaries presented here that several families who remained were very close to selling their estates and leaving Ireland for good, such as the de la Poers, Usshers, and Beresfords. However, a number of country houses were put up for sale in 1923. These included: Whitechurch, Glencairn Abbey, Pouldrew, Belmont, Ballinakill, and Camphire. The latter did remain in the Dobbs family so perhaps no buyer could be found as so many houses were on the market all over Ireland. A number of big houses were purchased by farmers and others and Emily Ussher

---

[396] Unpublished memoir by Harriet Bagwell (1853-1937), Dangan, Carrickmines, 1 January 1924. She was married to Richard Bagwell of Marlfield House. Thanks to Julian Walton for this reference.

has an interesting comment about this. She met a 'poor woman' in Fermoy and they discussed the burning of the Coote family home. The woman observed; 'No more charity, no more employment even!' And farmers around, who had bought neighbouring vacated country houses, 'did nothing for nobody'.[397]

In 1923 the *Waterford News* reported on the 'Event of the Season' – a hunt organised by 'the ladies Beresford'. The paper noted that the county was 'being hunted as thoroughly as in the palmiest days'. It was followed by a Hunt Ball described as the dancing event of the season.[398]

However, it appears that there was still a certain amount of lawlessness. Ballindud House was a small two-story mid-19th century house, which had been the home of Lieutenant Edward Barden in 1880. It was later acquired by Captain Carew, a commander in the Royal Navy. By July 1923 the house had been acquired by Cornelius Lynch, a cattle dealer who lived in The Glen, Waterford. In July 1923 Lynch was intending to make it his permanent home and had filled it with furniture. It was reported in the local press that he was not a member of the Farmers' Union and had no involvement in the labourers' strike. He was one of the first to pay the old wage rate to labourers demanded by the union.

The house was looked after by a caretaker who did not live on the premises. 'Evidence of the fire was first noticed at 7.30 this morning by a neighbour, Mr McCarthy. He immediately summoned the caretaker. When the caretaker arrived, the

---

[397] Emily Ussher, p. 40
[398] *Waterford News*, 7 December 1923.

241

building was completely enveloped in flames...the origin of the outbreak, is, to say the least, very mysterious.'[399]

The damage was estimated at £3,500 but the house was insured.

In January 1924 Mount Neill House was burned down. It was the home of John Morgan. A press report noted 'The fine old Irish mansion was completely gutted, and the damage estimated at between £3000 and £4000. The origin of the fire is unknown'.[400]

In January 1924 the Waterford Hunt organised a ball held in the City Hall. It was described as 'the most successful and enjoyable by far, witnessed in this city for many years. There was a genuine pre-war ring of jollity and care-freedom about the tout ensemble which has been absent from similar events for a noticeably long period'. Almost every hunt in the south of Ireland was represented. The hall was elaborately decorated with flowers and plants supplied from the gardens of some of the surrounding estates such as Curraghmore, Ballinamona, Glenville, and Woodlands. The Waterford architect Thomas Scully (who was involved in the reconstruction of a number of big houses burned in 1923) made paper cut-outs of hunting scenes and Lady Osborne Beauclerk made a large paper panel with a hunt chase in colour.

A dance in aid of the local Co-op was held at Cappagh House in February 1924 which was reported in the press:

> There was a large assemblage. They came from all quarters of the county and the large yard was packed with motor cars. The dancing was kept on till the morning. During the night the greatest pleasure was experienced,

---

[399] *Ballymena Weekly Telegraph*, 7 July 1923.
[400] *Birmingham Daily Gazette*, 3 January 1924.

and dances included all the latest innovations as well as quadrilles, lancers, etc. The large house was kindly lent by Mr Ussher...the spacious room afforded splendid accommodation for the purposes required. The music was rendered by the efficient Dungarvan Pierrot Band.

Margaret, Lady Davis-Goff of Maypark House claimed £300 for damage done to the house on 3 February 1924.[401]

In 1927 *The Tatler* magazine published a photograph of Col Power O'Shee chatting to members of the Waterford Hounds at his restored home at Gardenmorris.[402] In June of that year arms were seized from H W D Gallwey of Woodlands House for which he claimed £162.[403]

The *Irish Independent* of September 1927 published a full-page advertisement: 'Vote for Cumann Na nGaedheal'. The content gave a breakdown of the financial cost of damage done by 'Mr De Valera's gunmen'. The total figure amounted to £35,000,000. £1,945,201 was paid to owners of private properties. The Waterford court had claims of £474,767. For a period of five years up until 31 March 1928 additional charges were levied on every county at a sixpenny rate. That for Waterford city came to £33,813 and the county £9,687. Included in the advert was a long list of damaged properties including many country houses. Those for Waterford included: Gardenmorris, £17,119; Comeragh House, £14,300; Whitechurch, £1,738; Curraghmore, £1,980, and Ballinamona, £1,040.[404]

---

[401] WCCA WCC/GWA288.
[402] *Irish Tatler,* 9 February 1927.
[403] WCCA WCC/GWA288.
[404] *Irish Independent,* 14 September 1927.

New families moved into the old estates and they in time became part of the local big house society. The Irish Land Commission acquired several Irish estates. Strancally Castle was advertised for sale in 1946 and could have become the home of Evelyn Waugh who considered buying it. On 5 December 1946 he met the owners in Dublin: 'We lunched at Jammet's...then went to see the owners of Strancally Castle, a wistful, defeated old couple. The house looked lovely from their photographs, taken I suspect in Victorian times, but it is alarmingly remote'.[405] Waugh did not buy the castle and it was acquired by the Irish Land Commission. In a Dáil debate in 1958 Waterford T.D. Tom Kyne asked Erskine Childers, Minister for Lands, about an advertisement concerning the sale of Strancally. He wished to know why the land had not been divided amongst local people. The minister replied that 'the large castle with minimum area of accommodation land had now been sold. It would have been quite unjustifiable to demolish this fine residence which was not suitable for ordinary allotment purposes'. He said that he would consider local applicants when they disposed of the remaining 300 acres. The 160 acres that had been sold with the castle 'included land that could not be described as arable'.[406]

The Villiers-Stuart estate at Dromana also came to the Land Commission. In 1907 Henry Charles Villiers-Stuart (1867-1908) was interviewed by the committee on the improvement of forestry in Ireland. He told them: 'The future is too dubious for us except in the case of one's own demesne...Five years ago I thought I would plant it all [3,000-4,000 acres] but then things turned up

---

[405] Michael Davie, *The Diaries of Evelyn Waugh* (London, 1976), p.665.
[406] Sale of Strancally Castle and Lands-Dáil Éireann Debates, 29 October 1958. Vol.171 No2.

and I thought I would not get my money back'.[407] In 1957 the family sold the estate lands to the Land Commission, while a member of the family purchased the house. The Commission had a reputation as philistines, demolishing the country houses on the estates they acquired and devastating the demesnes and any ornamental features they contained. Emer Crooke feels this is an unfair assessment and that they made every effort to save the houses that were in good repair.[408] However, in the case of Dromana they demolished the fine stable block.

Writing in the 1950s, Denis Gwynn noted that Sir John Keane of Cappoquin had become the 'chief spokesman of those formerly Unionist landowners who had decided to adapt themselves to the new conditions and take a real interest in Irish public affairs'.[409]

Sally Phipps, in the biography of her mother the author Molly Keane, eloquently sums up the attachment to the country house and the relationship which existed between the landowners and their tenants and Irish people generally before and during the revolutionary period:

> Previous lives and deaths pervaded the fabric of the rooms. The Anglo-Irish needed this atmosphere to breathe. The shock of their suddenly torched homes was something their courage equipped them to deal with, but the loss of their particular rarefied atmosphere slowly broke their confidence and eroded their way of life. The burnings should not have been so rude a shock, but they were unprepared to pick up the signs. They lived in a half-

---

[407] Niall O'Carroll, *Forestry in Ireland-A Concise History* (Dublin, 2004), p.26.
[408] Emer Crooke, *White Elephants – The Country House and the State in Independent Ireland, 1922-73* (Dublin 2018), pp 123-152.
[409] *Irish Examiner*, 3 February 1956.

mythical place and they deluded themselves about the nature of Ireland...and because they mostly got on well with the people around them, and with those who worked for them, they thought they were loved. They were loved up to a certain point, but the Ireland they chose to ignore...nurtured in people's hearts by music, song, and poetry, was always there. It was usually submerged but from time to time it erupted and overturned all their loyalties.

They did not think of themselves as English. They were rooted in the land of Ireland.[410]

When Desart Court in Co Kilkenny was burned in 1923 its owner the 5th Earl of Desart   moved to England. However, the destruction of the house left a profound psychological impression: 'The wound is deep and there is no cure for it. The only thing is to go on and do one's work...but I sometimes feel that I can hardly bear it...I can't bear to think of Desart – it is sadness itself. All gone, all scattered – and we were so happy there'.[411]

Conclusion

Why were certain houses burned and others spared? The causes for the burning of big houses are complicated. Sometimes there is clear documentary evidence as to the reasons and the individuals or groups who carried out the task. The reason for burning Gardenmorris House is not clear. The past record of a landlord was no guarantee that a house would be spared/destroyed. Dromana was saved because they paid the IRA levy as did Curraghmore, but was threatened during the farm labourers'

---

[410] Sally Phipps, *Molly Keane – A Life* (London, 2017), pp 34-35.
[411] Iris Origo, *Images and Shadows* (London, 1971), pp 55-64.

strike in 1923. Sometimes it was simply a matter of luck that a property survived.

Emily Ussher gave her opinion in relation to the burning of Gardenmorris and other country houses:

> I read a newspaper report of some unfortunate gentleman, who asked the raiders whether they were going to burn him out because he was a Protestant. 'No', they replied, 'we have no religion'. Yes, the old lines of cleavage are disappearing and the O'Shees [Gardenmorris House] were not protected by their faith. Neither were they destroyed for land hunger because they had already sold their farms under the Wyndham Act and one can hardly imagine a mere park would have made the Act worthwhile. They were, of course, like their neighbours who suffered, old fashioned Unionists, but many such escaped unscathed, some of whom had no social virtues to recommend them. Merit in fact was neither here nor there and some of the best...were those who suffered the most. The most plausible explanation is that the whole 'divilment' was first conceived as part of a class war against Capitalists – an 'irregular' land bill in most cases – and that, towards the close of the struggle, when enthusiasm was getting to a low ebb, the unhappy members of the I.R.A. were told they must show something for the money they were getting and went then for the houses next them'.[412]

Emily Ussher was probably not justified in her opinion as to why houses were burned. The reasons varied from county to county. Sometimes the motive is clear, as in the case of the destruction of the homes of senators. The burning of Cappoquin has never been

---

[412] Emily Ussher, p.74.

satisfactorily explained but Cian Flaherty has recently found the answer in the Moss Twomey Papers. Cappoquin, Kingsmeadow House on the outskirts of Waterford, and another city dwelling were ordered to be burned in retaliation for the execution of republican prisoners in Kilkenny, Waterford and Roscrea. Flaherty has also uncovered evidence that Comeragh and Rockmount were burned by a party of Cork IRA led by Tom Barry, who it appears, later regretted the action.[413]

As we have seen, houses such as Ballynatray and Dromana were spared during the War of Independence, Ballynatray because the owners did a favour for the local IRA and Dromana not because the family were considered good landlords but because they agreed to pay the £100 IRA levy. Other houses such as Lismore Castle survived by chance when the Free State troops surprised the occupying IRA who did not have time to set it alight. It did however suffer considerable internal damage during the occupation by both sides.

Compared to other counties, Waterford was fortunate in relation to the small number of big houses burnt. The most architecturally significant such as Lismore Castle, Curraghmore, Mount Congreve, Dromana, and Whitfield were spared. In relation to house contents, the most significant losses were those from Comeragh and Gardenmorris. The latter was described after the burning as more like a museum than a domestic house because of the quality of the antique furnishings. Comeragh had the papers and artefacts of the great explorer John Palliser. The loss of archaeological artefacts from Whitechurch was significant. From an architectural point of view, we have no idea what the interiors

---

[413] UCDA, Moss Twomey Papers p69/92, 2nd Southern Division order No.2, 7 February 1923. Thanks to Cian Flaherty for this information.

of these two houses were like and the full details of what was lost in the fires. It is disappointing that we have no visual record of the interiors, such as those at Cappoquin House, which appears to have had fine 18th-century plasterwork.

Arland Ussher had his own opinions on the treatment of the Irish gentry during the revolutionary period. It surprised him that 'the Colonels' did not have their 'throats cut' as many of them had a low opinion of the general population, and he put this down to the 'innate decency and forbearance' of the people. He contrasted this with the level of violence usual in conflicts in other European countries. 'It is the more remarkable when one considers that the Northern Protestants were indulging, at that very moment, in a pogrom of Catholics falling not far short of East European standards of ferocity'.[414] He does admit that the country house owners suffered in the destruction of their houses, which often contained centuries of accumulated family history. He makes a generalisation that they were compensated and some over-compensated for the damage to their houses. As we now know, the compensation offered in no way covered the full cost of rebuilding houses and the process was protracted, putting off many owners from applying or persevering with the process. In a House of Commons debate about the Irish Grants Committee in 1927, Lieut Commander Kenworthy informed the house that 'several houses being rebuilt are much better than they were before', and that a friend of his 'a loyalist, has obtained a much better house paid for by the Free State Government than he had before'. Lieut Col. Howard-Bury rejected this statement, saying it

---

[414] Arland Ussher, pp 52-54.

was an exceptional case.[415] Ussher was sympathetic to both sides in the struggle and felt that at the time of writing (1944) it was time to live together in harmony for the general good of the country.

What about the present condition of the houses featured in this study? Fortunately, nearly all of them have survived, many with new owners. The great tragedy has been the disgraceful neglect and destruction carried out at Whitfield Court, an important listed building. After the collapse of a Celtic Tiger era development of the house and demesne, it eventually passed to NAMA. In the intervening years the fireplaces had been stolen, the interior fittings damaged or destroyed.

These houses are now accepted as part of our heritage and complex past and were for the most part built by Irish craftsmen. I hope this book has contributed to chronicling a significant period in their history when many of them were under threat of total destruction.

List of houses raided, looted, or burned

Annestown House
Occupied by IRA, 26 July to 3 August 1922
House looted and set on fire, 27 February 1923
House looted and damaged, 24 and 30 March 1923

Ballycoe House
Wrecked by Black & Tans, March 1921

Ballygally House

---

[415] http://api.parliament.uk/historic-hansard/commons/1927/may/25/irish-grants-committee [Accessed 8/11/2020].

Contents burned and house damaged, 1922

Butlerstown Castle
Occupied by IRA to 3 August 1922 and then by Free State troops, 3 August 1922

Cappoquin House
Set on fire, 19 February 1923

Curraghmore House
Riding School occupied by IRA 24-27 July 1922

Cappagh House
Raided for arms 1919
Threat to burn, July 1920
Occupied by IRA 11-18 August 1922
Nine plate glass windows destroyed 19-23 January 1923
Threat of burning, occupied by Free State, January 1923

Camphire House
Raided by IRA, 31 October 1922
Looted by Free State troops, 15 January 1923

Comeragh House
Set on fire 18 February 1923

Durrow House
Raided and looted, March, April 1922

Gardenmorris House
Raided for arms, Summer 1920
Set on fire, 22 February 1923

Glencorran House
Occupied by IRA, 1 November 1922-1 April 1923

Glenaheiry Lodge

Set on fire, 20 May 1920

Guilcagh House
Looted by armed men, 2 March 1923

Helvick House
Raided for arms, May 1919
Looted and damaged, May 1921-February 1922

Lackendarra Lodge
Occupied by IRA, May 1922-May 1923

Lismore Castle
Occupied by IRA, June- 10 August 1922
Occupied by Free State Troops, 10 August 1922 -January 1924

Milfort House
Occupied by IRA, July 1922

Mount Congreve House
Raided for arms, 16 July 1920
Occupied by IRA, 19 July 1922

Newrath House
Occupied by Free State troops, 18-21 July 1922

Parkswood House
Damaged by explosives, February 1920

Pouldrew House
Occupied by IRA, August 1922

Richmond House
Raided for arms, 1918

Rockmount House
Raided for arms, April 1920

Set on fire, 18 February 1923

Rock House
Looted and set on fire, 27 February 192

Tay Lodge
Raided for arms, 1920
Occupied by IRA, August 1922
Set on fire, 20 March 1923

Whitfield Court
Occupied by IRA, 21 July – 3 August 1922
Occupied by Free State troops, 3 August – 19 September 1922

List of RIC barracks destroyed, with owner's name and compensation claimed.*

Cappagh, Beverly Ussher, £1068.19.6

Colligan, Earl of Dartry, £1267.18.0

Annestown, Mary J Galloway, £1531.13.7

Portlaw, Mary F. Medlycott, £1430.18.1

Leamybrien, Caroline Fairholme, £1404.8.0

Lismore Courthouse, Duke of Devonshire, £5045.15.2

Stradbally, John George Beresford, £1673.8.6

Glenaheiry, Lord Ashtown, £2000.0.0

Clashmore? Earl of Huntingdon, £1623.8.1

Kill, Col Power O'Shee,

*Source: Waterford Co Council, Notices of claims for Compensation or Criminal Injury 1920-1946. WCCA WCC/GWA288.

Select Bibliography

Primary Sources

Manuscripts

Marquis of Waterford Archive
Keane Archive
Dawnay Archive
Congreve Archive
Ussher Archive
de la Poer Archive
Waterford County Museum
Waterford City and County Archives
National Archives of Ireland
National Library of Ireland
University College Dublin Archives
Bureau of Military History
National Archives Kew

Newspapers And Periodicals

Waterford News, Waterford Mail, Waterford Standard, Munster Express, Dungarvan Observer, New Ross Standard, Wicklow People, Leinster Reporter, Freeman's Journal, Irish Examiner, The Nationalist, The Irish Times, Evening Herald, Sunday Independent, Limerick Reporter, Belfast Newsletter, Ballymena Weekly Telegraph, Northern Whig, Londonderry Sentinel, Cambridge Independent Press, The Dover Express, Derbyshire Advertiser, Portsmouth Evening News, Nottingham Express, The Irish

Canadian, The Scotsman, The Tatler, The Irish Tatler, The Pictorial World.

Published Works

Anson, Lady Clodagh, *Book - Discrete Memoirs* (London, 1931).
-*Another Book* (London, 1937).
-*Victorian Days* (London, 1957).

Burkes Landed Gentry of Ireland (London, 1912).

Brady, Donald, *Essays from Lismore* (Dungarvan, 2014).
-*Una Troy 1910-1993, Her Life and Work* (Dungarvan, 2010).

Bowen, Elizabeth, *Bowen's Court* (London, 1942).

Bence -Jones, Mark, *Twilight of the Ascendancy* (London, 1987).
-*Life in an Irish Country House* (London, 1996).

Bury, Robin, *Buried Lives - The Protestants of Southern Ireland* (Dublin, 2017).

Byrne, Brendan, "Law, Order and the R.I.C. in Waterford 1920-21: A Chronology' *Decies*, *55*, 1999, pp 117-126.

Clark, Gemma, *Everyday Violence in the Irish Civil War* (Cambridge, 2014).

Crooke, Emer, *White Elephants -The Country House and the State in Independent Ireland, 1922-73* (Dublin, 2018).

Countess of Fingal, Elizabeth, *Seventy Years Young* (Dublin, 2009).

Curtis, L Perry, 'The Last Gasp of Southern Unionism' *Eire-Ireland* Vol 40, 2005, pp 140-188.

De Vere White, Terence, *The Anglo-Irish* (London, 1972).

Dooley, Terence, *The Decline of the Big House in Ireland - A Study of Landed Families 1860-1960* (Dublin, 2001).

-*Burning the Big Houses, The Story of the Irish Country House in Time of War and Revolution*, (New Haven &London, 2022)

-'The Burning of Irish Country Houses 1920-23' *Atlas of the Irish Revolution*, (Cork, 2017), pp 447-453.

Dun, Findlay, *Landlords and Tenants in Ireland* (London, 1881).

Dowd, Marion, *The Archaeology of Caves in Ireland* (Oxford, 2012).

Donnelly, J. S. Jr., 'Big House Burnings in Co Cork During the Irish Revolution, 1920-21', *Eire-Ireland*, Vol 47, 2012, pp 141-197.

Farrell, M.J., *Two days in Aragon* (London 1941).

FitzGerald, Barbara, *We Are Besieged* (London, 1946).

FitzGerald, Ivan, 'The Power O'Shee Family, Gardenmorris, County Waterford', *Irish Genealogist*, XIV, I (2014) pp 14-22

Fraher, William, *A Calendar of the Minutes and Records of Dungarvan Town Commissioners and Urban District Council, 1855-1950* (Dungarvan, 1991)

Girouard, Mark, 'Whitfield Court, Co Waterford', *Country Life*, 7 September 1967, pp 522-526.

Habja, Anna Maria, *Houses of Cork, Vol. I.-North* (Clare, 2002).

Hobbs, John V., 'The Troubles in Mid-Waterford; A Family Perspective', *Decies 76*, 2020, pp 175-183.

Keane, Frida, *The Valley is too Lush* (Dublin, 2015).

Mulley, Clare, *The woman who saved the children, A Biography of Eglantyne Jebb; Founder of Save the Children* (London, 2019).

Murphy, Seán and Síle, *The Comeraghs, Gunfire and Civil War* (Middleton, 2003).

MacEoin, Uinseann, *Survivors* (Dublin, 1980).

McCarthy, Pat, The *Irish Revolution 1912-23 - Waterford* (Dublin, 2015).

Mooney, Tommy, *Cry of the Curlew* (Dungarvan, 2012).
_ *Deise Divided - A History of the West Waterford Brigade I.R.A. and the Civil War* (Kilkenny, 2014).

O'Byrne, Robert, *Left Without a Handkerchief* (Dublin, 2022).

O'Connor, Elizabeth, *Dead Star's Light* (London, 1938).

O'Ceallacháin, D., 'Land Agitation in County Waterford. 1879-1882', *Decies 53*, 1997, pp 91-131.

O'Macháin, Pádrig, 'Patrick Carmody, Irish Scholar', *Decies, 53,* 1997, pp 132-135.

O'Reilly, Terence, *Rebel Heart - George Lennon Flying Colum Commander* (Cork, 2009).

Origo, Iris, *Images and Shadows* (London, 1971).

O'Carroll, Niall, *Forestry in Ireland - A Concise History* (Dublin, 2004),

O'Connor, Emett, *A Labour History of Waterford* (Kildare, 1989).

Power, Patrick C., *History of Waterford City and County* (Cork,1990).

Power, Rev. Patrick, *Waterford and Lismore - A Compendious History of the United Diocese* (Cork, 1937).
-'Exploration of Bone Caves in Co Waterford', *Irish Naturalist's Journal*, Vol. 2, No 6. November 1928, pp 122-123.

Power, Bill, *White Knights, Dark Earls, - the Rise and Fall of an Anglo-Irish Dynasty* (Cork, 2002).
-*Doomed Inheritance, Mitchelstown Castle, Looted and Burned, August 1922* (2022).

Phipps, Sally, *Molly Keane - A Life* (London, 2017).

Symes, Glascott, *Sir John Keane and Cappoquin House in time of war and revolution* (Dublin, 2016).

Sargent, Harry R, *Thoughts Upon Sport* (London, 1895).

The Hurler on the Ditch (Emily Ussher), *The Trail of the Black & Tans* (Dublin, 1921).

Ussher, Arland, T*he Face and Mind of Ireland* (London, 1949).

Walton, Julian, 'Butlerstown Castle', *Unlocking Butlerstown*, (Waterford, 2016), pp 60-63.

Wydenbach, Joanna, 'Emily Ussher and *The Trial of the Black & Tans'*, *Aspects of the Irish Book from the 17th Century to the Present Day*. Revue LISA/LISA e-journal, January 2005, pp 22-28.

Theses And Unpublished Works

Flaherty, Cian, 'Lucky escapes, rising damp or something else entirely? Why so few county Waterford 'big houses' were burned during the Irish Revolution'.
_'The triple misfortune of Richard Power O'Shee; aspects of Civil War unrest in Waterford 1922-1923. (MPhil, Trinity College Dublin, 2019).

Dobbs, Mildred, 'Sojourns of A Spinster', 1933. Private collection.

Ussher, Emily, 'The True Story of a Revolution: Life at Cappagh from the Spring of 1914 to the Spring of 1925, when all ended in a happy wedding', 1925. Private collection.

de la Poer, Mary Olivia, 'Diary 1921-1923'. Private collection.
de la Poer, Rivallon, 'Diary 1922-1923'. Private collection.

Lady Osborne Beauclerk, Beatrix, 'Account of a visit to Curraghmore and Derreen, 1923'. Private collection.

Abbreviations

RIC   Royal Irish Constabulary

IRA   Irish Republican Army

WS   Witness Statement to Bureau of Military History

IMA   Irish Military Archives

TNA   The National Archives, London

NAI   National Archives of Ireland

ITGWU   Irish Transport and General Workers' Union

WFA   Waterford Farmers' Association

WCCA   Waterford City and County Archives

BMH   Bureau of Military History

UCDA   University College Dublin Archives

HC Debs   House of Commons Debates

Index

Castleboro House, 150
Ceylon, 3, 89, 97
Chearnley, Henry P, 1, 15, 20, 168-9
Chearnley Family, 19, 36
Chearnley, John Henry, 167
Christ Church Cathedral, 22
Clashmore, 11, 173, 210, 213, 254
Cloncoskeran House, 2, 12, 18-9, 81-4
Cloncoskeran Castle, 136
Coolfin House, 40
Comeragh House, 18, 71, 72, 93, 150, 184, 186-90, 197-199, 201
Coolnagour House, 2
Coolnasmear, 31, 46
Cody, Jack, 204
Costen & Sons, 195
Crooke, Emer, 245
Currey, Chetwynd, 12
Currey, Fanny, 204
Curraghmore House, 1, 5, 9-10, 13-14, 16, 64-7, 103, 107, 108, 113, 115, 126-30, 132-3, 135, 242-3, 246, 248, 251
Curraghmore Hunt, 10, 18

D

Dáil Eireann Land Courts, 3
Dalton, Tom 58
Dalton, Frank, 183
Dawnay Family, 116
Dawnay, Lady Susan, 116, 120, 138
De Bromhead, Harry, 100
De Bromhead Family, 7
de la Poer Family, 7, 134, 141-4, 150, 153-4, 158, 240
de la Poer, Mary, 7, 94, 138, 141, 148-9, 193, 209
de la Poer, Count, 9
de la Poer, Rivallon, 139
de la Poer, Edmund James, 138
de la Poer, Francis, 151
Devonshire Arms Hotel, 211
Desart Court, 193, 246
Dempsey, Jeremiah, 186
Derryluskan, 184
Derrinlaur, 142, 150

Golden, Sergt, RIC, 79, 80
Grange Volunteers, 25
Grant Ussher, Beverly, 23
Graves, Elizabeth, 106
Graigueshoneen, 13
Grove House, 145
Gurteen, le Poer, 5, 9, 70, 103, 138, 140-59, 193
Gubbins, Marcus Stamer Beresford, 125, 203-4
Gwynn, Denis, 245

H
Hackett, James, 183
Hales, John, 175
Hall, Mr, Bleach House, 223
Hall, Mrs Bleach House, 224
Hayden, John, 58
Hastings, Francis Henry Theophilus, 213-4
Harrington, Mary, 121
Harney, Bridget, 197
Headborough House, 2
Heaslip, Commandant, 137
Helvick House, 86, 90, 97, 165, 252
Hickey Sergt Michael, 48
Hickey, Michael, 231
Hicks, Kathleen, 111
Hearne, John, 203, 218
Hogan, Kate, 186
Hogan, Patrick, 174
Hobbs Family, 37-8
Hobbs, John, 37-8
Hobbs, Mrs, 38
Home Rule, 13, 20, 22, 25, 27-8, 86
Holroyd - Smyth, Lady Harriet, 3, 172
Holroyd - Smyth, Family, 67, 171-2
Holroyd - Smyth, Alice, 173
Holroyd - Smyth, Capt. Rowland Henry Tyssen, 171
Howard - Bury, Lieut. Col., 249
Hudson, John Thomas, 86-8, 220
Hunt, Phineas, 216
Hunt, Arthur, 37, 179, 197, 200-1
Hunt, John, 2, 83

Hutcheson, Maud, 46
Hurley, John, 180
Huntingdon, Earl of, 213, 254
Hyde, Seán, 70

I

Irish volunteers, 30, 33-4
ITGWU, 56-7, 64, 259
IFU, 56
Irene Ponsonby, Lady, 108

J

Jebb, Emily Horsley, 23
Jebb, Eglantyne, 23
Jebb, Dorothy, 23
Johnstown, 52-3

K

Keane, Sir John, 3, 31, 56, 62-3, 69, 170-1, 176, 179-80, 182, 233, 235, 245,
Keane, Harry, 17
Keane, Frida, 171, 174, 177, 222
Keane, John, 175
Keane, Alice, 205
Keane, Molly, 245
Keane, Lady, 179
Keane, Michael, 17
Keane, William, 39-40
Kingsmeadon House, 178, 248

L

Langley Family, 216, 218-19
Langley, Charles, 37, 188, 190, 216, 218
Langley, Peter, 217
Langley, Elizabeth, 216
Land Commission, 85, 167, 244-5
Lansdowne, 5th Marquess, 126, 135
Lansdowne, Lady, 96, 126, 132, 208
Lansdowne Family, Bowood House, 134
Land League, 10, 18, 216
Lackendarra Lodge, 19, 36, 148, 167, 252

Power, P. J. MP, 18
Power, E. N., 36
Power, Jim, 237
Power, Jimmy, 39
Power, Michael, 66, 191
Power Trench, Robert, 4th Baron Ashtown, 77
Power, Charles, B.L., 92
Power, Paddy Joe, 137
Power, Martin, 169
Power, Canon Patrick, 214
Power, Richard, 213
Ponsonby, Lady Irene, 108
Pouldrew House, 110, 115, 122-3, 129, 131, 240, 253
Pouldrew, Mills, 132
Power O'Shee Family, 191, 192
Power, O'Shee, Nicholas, 10, 41, 192, 194-6, 243, 254
Power, O'Shee, Col Richard Alfred, 191
Power, O'Shee, John, 192
Power O'Shee, Major Patrick, 195
Power O'Shee, 1, 197
Poole, A. H., 127
Portlaw, 40, 65, 66, 110, 117, 127, 129, 139, 131-2, 166-7, 253

Q
Quin, Joseph, 51
Quin, Col., Castletown House, 69
Quinlan, T., 62, 150
Quinlan, Tom, 150
Quin, Elizabeth, 217
Queally, William, 168

R
Rathgormack Tenants National League, 15, 216
Raphael, 43, 54
Rennison, Rev. William H., 128, 131
Reilly, W, 189
Reilly, Sgt. Patrick, 73
Redman, Sidney, 48
Redmond, John, 29, 75
Redmondstown, 103, 106
Richardson, General George, 25, 27

W

Waterford Hunt, 17, 242
Waterford Hounds, 15, 243
Waterford Farmer's Club, 10
Waterford Farmer's Association, 56
Waterford Sinn Féin Executive,
Waterford County Council, 46, 74, 78, 82, 144
Walsh, Mrs, 26
Walsh, Willie, 58
Walsh, Mary, 58
Walsh, Father James, 66
Walsh, Annie, 197
Walker, Maggie, 124
Walker, Doctor David, 130, 167
Walker, Miss, 201-2
Walker, Mary, 203
Waugh, Evelyn, 244
Westropp Fleming, Rev. William, 40
Wexford, 57, 71, 150, 152, 196
Whelan, Jack, 36
Whelan, Pax, 36
Whitechurch House, 161, 213-5, 240, 243, 248,
Whitehead, Emily, 101, 103, 160-1, 237
Whitehead, Christopher, 237
Winters, William, 41
Williamson, Lizzie, 74
Wilton Castle, 152
Williams, Jack, 198
Widger, Joseph, 34
Woodstown House, 18
Women's Land Army, 23
Woodlands House, 242, 243
Woodpark House, Co. Clare, 95
Wyndham Land Act 1903, 1, 4, 247
Wyndham Quin Family, 148

About Waterford County Museum

Waterford County Museum is a volunteer run museum dedicated to preserving the history of County Waterford, Ireland. Based in the town of Dungarvan, the museum is open to the public throughout the year, admission is free of charge. The museum operates a very active volunteer community archaeology group. A number of lectures, educational events and exhibitions are run by us during the year. We also publish books and e-books relating to County Waterford history. You can keep up to date with museum news and happenings at:

Email: history@waterfordmuseum.ie

Web: www.waterfordmuseum.ie

Twitter: @waterfordmuseum

Facebook: @waterfordcountymuseum

Other Books in the Series

This book is part of a series of Waterford history books that the museum is republishing as Ebooks or making available to print on demand on the Amazon web site. For a complete list of our books search for "Waterford County Museum" on Amazon. Other books in the series include:

The Comeraghs, Gunfire and Civil War

by Seán and Síle Murphy

The story of the War of Independence and Civil War in Dungarvan and West Waterford in the words of the veterans. This important work was originally published in 1980 as *The Comeraghs, Refuge of Rebels*. In 2003 a revised and expanded version was published under the title *The Comeraghs, Gunfire and Civil War*. The 2020 edition has been further updated with additional content including notes from the original interviews and 31 photographs. The book's importance derives from it being compiled using the first-hand accounts of the Co. Waterford veterans who participated in the struggle for Irish independence. The republication of this seminal history of the Déise Brigade IRA from 1914 to 1924 is a collaboration between the authors, Seán and Síle Murphy, Waterford County Museum and the Commemorations Committee of Waterford Council.

Desperate Haven: The Poor Law, Famine, & Aftermath in Dungarvan Union

by William Fraher, Bernadette Sheridan, Seosaimh O'Loinsigh, & William Whelan

Originally published in 1996, this book is the definitive study to date of the Great Famine (or Irish Potato Famine) and its effects in the towns and villages of West Waterford, Ireland. This long out of print and much sought-after volume was the product of more than 5 years of research by Dungarvan Museum Society (now Waterford County Museum). It provides a fascinating insight into the lives of the poor in mid-19th century Ireland, the response of the authorities to the unfolding tragedy and the conditions which saw many Irish people create new lives for themselves in America, England, Canada, Australia and elsewhere. Tracing the development of the Dungarvan Poor Law Union from its establishment in 1839 to its abolition in 1920, the workhouse figures prominently in the story. The chapters covering the Famine period are based on the minute books of the Dungarvan Board of Guardians, the Famine Relief Papers in the National Archive, and contemporary newspapers. The book examines in detail the lives of the workhouse inmates, with sections on diet, education, work, the workhouse farm, religion, the treatment of women and children. There are also chapters on the effect of the Famine on the fishing industry, and on emigration from West Waterford during and after the Famine. At the height of the Famine 4,000 men, women and children from all over West Waterford were housed within the workhouse and auxiliary workhouses of Dungarvan. Thousands more were dependent on soup kitchens and 'outdoor relief' to prevent themselves starving. For specialist historians and genealogists, it is hoped that the book will be of assistance in prompting further research. For the general reader, and particularly for those whose origins are in the locality, it is hoped that it will provide insights into a tragedy which even yet marks the area after the passage of over a century and a half.

A History of Dungarvan in 33 Illustrations: The Grattan Square Heritage Plaque Project

by William Whelan & Rachael Power

A handy introduction to major events, people and industries from Dungarvan's past. This 'Greatest Hits' of Dungarvan history had an unusual genesis. It started life as a project to lay commemorative plaques in Grattan Square, Dungarvan. The story behind each plaque was originally told in a series of articles written for the local newspapers. These articles by Willie Whelan, have now been compiled into this book. We have included the original illustration for each plaque drawn by Rachael Power.

Illustrated History of Dungarvan

by Edmond Keohan

Originally published in 1924, this first Dungarvan history book set the standard for future local historians. It is an important eyewitness account of the town's Victorian, Edwardian & revolutionary periods. Keohan used all his journalistic skill to provide an entertaining and very readable eyewitness account of the Dungarvan from over a hundred years ago. This new much expanded edition published by Waterford County Museum includes an author biography by William Fraher, photos from Keohan's photographic career, a tourist guide to Dungarvan from 1917 and a history of Abbeyside Castle published in 1916.

This volume also contains annotations to the original work by Cian Flaherty and William Whelan. These annotations provide definitions for terms no longer in common use and notes occasions when Keohan may have been incorrect in his historical suppositions. This is no fault of the author as he was working with the material available at that time.

The real strengths of the book are the chapters covering the 19th and early 20th centuries when Keohan provides us with an eyewitness account of events that shaped the town and country to this day.

Stories of growing up in an Irish village told with a "blend of history, tradition and humour". Siobhán Lincoln records the social history of Ardmore village in County Waterford, tales of school days, dances, fishing, work, language and tradition. This book will be of interest to anyone who wants a picture of life in rural Ireland from the late 19th century to the dawning of the Millennium.

Ardmore: Memory and Story: The history, traditions and stories of an Irish village.

by Siobhán Lincoln

From the foreword by Fergal Keane: "The past slips away from us quietly. We are too consumed with the drama of the present to notice the departure of old ways and traditions. In an age of economic growth without parallel in the history of the state, we are all urged to speed into a bright new future. The places we came from, the landscape of our past recedes and is in danger of being lost. And so when a remarkable book appears like that now offered by Siobhán Lincoln it is important that we pay it proper attention. It is said that every village in Ireland has a historian: I can't vouch for that but know that Ardmore is blessed to have a woman like Siobhán who is so passionate in the cause of saving memory for the coming generations."

Printed in Great Britain
by Amazon

a304dac8-45dc-449c-8cc7-c60352d92057R01